Arab Folktales from Palestine and Israel

Raphael Patai Series in
Jewish Folklore and Anthropology

A complete listing of the books in this series can be found at the back of this volume.

General Editor:

Dan Ben-Amos
University of Pennsylvania

Advisory Editors:

Jane S. Gerber
City University of New York

Barbara Kirshenblatt-Gimblett
New York University

Aliza Shenhar
University of Haifa

Amnon Shiloah
Hebrew University

Harvey E. Goldberg
Hebrew University

Samuel G. Armistead
University of California, Davis

Guy H. Haskell
Emory University

Arab Folktales from Palestine and Israel

Introduction, Translation, and Annotation by Raphael Patai

Wayne State University Press Detroit

02 01 00 99 98 5 4 3 2 1

Library of Congress Cataloging-in-Publication Data

Arab folktales from Palestine and Israel / introduction, translation, and annotation by Raphael Patai.
p. cm. — (Raphael Patai series in Jewish folklore and anthropology)
Includes bibliographical references and index.
ISBN 0-8143-2710-9 (pbk. : alk. paper)
1. Arabs—Israel—Folklore. 2. Arabs—Palestine—Folklore. 3. Tales—Palestine. 4. Tales—Israel. I. Patai, Raphael, 1910- . II. Series.
GR286.2.A72A72 1998 98-11614
398.2′089927—dc21

Designer: Mary Primeau

This book is done with the assistance of a fund established by Thelma Gray James of Wayne State University for the publication of folklore and English studies.

Contents

Introduction 1

Part One: 1910–11

1. The One-eyed Ghoul 31
2. Allāh's Dispensation 37
3. The Jinn's Gratitude 45
4. The Price of the Bride 51
5. The Virtuous Maiden 59
6. The Banished Prince 69
7. The Emir's Daughter 79
8. The Unfaithful Wife 89
9. The Two Blind Women 95
10. Each Man Suffers Disasters 101

Part Two: 1946–47

11. The Lightest of the Light, the Heaviest of the Heavy, and the Fattest of the Fat 109
12. Ṭalāja of the Twenty and the Chicken 117
13. Cunning . . . and Cunning 123
14. The Locust and the Sparrow 135
15. Tambar Tītī 141
16. The Return of the Light 147
17. The Bird of Power 155
18. The Dull-witted Fisherman 165

Part Three: 1982–84

19. The King and His Wife 175
20. Ghouls in Switzerland 183
21. The One-eyed Giant Shepherd 197
22. Ḥasan the Sharp-witted 203
23. The Prince Who Turned into a Deer 209
24. Pomegranate Seed 217
25. The Uncles and Their Nephew 225
26. Seven Brides for Seven Brothers 233
27. Wadīʿah 239
28. The Two Hunters 247

Afterword 255
References 259
Type Index 261
Motif Index 263
Index 265

Introduction

1

One of my earliest memories from Arab Jerusalem dates back to 1933 when, on a Ramaḍan night, my friend Sheikh Aḥmad al-Kinānī took me to a café in the Old City, to listen to a *qaṣṣāṣ* (storyteller). "This *qaṣṣāṣ* is a famous one," Aḥmad told me. "He is from Damascus, and every Ramaḍan he comes for one week here, spends another week in Jaffa, and a third one in Nablus." His fame was certainly powerful enough to attract a large audience to the café, which was so full when we arrived some two hours after sunset (first Aḥmad had to break his fast with a large evening meal) that we barely could find seats. My knowledge of colloquial Arabic was at the time rather limited. I did not understand much of what the storyteller said, so that my attention wandered, and I concentrated on the people sitting around rather than on the performer. I still remember how impressed I was by the rapt attention with which the all-male audience listened to his stories. They all sat on low backless chairs around tiny tables; many of them smoked ("drank") narghiles, alternating with small cups of black coffee. They all bent forward eagerly so as not to miss a word, virtually hung on the lips of the *qaṣṣāṣ*, reacted to everything he said with instant changes in their facial expression, with movements of their hands, heads, and shoulders, and capped nearly every sentence of his with a choral refrain of approving or disapproving outcries. I still remember that most of their expletives invoked the name of God; *Billāh!* could most frequently be heard.

The listeners' participation in the story was so intense that the *qaṣṣāṣ* seemed to be leading the audience as if it were a large orchestra, and the whole scene was one of group action rather than of a solo performance. The repertoire of the storyteller was so rich, Aḥmad assured me, that he could go on night after night and all night throughout the month of Ramaḍan without repeating himself. We sat through story upon story, as it grew later and later, but the audience never seemed to have enough. It was past midnight, and I grew tired and sleepy. Aḥmad was wide awake, as fascinated by the stories as all the rest of the audience, but when I asked him whether he minded if I went home, he, with his natural

Arab courtesy, insisted on keeping me company on my way. While walking through the silent and fragrant Jerusalem night, I asked him whether the stories the *qaṣṣāṣ* related were those of the *Arabian Nights.* Aḥmad smiled at my ignorance. "No *qaṣṣāṣ* worth his name," he said, "would tell his audience stories available in books. None of the stories of this *qaṣṣāṣ* has ever been printed."

That was more than sixty years ago. Since then, who knows how many of the stories of that *qaṣṣāṣ,* and of the venerable tribe of *qaṣṣāṣīn* in general, have been forgotten and forever lost?

2

This volume presents three groups of Arab folktales recorded at three different times and under very different circumstances in Palestine and Israel.

The first group of ten tales is a selection from among sixty-four recorded in 1910–11 by the German theologian and Palestine scholar Hans Schmidt with the help of Jirius Abū Yūsif, a teacher at the Evangelical School in Jerusalem. They were subsequently published in the Arabic original (in a phonetic transliteration) with a German translation by Hans Schmidt and Paul Kahle in a volume titled *Volkserzählungen aus Palästina.*[1] Jirius was a native of the village of Bi'r Zayt in the hill country of southern Samaria, and it was there that Schmidt recorded the folktales. My translations of the ten stories I have chosen are based on the Arabic originals, with which Schmidt's German renderings took certain liberties.

The second group consists of eight stories that were read over the Jerusalem Radio in the winter of 1946–47 by Dr. Isḥāq Mūsā al-Ḥusaynī, Fāyis al-Ghūl, and Ilyās Shihāda. I received the typewritten Arabic transcripts of these tales by courtesy of my late friend Edwin (later Viscount) Samuel, who served at the time as head of the Palestine Broadcasting Service. In the typescripts, the stories were identified either as "from the tales of the folk, recorded and read" by one of the three men named, or as "written and read" by one of them. The latter group, however, differs neither in style nor in content from the former, so that it can be assumed that the broadcasters of both types of stories took their material from the mouths of popular storytellers and that all eight pieces are genuine Palestinian Arab folktales.

The third group of ten tales I selected from among a large number of folktales sent to me by the Israeli folktale researcher Yoel Perez of

Yodfat, who recorded them in 1982–84. The narrators of nine of these tales were members of various nomadic, or formerly nomadic and subsequently settled, Arab tribes in Israel, in the Galilee. The tenth (number 25 in this volume) was recorded by Yehudah Katz in the Negev, in southern Israel. Yoel Perez had the tapes transcribed and kindly put copies of these Arabic transcriptions and their Hebrew translations at my disposal. In turning these texts from the Arabic originals into English, I was helped by my late friend Laṭīf Khayyāṭ, Arabic expert of the Oriental Division of the New York Public Library, who in 1990 tragically succumbed to a heart attack.

The three groups of folktales, despite the time-distances separating them, represent a unit in that they are tales that were, and in part still are, elements in the cultural heritage of a small corner of the Arab world, that of Palestine-Israel. In presenting them in this volume, I have three salient purposes in mind. One of my objectives is to demonstrate the surprisingly wide range in storytelling skills manifested in the tales. At one extreme of this range are found simple, inept, and primitively presented tales, confined to a single fragmentary scene, hesitantly told, with a limited vocabulary, vague references, confused time sequence, much repetition, faulty logic, and inner contradictions. Tales of this type create the impression that there took place a decline of the storytelling art, that they represent a last phase in a great tradition about to disappear. Several of the tales recorded in the 1980s by Yoel Perez are of this type. But it would be a mistake to assume that the decline has begun in recent years only. The fact is that quite a few of the Palestinian folktales collected by Hans Schmidt as early as 1910–11 also belong to this category. It therefore appears that certain *qaṣṣāṣīn,* endowed perhaps with lesser powers of retention, reproduction, and formulation, must have functioned for at least two or three generations, and probably much longer than that, alongside their more gifted brothers and sisters in the Arab world. Or, to put it differently, beside talented, professional storytellers there have always been amateurs with limited abilities but with an urge to tell stories for the entertainment of their children, grandchildren, relatives, and friends.

At the other end of the continuum are found complex, carefully structured and developed sequential tales, reminiscent in certain respects of the famous *Thousand and One Nights,* rich in vocabulary, detail, motivation, and plot. These stories are eloquent testimony to the survival, and more than that to the vitality, of the great tradition of Arab storytelling art not only among the Arabs of Palestine in the pre–World War I era but also in the present-day Arab population of Israel (especially among the Bedouin and ex-Bedouin), despite the greatly changed conditions in which they now live in the Jewish state.

My second purpose is to present English translations of Arab folktales in the very style in which they are (or were) told in the original Arabic. Such a literal translation of Arab folktales has been long overdue, since the existing English collections of Arab folktales typically present them in stylistic reworkings from which the English reader cannot derive a true idea of how the story sounds in the original, what narrative devices it utilizes, how it expresses what it intends to say, what kind of cultural atmosphere it reflects, and what conceptual and emotional images it conjures up in the minds of its listeners.

The extent to which a reshaping of style and even of contents is the rule in the available English renderings can best be illustrated by recalling what has been done to the *Thousand and One Nights,* better known as the *Arabian Nights,* the most famous of the classical Arab folktale collections. The unwarranted liberties taken by translators have recently been pointed out by Husain Haddawy, who goes so far as to term the work of these translators "hack versions." Let me reproduce here only one of his examples. Haddawy quotes a passage in Richard Burton's still most popular translation and opposes this to his own literal rendering. I am placing the two versions side by side:

Haddawy

The curtain was unfastened, and a dazzling girl emerged, with charm, wise mien, and features as radiant as the moon. She had an elegant figure, the scent of ambergris, sugared lips, Babylonian eyes, with eyebrows as arched as a pair of bent bows, and a face whose radiance put the shining sun to shame, like a great star soaring in the heavens, or a dome of gold, or an unveiled bride, or a splendid fish swimming in a fountain, or a morsel of luscious fat in a bowl of milk soup.[2]

Burton

Thereupon sat a lady bright of blee, with brow beaming genial brilliancy, the dream of philosophy, whose eyes were fraught with Babel's gramarye, and her eyebrows were arched as for archery; her breath breathed ambergris and perfumery and her lips were sugar to taste and carnelian to see. Her stature was straight as the letter I, and her fame shamed the noon-sun's radiancy; and she was even as a galaxy, or a dome with golden marquetry, or a bride displayed in choicest finery or a noble maid of Araby.

As is evident, Burton practically rewrote this entire passage; deleted such typical Arab similes as "radiant as the moon," "unveiled bride," "splendid fish," and "a morsel of luscious fat"; and added instead several ideas and images that he knew, or imagined, would make a greater impression on his English readers. In any case, it is clear that he did not in the least feel compelled to hew close to the original. His *Arabian Nights,* as Haddawy put it, "is not so much a true translation of *The Nights* as it is a colorful and entertaining concoction." Of course, Burton's rendering does convey some general ideas of what the Arabic original says, but it does little else. How these ideas are articulated in the original, what verbal devices are used by the tale to create interest and tension, how by being succinct and occasionally telegraphic in expression it forces listeners or readers to supply details from their own imaginations—these and many other characteristics of the original Arab art of storytelling are all but lost in the rendering.

Burton's translation was prepared more than a hundred years ago. But the urge to English the Arabic folktale has persisted down to the present. Take, for instance, Inea Bushnaq's handling of the opening lines of the Palestinian Arab folktale she titles "Seven Magic Hairs," of which the original Arabic is available in the Schmidt and Kahle collection of 1918. Again, I put the two versions side by side:

Literal Translation	*Bushnaq*
A sultan had two wives. The first one brought forth a boy, and her co-wife brought forth two boys. The first woman died, the other remained. This one said, "I want to kill the son of my co-wife, and free my sons from him." That one loved horses, and had a colt brought up by the jinns, faster than lightning. On a day of the days he came home, the colt was crying. He said to him, "What have you?" He said, "The wife of your father cooked three geese, two for her sons, and one poisoned for you."	A sultan had two wives. The first had one son, the other two. When the first wife died, the other said to herself, "I must free my sons of my rival's child." It so happened that this boy burned with a love of horses. He had raised a colt from the stables of the Djinn which raced faster than lightning. One day when he came home, what did he find but his favored colt shedding tears like a man. "What is the trouble?" he asked. And the colt said, "Your father's wife has stewed three geese, two for her own sons, and a third, a poisoned one, for you."[3]

It is easy to see that the original is much tighter and more rhythmic than Bushnaq's translation and that it has a more consecutive way of saying what it wants to say. Nor is it encumbered by the embellishments of a romanticizing English style ("burned with a love of horses"; "shedding tears like a man"). Lost in the translation, moreover, is the typical Arab manner of expressing a decision by saying (or thinking), "I want to . . ."

I should add that this is a relatively innocuous example of translators' liberties taken with the Arabic text. Many instances in the work of other translators or anthologists, who deviate much farther from the original, could easily be adduced. One more example will show how a "free" translation can occasionally hide a mental construct that forms an important element in popular thinking. A Palestinian Arab folktale relates the internal conflict going on in the heart of a young man commanded by his father to kill his sister, who was suspected of immoral behavior. The youth tracks down his sister and she, trusting him, falls asleep next to him. This is what happens:

Literal Translation	*Bushnaq*
When she fell asleep, Satan came and said: "O people, shall I slaughter her? O people, shall I let her live?" The Merciful One defeated Satan. He let her live and went away.	When he [the youth] saw her like this, the Compassionate One moved his heart, and he said, "I cannot kill her—I must let her live." [4]

In the original version the youth's contest of conscience is objectified: it is not he who struggles inwardly to decide whether or not to kill his sister, but Satan who appears and ponders whether or not the girl is to live. Allāh overcomes Satan, directing him to let the girl live. Satan departs, and she is saved. This is the typical manner in which the Arab folktale presents the internal struggle taking place within an individual contemplating an evil act: the combat of two outside forces struggling to gain control over his mind. In the foregoing scene, the externalizing of the responsibility for a fateful action serves one additional purpose: it acquits the youth of having disobeyed the command of his father, because it was God's decision that he do so. This shifting of guilt away from the human agent is a device as old as the Bible: when Abraham is about to sacrifice his son Isaac on Mount Moriah, his hand is stayed by an external force, "an angel of the Lord" (Genesis 22: 11–13). All this is lost in the Bushnaq rendering.

What I have tried to do in this book is to present a selection of Palestinian-Israeli Arab folktales translated as faithfully to the original as possible, thus preserving much of the stories' original atmosphere and allowing what the German biblical scholar Hugo Gressman once called Palestine's *Erdgeruch* ("earth-smell") to come through their English garb. I have persisted in this aim even at the cost of occasionally having to use turns of phrase, expressions, and sentence structures that must sound rather unidiomatic in English. I believe the translation of a folktale should be given not as if it had originally been written in the target language but rather as it must have sounded in the mouth of the original storyteller and as the people who listened to it heard it in their own tongue. The many comments and annotations that I have appended to each of the stories seek to elucidate for the Western reader what this telling-and-listening experience must have been. An authentic literal translation such as I have attempted here requires extensive explications of words, turns of phrase, narrative and descriptive details, and allusions that otherwise would remain cryptic in their lapidary concision. The intended listener of these tales would, of course, have instantly grasped every reference. The Western reader is likely to be baffled by many of them. My notes are intended to supply the reader with the necessary linguistic and cultural context for understanding and enjoyment.

3

My third and most important purpose in this volume is to present the Arab folktale as an invaluable source of knowledge of the mental world of traditional Arab culture. This aim requires some elucidation.

I am fully aware that to try to reach conclusions from folktales about the *mentalité* of the society in which they are (or were) current is at best a risky undertaking. After all, the folktale is the creation of popular fantasy, where the imagination is allowed to run wild, or at least to roam freely, unrestrained by the norms of reality, and where whatever is impossible in real life is not only possible but bound to happen. The folktale is populated by animals and even objects that talk; by flying carpets, horses, and camels; by dwarfs, giants, monsters, demons, and ghouls who are cunning and yet foolish, who alternately threaten and help humans. In the folktale, human beings and demons marry each other and procreate; people fall ill or are killed and miraculously recover; poor men find treasures and grow rich, beggars become kings and kings beggars, caves open and close, and we are taken on visits to strange worlds under the ground and beneath the sea. Given these fantastic settings, would it not be reasonable to assume that the folktale moves in realms that bear no relation at all to the actual world of those who tell the tales and those who hear them?

In seeking an answer to this question, we can be helped by considering for a moment that latter-day cousin of the folktale, science fiction, which has, in effect and to a significant extent, replaced the folktale in the modern world and which has a function similar to that still served by the folktale in traditional societies down to our own day. Writers of science fiction depict worlds that are as different from our own actual environs as they can imagine them. Especially when it comes to describing living beings from those other worlds, authors of science fiction aim for the strikingly strange—and yet their inventions are no more than variations on themes well known from this familiar old world of ours. Beginning with the classics of the genre, such as the novels of Jules Verne, H. G. Wells, and Camille Flammarion, and down to the latest masterpieces of the craft, which take us on great voyages aboard the starship *Enterprise* or invite us to join Arthur C. Clarke's *2001: A Space Odyssey,* the situations and creatures we encounter, while appearing to depart from what we know in our own world, actually show a remarkable similarity to it.

In those faraway (or future) worlds, we find machines that look and act like human beings (an idea that goes back to the medieval Golem legend and was most impressively utilized in the 1920s in Fritz Lang's classic film *Metropolis*). We see creatures that resemble humans with occasionally major, but usually minor, differences. Mr. Spock of the planet Vulcan, despite his pointed ears and the force of logic in his thinking, is in most respects like an earthling. The inhabitants of *The Planet of the Apes* are entirely human in behavior and even in appearance, except that their faces combine human and simian features. H. G. Wells's old, and by now venerable, invaders from Mars also have quasi-human bodies, including a susceptibility to disease borne by earthly microbes, as well as very human attitudes and ambitions, such as an imperialistic desire to colonize the planet Earth. Where we have five fingers on our hands, the aliens of Steven Spielberg's movie *Close Encounters of the Third Kind* have only three, if I remember correctly, but hands and fingers, of course, they must have. If they are depicted as superior to us, visitors from remote worlds transmit thoughts directly rather than communicating by speaking, but brains capable of thinking, and some method of interpersonal communication, they, of course, must possess.

What we learn from contemplating the products of science fiction is, in brief, that even the most ingenious writers of the genre, when they set out to imagine worlds other than ours and to invent creatures different from those existing on this planet, inevitably build on what they are familiar with and then transform it somewhat so as to create something new. But they cannot break the constraints of the conceptual framework within which humankind thinks and acts, and in the end they can imagine nothing more than fresh variations on familiar patterns.

There is no reason to assume that the creative limitations under which science fiction labors should not hold for the folktale as well. The inventors, enrichers, transmitters, and reciters of folktales may not have set out purposely, as do science fiction writers, to transcend their own conceptual environment, but—however far afield they let their imaginations run—they willy-nilly have had to work with the building blocks found in the physical, social, and emotional worlds of their surroundings.

Some very simple examples illustrate this point. The familiar folktale about Little Red Riding Hood (Aarne-Thompson Tale Type 333 "The Glutton [Red Riding Hood]") tells of a young girl who goes out to visit her grandmother, is devoured by a wolf posing as the grandmother, but is subsequently rescued alive when the wolf's belly is cut open. At first glance, this is sheer fantasy. Yet several elements are taken from the actual milieu of which the tale was a product or in which it circulated. The tale could not have come into being except in a milieu in which there were forests inhabited by wolves representing a danger to children, in which there were hunters equipped with weapons including knives, in which people wore certain kinds of garb, in which grandmothers did not live in the same houses as their granddaughters, in which a young girl occasionally was sent out, or was allowed to go out, of the house to visit a relative. (This last mentioned feature would, for example, exclude a traditional Arab environment as the place of origin of this story.)

Similarly, the folktale about Snow White and the Seven Dwarfs (Tale Type 709 "Snow White") could have originated and circulated only in a climate in which there was snow and in a society in which people were white-skinned, where there existed princes and princesses and stepmothers and stepdaughters, and with a material culture including such things as mirrors, poisons, and coffins. Such features, taken from reality, constitute the baseline or infrastructure of the folktale, and it is to them that are then added the marvelous details that take it out of the realm of the real and place it in that of the imaginary. The reality is that wolves run in forests and occasionally attack and eat children. The added fantasy element is that this particular child, after having met a talking wolf and having been eaten by him, remains alive in his stomach and emerges from it unscathed. The reality is that if you swallow poison, you die; the fantasy increment is that the princess, after having expired of the poison, comes back to life.

A similar dual process—of building a story upon the real and adding imaginary features to it—is found in those aspects of the folktale that reflect family relationships. If a folktale tells about a stepmother who hates, drives out, or tries to kill her stepdaughter, it is evident that it has originated in a society in which it was customary (or happened frequently) that a man whose wife died would marry a second time, and that the attitude of his second wife to the daughter of the first was one of jealousy, dislike, or even hatred. This is the scaffolding of the folktale, which then embroiders it, exaggerates it, and transfers the action from the real to the imagined. But no tale about stepmothers and stepdaughters could have come from a society in which there were no households consisting of father, stepmother, and stepdaughter. To take one more example, this time one that brings us back to the world represented by the stories in this book, in Arab folktales we often hear about jealousy (or hatred) among co-wives and among the children of co-wives. We are also told about the unhappiness of the unloved wife whose husband shows a preference for her co-wife. As one would expect, tales of this type are found only in a polygynous society. This observation can be generalized: the setting in which events related by the folktale take place inevitably reflects the sociocultural environment of the storytellers and their listeners.

We can go one step further. If folktales reflect their social, cultural, and material milieu, it stands to reason that attitudes, inclinations, values, ambitions, hopes, and fears should also be so reflected, that they should be part of the baseline upon which the folktale builds or, to put it differently, should be inherent in the folktale as elements of its very structure. Take the stories that, beginning with a father who sets out to find a bridegroom for his daughter or a bride for his son, go on to recount the complications resulting from this well-meant paternal undertaking. Evidently, such a scenario could not figure in the folktale repertoire of a society in which it would be unheard of for a father to decide whom his daughter or son should marry. Moreover, it tells us not only of a society in which the father selects spouses for his children but also of one in which the young people find it right and proper that their father should make this important decision for them. The approbation with which the tale treats the father's search for spouses for his children reflects widespread, if not universal, approval of this feature of the social order and testifies to its being upheld as a cultural value.

The worth accorded to human life relative to individual and/or family honor is another case in point. In many Arab folktales, a man kills his wife or daughter or sister because he finds out that she has committed a moral offense, meaning that she has transgressed the extremely strict traditional Muslim-Arab code of female sexual conduct. Again, the folktale's tacit or explicit approval of the taking of life in such cases reflects society's consent to this practice, an acceptance well known from many actual incidents occurring in the tradition-bound parts of the Arab world. But even if such evidence were not available, the folktale material would in itself provide a basis for concluding that in the eyes of those who are the product of traditional Arab culture, the life of a woman guilty of such an offense is forfeit.

4

To repeat: once we peel away the miraculous casings in which the folktale comes wrapped, we find that the events related in it, the actions of its protagonists, and their presuppositions contain significant pointers to the sociocultural patterns of the society in which the tale is at home.

With this linkage in mind, let us now have a look at some of the more significant features of Arab culture as these appear in light of the Arab folktale. Before proceeding, however, an obvious point must be made: the folktales included in this book do not mirror the most recent trends in Arab societies; rather, they reflect conditions as they existed in Arab countries up to a few decades ago and as they continue to exist in the most traditional sectors of the present Arab world.

Bruno Bettelheim in his delightful midrash on the fairy tale has called attention to what he considers one of its most important functions. Fairy tales, he writes, "offer figures onto which the child can externalize what goes on in his mind, in controllable ways. Fairy tales show the child how he can embody his destructive wishes in one figure, gain desired satisfactions from another, identify with a third, have real attachment with a fourth, and so on, as his needs of the moment require."[5] While I am not quite sure whether and how fairy tales accomplish all this, Bettelheim is undoubtedly right in recognizing that figures appearing in fairy tales often work as externalizations and concretizations of strong emotions.

This process of externalization and concretization is pronounced in the Arab folktales. Perhaps its clearest instance is the Arab folktale's presentation of the internal struggle taking place in the breast of the hero before he decides whether or not to commit an evil act. In many an Arab folktale, when the protagonist must choose between good and evil, the story brings on the figure of Satan to carry out the wicked deed or introduces Allāh to intervene in the nick of time to drive away Satan and allow the hero to let his intended victim live. Above I discussed such an incident contained in a Palestinian folktale recorded in 1910–11.

What such scenes tell us is that when a person enculturated in an Arab milieu is tempted to commit an evil act (such as murder), or actually commits such an act, he finds reassurance in projecting the motivations that prompt him to perform the deed. The responsibility for the evil act is removed from the individual who commits it and is deposited instead in a superior outside power. This enables the human agent to feel that he himself was merely an instrument of Satan, who overpowered him, and that he therefore bears as little guilt for the murder as does the sword or the gun that inflicted the mortal wound.

Had Bettelheim been acquainted with folktales of this type, he probably would have said that this shifting to a higher external power of the responsibility for an act one commits even though one knows it to be wrong is a mark of infantile fixation in a prepubertal stage of emotional development. I would not go that far but would rather interpret it as a capacity (or inclination) to escape into the world of traditional religious beliefs and to find relief there from the otherwise too painful recognition of one's own propensity to evil.

While this would seem to make it easier to commit a wicked act, the same thought process can also have an opposite effect. By transforming the inner conflict into a confrontation between Satan and Allāh, the balance is definitely tilted in favor of the good, Allāh being, of course, much more powerful than Satan. If a man does an evil act despite his belief that his doing or not doing it depends on a face-off between Satan and Allāh, he will in effect have denied the superior power of Allāh, and thus his crime of murder becomes something much worse: it turns into the grievous sin of *kufr,* of unbelief.

Another area into which many Arab folktales afford insights is that of family relationships. For those used to viewing the position of the Arab woman within the family in the light of the *Sharīʿa,* the traditional Muslim religious law, one of the most surprising aspects of the folktales is the picture they present of the actual day-to-day interaction of daughter and father, and wife and husband. In most sectors of the Arab world, the *Sharīʿa* as well as the *ʿurf,* the customary law, and even more so the unwritten and uncodified tradition are the basis of women's subordinate status vis-à-vis both father and husband. (However, see tale 22 below, note 2 on the daughter's position among the Bedouin.) According to the code, as long as a woman lives in her father's house, she is subservient to him. He controls her, and, most important, he decides when and whom she marries. Once married, she becomes a subordinate of her husband, who now exercises control over her and, again most importantly, can divorce her not only at will but at whim and upon a moment's notice.

It is against this traditional place of women that Arab feminists have been struggling for decades in the more advanced (in the sense of less tradition-bound) Arab countries. The dozens of books and studies published in recent decades by Arab feminists paint a dismal picture of the oppressed condition of the Arab woman as a foil to their demands for her liberation and the acquisition of rights. Most of these writings (some of which are by men) are available only in Arabic, but two of them, published in English, should be mentioned here: the Moroccan scholar Fatima Mernissi's *Beyond the Veil: Male-Female Dynamics in a Modern Muslim Society*[6] and the Egyptian physician Nawal al-Saadawi's *The Hidden Face of Eve: Women in the Arab World.*[7]

In the light of the folktale, this picture has to be modified. At the very least, we are put on notice that the subordination of the Arab woman in her father's and husband's houses was far from being a universal state. We learn that along with downtrodden daughters and wives there existed women who not only knew their own minds but managed to have their will, and who were decisive actors and factors in the affairs of the family.

As far as the daughter's position in her father's house is concerned, we hear in many tales about girls—daughters not only of kings and emirs but also of merchants and blacksmiths—who refuse to accept the bridegroom selected for them; who, despite their fathers' most strenuous efforts to keep them out of sight of all males, find opportunities to become acquainted with youths; who fall in love with men they chance to meet or only glimpse from a distance; who openly defy their fathers and run away from home.

Two explanations are possible for the frequency of folktales on this subject. One is that they are wish-fulfillment stories, representing what the womenfolk in the Arab world would have liked to happen. If this is the case, the tales testify to a widespread desire among Arab women, long preceding any modern feminist stirrings, for emancipation from traditional patriarchal control and represent this desire as having been actually achieved by their heroines.

The other possible explanation is that the tales reflect the real situation, showing that the position of women in their paternal families was actually at variance with the traditional place upheld as correct by the menfolk in most of the Arab world. If this second explanation is valid, it would mean that even within the traditionally upheld *patria potestas,* many Arab girls have for generations enjoyed considerable freedom and self-determination.

The same picture emerges from Arab folktales that touch on the relationship between spouses. In most Arab folktales in which husband and wife figure, the wife is the dominant partner, the one who takes the initiative, who suggests tasks that the husband subsequently carries out, who is cleverer than he, who tells him what to do and what not to do, who manages him and the house—who leads while the husband follows.

The two explanations are possible, but a moment's reflection will show that the second must be the correct one and that the stories mirror the actual situation, which is often in conflict with official ideology. Were the stories merely wishful thinking, they would have to be the creation of women and would express the women's point of view. This, however, is unlikely. Even though many of the storytellers were and are, in fact, women, classically exemplified by the renowned Shahrazād (formerly usually transliterated Scheherezade), the public role of teller of stories has been predominantly played by male performers who, on Ramaḍan nights and other occasions, disseminated folktales to large audiences in cafés and other gathering places where the listeners were exclusively male. Stories told for generations by male *qaṣṣāṣīn* to male audiences are unlikely to be the medium for the expression of female hopes. They are much more likely to represent the men's mental image of womenfolk in family and society. It would therefore seem reasonable to assume that these folktales, if they do not precisely endorse acts of disobedience, not to say rebelliousness, on the part of wives and daughters, at least reflect men's awareness of women's state of restiveness under male power. If this is the case, a new look at women's status in premodern Arab society is definitely called for.

Of course, none of this means that the position of women in the Arab family was comparable to the place women have achieved in recent decades in the West. There is an ample supply of folktales that mirror the power of the father over the daughter and of the husband over the wife. In fact, some tales tell about the ultimate weapon wielded by a husband against a strong-willed and recalcitrant wife: instant divorce. But even this drastic step is not always the end of the story; in some tales the wife still finds a way of proving herself to be in the right.

The same ambiguity in the power relations between the sexes is reflected in those Arab folktales in which the protagonists are brother and sister. In the stereotypical Arab family, the brother is, next to the father, the guardian of his sister's honor. It is his duty to restore the family's honor by killing his sister should she commit a sexual offense. Arab feminists have bitterly denounced this sex-centered honor complex, which is indeed described explicitly in a number of folktales.

If, in real life, the brother were actually the stronger of the two, one would expect the folktale to feature brothers who protect their sisters, rescue them from danger, and so on. The fact, however, is that Arab folktales give precisely the opposite impression. We hear in them of brothers who fall into trouble and sisters who save them, of brothers who have to be cared for by their sisters, of girls who lead their brothers out of awkward predicaments.[8] Again, these stories complicate our view of the Arab family and suggest a real-life situation in which girls are seen as more resourceful than their male siblings and in which men rely on the womenfolk.

Yet another aspect of family relations illustrated in the folktale is the attitude of children toward parents. That the child should be depicted in the Arab folktale as obedient and respectful is exactly what one would expect; after all, filial love, esteem, and deference are essential features of traditional Arab mores. What one would not anticipate, and what in fact comes as something of a surprise, is that the Arab folktale frequently tells about children who revere (and presumably love) their parents, even though these parents plan, or actually try, to put them to death. As far as I know, this is an unusual feature in the world of the folktale. In other cultures, too, we hear of parents behaving cruelly to their children, of mothers (and more often stepmothers) trying to kill their daughters (stepdaughters).[9] But that the child-victims should nevertheless continue undiminished in their filial devotion is, I believe, exceptional and foreshadows modern perspectives on child psychology.[10] Yet in several Arab folktales this is precisely the case.

One can do no more than guess at the explanation of why this feature should be a constituent element in the Arab folktale. Filial piety, devotion of son to father and of daughter to mother, may be a more powerful factor in the emotional life of young persons brought up in a traditional Arab family than it is in, say, a modern Western family. In the

Middle East, such unshakable loyalty, respect, and love may be a heritage from biblical times, with the dark myth of Abraham's willingness to sacrifice his son Isaac as commanded by God, and the later midrashic embellishment according to which Isaac himself exhorted his father to carry out God's command. Implied in that story is the undiminished filial affection of Isaac despite the traumatic experience of seeing his father about to plunge his knife into him on Mount Moriah. This near-infanticide seemed of such importance to the early Muslim Arabs that they eventually substituted their own ancestor Ishmael for the biblical Isaac as the *dhabīḥ* ("sacrifice"). Indeed, the son willingly offering himself as a sacrifice to be slaughtered by his father has become a powerful symbol of filial love in the entire Arab world. It is quite possible that this myth has left its traces in the Arab consciousness, expressing itself in folktales whose plots turn on the indestructible love of children for their parents, regardless of the parents' behavior.

5

I have already referred, above, to folktales that tell of the relationship between co-wives. Problems between father and daughter, stepmother and stepdaughter, brother and sister, and husband and wife are, of course, common in many folktales from around the world. But tales of clashes between co-wives and the difficulties created by plural marriages are specific to polygynous societies such as still exist in the conservative sectors of Arab countries.

Again, these stories reflect actual situations encountered in families consisting of a husband and two or more wives and their children. Problems of polygyny and concubinage are as old in the Middle East as biblical times. We all know of Abraham, his wife Sarah, and his concubine Hagar, and of Jacob and his two wives and two concubines. In the Arab folktale the typical situation depicted is one in which the husband loves one wife and neglects the other. This, too, is familiar to us from the biblical stories about Jacob, who loves Rachel and ignores Leah. In the Arab folktale sympathy invariably lies with the neglected wife, the favorite wife often being depicted as evil. It is always the second wife whose entry into the family causes the first wife pain and suffering; this fact is reflected in the term designating the former: *ṣarah* in Hebrew and *ḍarrah* in Arabic, both of which words have the primary meaning of "[female] enemy."

The competition between two co-wives is often passed on to their children. Here, too, the folktale sympathizes with the son or the daughter of the neglected wife and depicts the sons and daughters of the favored wife as wicked. Or it presents the son of the neglected wife as clever and talented and her daughter as beautiful, while the children of the favored wife fall short in physical and mental traits. Given these stark differences, it is inevitable that there should be clashes between the two sets of children, to the extent that occasionally the children of the favored wife try to kill their half-siblings. Again, a biblical antecedent exists in the story of Joseph and his ten half-brothers.

It is a well-known fact that in those conservative sectors of the Arab world where polygyny is still practiced, children of the same wife feel much closer to each other than they do to the children of their father's other wives. Occasionally they even form a sort of clique with strong bonds. The most famous modern example of this tendency is found in the royal family of Saudi Arabia. The greater harmony expected to prevail among children of the same father and the same mother is referred to in several Arab folktales, in which a father sets out to find for his seven sons seven brides who are "of the same back and the same belly,"[11] that is, of the same father and the same mother.

When the Arab folktale deals with marriage, it usually does so in a single sentence in which, for example, the mother of the youth tells the girl's father that she wants her son to marry his daughter, the girl's father agrees, and the two young people marry. Or, again in a single sentence, the girl and the youth chance to set eyes on each other, "desire" each other, and marry. Whether the initiative comes from one of the young people themselves or from their parents, there is no passage of time and narrative between the first sight and the accomplished union.

An example is tale 3, recorded in 1910–11 in Bi'r Zayt. In it we hear that the boy's mother went to the sultan, "asked for him the daughter of the sultan. . . . The sultan gave her to her." In the same story the youth informs the *qadi* that he wants to marry a girl who knows her seventh grandfather, whereupon the *qadi* "gave him his own daughter to wife." In a folktale recorded in Israel in 1982 (tale 20), a youth and the king's daughter glimpse each other from a distance: "The king's daughter desired the boy and the boy desired her," and before exchanging as much as a single word both decide that they want to marry. Likewise in another story (24), also recorded in Israel in 1982, a king's son sees a girl, at once falls in love with her, and succeeds in marrying her. This single-sentence progression from first glance, by way of "desiring" or falling in love, to marrying is a characteristic and frequently repeated pattern in the Arab folktale.

One might think that this narrative telescoping of events is nothing more than gross folkloristic exaggeration. But this is not the case. Reports of actual events show that such express procedures were quite typical of the way in which "boy meets girl" led to "boy marries girl" in Arab society, especially in its rural segments. Hilma Granqvist, in her classic *Marriage Conditions in a Palestinian Village,* describes several marriages that took place in the 1920s and 1930s among Palestinian fellahin and that follow this pattern, which she found quite characteristic. Often the exchange of one sentence was sufficient to lead from the idea of a marriage to its accomplishment. As one of her informants reported, "He who comes and says, 'I want to have from you a filly that eats with its hand.' He who is wise understands [and replies], 'Welcome.' "[12] What this laconic description means is that a representative of the young man comes to the father of the girl and indicates in a figurative phrase that he is asking for his daughter, the father understands it and agrees, and therewith the marriage between the two young people is sealed.

In another case reported by Granqvist, as many as three or four sentences were exchanged between the woman representing the boy and the parents of the girl, after which the woman went back and reported to the boy's parents: "The thing is attained. Her father has given her and her mother has given her."[13] In yet another instance, the representatives of the man went to the woman's house and spoke to her in the evening, she agreed, and next morning they went to buy her the wedding outfit.[14]

The same high-speed progression from first meeting to marriage can take place when a youth and a girl happen to meet without an intermediary. Granqvist gives such a case: A Bēt Sāḥūr girl, Ṣabḥa by name, met a coachman, Mahsi, at the market in Bethlehem. "They began to talk to each other. He said to her, 'Come, lay thy hand in my hand and let us go eastwards [beyond Jordan] and leave this country and go!' They left this country."[15] Evidently what happened was that the young people met by chance in the marketplace and started to talk, whereupon the youth suggested that they elope, which they forthwith proceeded to do.

Falling in love at first sight followed by an instant decision to marry can happen even when the suitor is not a fiery youth but an elderly man. As quoted by Granqvist, an oldster in Arṭās (the Palestinian village she studied) admitted, "I saw her at the market selling milk. I desired her for my own old age, and not for my son." [16]

Because in traditional Arab marriage the bridegroom (or rather his father) had to pay a bride price to the father of the bride, marriage had a distinct financial aspect. This occasionally could lead to the replacement of one woman by another, as if marriage were a joining of interchangeable partners. A case in point is reported by Granqvist: ʿAlī Sālem wanted to marry Fatme and gave seventeen pounds as part of the bride price. But her paternal uncle wanted her for one of his own sons, and while ʿAlī Sālem was away in Jerusalem, they celebrated a betrothal feast for her and her paternal cousin. When the enraged ʿAlī Sālem protested, they told him he could have instead of her the bride's mother's sister. "He said, 'No!' They said, 'Then thou wilt lose thy money.' Defeated by the trick, he said, 'I take her.' " [17] Having to choose between losing his prepaid bride money and accepting an older woman, ʿAlī Sālem consented to take the wife he did not want.

Two generations before Granqvist, Ermete Pierotti observed among the Arabs of Palestine that in making arrangement for their children's marriages, "the fathers only look at their own interests; and the children submit to marriage, not with any religious feeling or emotion of the heart, but as a matter of business." [18] Observations such as these convey the impression that the traditional Arab attitude to the selection of a marriage partner was a distinctly practical one, and this is borne out also by the laconic manner in which the Arab folktale refers to marriage.

This, of course, does not mean that love between young people was present only in those relatively rare cases in which boy met girl outside the constraints of parental choice. Generally speaking, however, it can be said that the youngsters whose marriages were arranged by their parents in traditional Arab society were so inexperienced, and to such an extent under the domination of their elders, that to fall in love, or to conceive a preference for one particular young person of the opposite sex over another, was largely beyond their horizon. Practically all the observers who discuss marriage among the Arabs in the early twentieth century are in agreement regarding what happened in the great majority of marriages: the two sets of parents made their decision on the basis of social, economic, familial, and prestige considerations; they informed the boy and girl only at the last moment; and the two youngsters, used to submitting to their parents, did what they were told.[19] Granqvist's own conclusion is that "the consent of the bride and bridegroom is of little consequence."[20]

These conclusions were borne out by a study of the position of women and marriage patterns carried out in the 1970s in a group of adjacent hamlets in Samaria, to the north of the city of Tul Karem, by the Israeli anthropologist Joseph Ginat. He found that the decision about whom a girl would marry was taken in 34 percent of the cases by both her parents, in 32 percent of the cases by her father alone, in 1 percent by her mother alone, in 10 percent (where the the father had died prior to the selection of a marriage partner) by the girl's other relatives (brothers, uncles, guardians), in 18 percent by the girl jointly with her parents, and only in 5 percent by the girl herself.[21] These data give quantitative support to Granqvist's findings. As for young men, the pattern is very similar: in 65 percent of the cases studied, it was the parents who decided the selection of marriage partners for their children of both sexes.[22]

Ginat's study also provides additional data to show that even as late as the 1970s, the practical attitude toward marriage evidenced by the folktale could lead to an interchangeability of brides or bridegrooms. Among the case histories Ginat reports is one in which a youth, Ṣabrī, had premarital intercourse with a girl, Lea, and impregnated her. Lea's father wanted Ṣabrī to marry Lea, but Ṣabrī's uncle explained to him that Ṣabrī was to marry his (the uncle's) daughter and proposed one of Ṣabrī's younger brothers as a substitute. As various difficulties impeded this arrangement, Lea's father despaired of a solution to his daughter's disgrace and killed her by striking her on the head with a hoe while she slept. Such an action was fully in accordance with the consensus in the hamlets regarding a father's right to restore the family honor in this way. The father's "deed was not condemned, most people believing that he had done right."[23]

Substitutions of one brother for another figure in the folktale as well. In story 20 (recorded in Israel in 1982), the bridegroom chosen by an emir's daughter is killed, whereupon the girl says to her father, "The one I wanted died. This is his brother." And "her father made a marriage contract with the brother."

Thus, both the folktale and real-life observations testify to the nonchalance with which the individuality of young people entering marriage has generally been regarded in traditional Arab society. The important matter is the marriage alliance itself, binding two families and establishing a permanent link between them; precisely which boy and which girl represent the two families in these newly forged ties is of secondary importance. Either the groom or the bride can be replaced by an alternate occupying an equivalent position in his or her family.

Granqvist's and Ginat's studies have shown that in the great majority of cases, it is not the young people themselves but their parents, other relatives, or guardians who decide whom they will marry. This, of course, is reflected in the folktale, which presents a girl refusing to accept her father's choice of a suitor as a very rebellious, headstrong, and even unfilial child. Parents strike the bargain; daughters and sons acquiesce. The rather arbitrary nature of the choice, decided by the parents in an apparently offhand manner, renders the transaction somewhat similar to selling or buying a horse ("a filly that eats with its hand").

The transactional character of matchmaking was (or is) most pronounced in those not infrequent cases where, in order to save the ruinous expense of a bride price, the groom's parents give the parents of the bride a daughter of their own to be married to the bride's brother. Such *badal* (substitute or exchange) marriages were once very common in the Palestinian Arab rural population. There was even a pithy formula for initiating it. The two men would say to each other: "Take my sister and give me your sister."[24] Ginat found that from 1967 to 1974, of the marriages that took place in the Samarian hamlets he studied, 17.5 percent were *badal* marriages.[25] The familial—that is, nonindividual—nature of these marriages is attested to by the fact that the two unions remain linked; if one of them breaks up, the other automatically does so, too.[26] Granqvist reports that in Arṭās there were several cases of such *badal* marriages in which not only two but three and even four couples were involved.[27]

All this, however, does not mean that a wedding in traditional Arab society was not an important occasion. In fact, the wedding was the greatest festive event in the lives of individuals and families, involving a sequence of ceremonies and observances that could extend over several months, often obliging both families to incur extravagant expenses and constituting classic examples of conspicuous consumption for the sake of augmenting family prestige in the eyes of the village or the tribe. The pomp and circumstance surrounding the wedding itself are only apparently contradictory to the dispatch with which a marriage was decided upon. The minimizing of emotional involvement and the speediness of the process leading from "boy meets girl" to "boy weds girl" are counterbalanced by a maximizing, as it were, of the wedding itself and by the traditionally prescribed incorporation of the new relationship of the two families into the social structure of the village or tribe. In the West, generations of novelists have focused on the joys and tribulations of courtship, treating what comes later as a negligible consequence. This convention has been characterized by E. M. Forster, in *Aspects of the Novel,* as "the idiotic use of marriage as a finale." [28] By contrast, in the Arab world, what passes between the meeting and the winning is passed over as an unimportant preliminary to the great event of the wedding itself and the ensuing developments within the newly constructed family.

6

One of the most difficult problems facing the interpreter of the Arab folktale concerns the theme of homicide and violent death. As Arab folktales have it, the death penalty is imposed for all kinds of crimes and violations of the prevailing code, and people are killed by human or extrahuman agencies for a great variety of actions that in Western culture would be considered minor infractions. We hear of persons put to death for stealing, for contravening accepted sexual mores, for disregarding curfew regulations, for disobeying instructions issued by an emir, and for offering bad advice to a ruler. The threat of capital punishment hangs over even smaller offenses. And, with apparent approval, the stories relate the executions suffered as a result of jealousy, envy, avarice, as well as lesser shortcomings which, among others, would be judged nothing more than minor character flaws. In the social order depicted by the Arab folktale, then, violent death inflicted by one person upon another is as common an occurrence as traffic deaths are in modern Western society.

Does this aspect of the Arab folktale, too, reflect the real situation? Does, or did, Arab society actually accord lesser value to human life than it is given even in today's violent American society? Or does the Arab folktale in this case bear little relation to reality?

No unequivocal answer can be given to these questions. One thing, however, is clear: in the traditional Arab moral code, some violations are treated much more severely than they are in the Western world. Especially in the sexual realm, a considerable difference exists. If a woman of the traditional sectors of Arab society (e.g., in Saudi Arabia or in Iraq) is caught engaging in unlawful sex (which means all sex outside legal marriage), she is considered to have earned the death penalty, which is administered by members of her paternal family. Men have much more sexual freedom than women; nonetheless, if a man is apprehended in a carnal act with a married woman or with an unmarried girl still under the tutelage of her paternal family, he, too, forfeits his life, and it is considered proper for a member of the woman's family to put him to death. The execution of a Saudi Arabian princess and her lover, portrayed in the film *Death of a Princess,* made this situation well known in the Western world. Many cases like it are known to have happened down to the present time in the conservative sectors of other Arab countries as well.

Equally contrary to the Western sense of justice is the killing of persons in blood revenge, another practice still taking place in tradition-bound sectors of various Arab countries. If a man commits a murder, the relatives of the victim have the right, and in fact are expected, to kill him. If the murderer manages to escape, the victim's menfolk, in their capacity as avengers of blood, are considered justified, indeed are honor-bound, to kill a relative of the murderer in accordance with the age-old adage *Damm buṭlub* [*yaṭlub*] *damm* ("Blood demands blood"). To leave the death of a kinsman unavenged would destroy the honor of his entire family. It may be noted that blood revenge, like many other traditional customs in the Arab world, has its biblical antecedents, except that biblical law permitted the avenger of blood only to kill the murderer himself, not to slay a relative of the murderer.

It should be emphasized that such private executions for a sexual offense or in retaliation for a murder have for several decades been on their way out even in the most tradition-bound parts of the Arab world. But the folktales do not, of course, reflect the most recent developments in Arab customs, nor do they incorporate the latest laws imposed by modern governments in Arab countries. They mirror life as it existed up to a few decades ago. Therefore, it is probable that the casualness with which the folktale handles the killing of persons found guilty of a wide range of offenses, or of persons who have the misfortune of being blood relations of such individuals, is a true image of actual attitudes prevailing up to the recent past.

What has been said about death as punishment for various transgressions holds also for death in general. In the Arab folktale, death is, so to speak, an everyday occurrence. While the protagonist of the folktale does, of course, survive, many of the other actors die, and their deaths are usually reported in a matter-of-fact way, as events of no great consequence, about which nothing could be done, and which have to be accepted by the survivors as part of life. It is likely that this cavalier posture is the reflection of similar views about death held by Muslim Arabs for many centuries. Part of their attitude is anchored in traditional Muslim fatalism: death, like all major events in a person's life, is predetermined, it is *maktūb,* and railing against it is useless. Among the other factors that go into what could be called a "soft" attitude toward death is the firm Muslim belief in the pleasures of Paradise awaiting the pious, also the recognition of the precariousness of existence within a natural and social environment full of hazards and, until very recently at least, the resigned acceptance of human impotence in the face of illness and the consequent high rates of infant and general mortality and low life expectancy. Precisely because the average age reached by people was very low, the rare person who did attain high old age was honored, even venerated, and—in contrast to the prevailing practice in the Western world where everyone tries to appear younger than he or she really is—people liked to exaggerate their age. The ideal balance between doing the best one can toward survival in this world and being prepared for death any and every day is beautifully expressed in the old Arabic proverb: *Taʿmal li-dunyāka kaʾannaka taʿīshū abadā, wa-taʿmal liʾākhiratika kaʾannaka tamūtu ghadā* ("Work for this world of yours as if you were to live forever, and work for the Other World of yours as if you were to die tomorrow").

One more related matter needs to be considered. For many centuries most Arab societies and polities lived under extremely autocratic rule. The caliph, the sultan, and the emir were masters over the life and death of their subjects, who had no recourse against the ruler's verdict. The words put in the mouth of the caliph by the old Arab story, "I see heads here that need cutting," sum up succinctly how people understood the ruler's power over them. Although unlimited indulgence in autocratic rule has long vanished from the Arab political scene, the folktale has preserved its memory and still speaks of emirs and kings whose whims spell the difference between riches and poverty, between happiness and misery, and even between life and death.

However, if the Arab folktale suggests that the death of a close relative caused the survivors less trauma than it would in the West, this does not mean that death is passed over easily or carelessly in actual Arab folk life. True, the folktale shows that just as marriage is not an occasion for major emotional upheaval, neither is bereavement. The same laconic brevity with which the folktale portrays marriage characterizes its references to death. Nevertheless, the passing of a member of the family is the occasion for major and protracted ceremonial observances, paralleling to some extent those of marriage. Thus, while the stories contained in this volume present numerous examples of a brief, matter-of-fact reporting of death followed by an instant transition to the next scene, event, or subject, numerous studies of Arab folk life show that death is invariably accompanied by formalized, often violent mourning rituals, whether performed by female relatives of the deceased or by hired professional female mourners. That these vociferous demonstrations of grief are only partly spontaneous is made evident by the fact that they are confined to the women, while the men behave impassively, walking about with a somber mien but otherwise evincing no sign of their feelings.

Granqvist relates that after the death of Sheikh Sālem Ethman of Arṭās, twenty women came from the neighboring village of al-Khadr to weep and lament over him. "Weeping loudly, they loosed their hair, jumped up and down on the earthen floor, whirled about, slapped their faces, all the while singing their mourning songs. Thus did the twenty stranger women, and Sālem Ethman's mother and his sisters and his wives, and all the women of his flesh and blood." Part of the traditional mourning rite calls for the women to pull and even tear out their hair, beat their breasts alternately with the left and the right hand, blacken their faces and hands with soot, and sometimes even put dust and ashes on their heads. The closest female relatives of the deceased strike their faces and tear at their hair until someone intervenes, catching hold of their hands at the crucial moment to prevent them from injuring themselves. "A woman takes pride in expressing her violent sorrow. And she knows it will be spoken of in the village: 'She beats herself hard.' "[29]

As this description shows, not only marriage but death, too, is a social occasion. It has traditionally mandated patterns of behavior, a complex sequence of rites and rules that must be observed, and an opportunity for the women to display their ability to excel in performing the traditional songs, outcries, movements, dances, whirlings, and self-woundings appropriate to the occasion. Under the influence of these traditionally sanctioned and prescribed performances, whatever sorrow and sense of loss are actually felt are submerged and stripped of their emotional poignancy. That this indeed is the case is eloquently demonstrated by the folktale. Death, like marriage, is faced stoically as a station in human life through which everyone must pass. Moreover, in the conditions of uncontrolled mortality that have characterized traditional Arab life, death is a contingency that may occur at any moment, an event that has to be accepted as an ineluctable part of a precarious human existence.

A final brief comment is needed about the impact of the modern environment on the Arab folktale, which can be felt especially in those Israeli Arab tales that were recorded in the 1980s. These stories, like their predecessors collected many decades earlier, are replete with miraculous features. One still encounters male and female ghouls, jinns, *ʿafrīts,* people living in the depths of the sea, horses and camels that fly, animals that speak, humans who are transformed into animals, magic hairs, caves that open and close at a verbal command and hold fabulous treasures—in other words, the whole panoply of the classical Arab folktale. At the same time, the protagonists of these stories live in the modern world, travel by airplane, study in universities, use modern technical features such as heated wires to blind the monstrous man-eating Arab counterpart of the ancient Greek Polyphemus, communicate by radio, check into hospitals, drive motor vehicles, and so forth. These modern tales find nothing incongruous in relating the adventures of a youth and a girl who fly in a plane from their Arab city headed by an emir to a city in Switzerland, rent a house there, and then encounter in that house a snake who is a ghoul, a whale who is human, and other such beings taken straight from the old Arab wonderworld (see story 20).

In fact, it is the genius of the modern Arab folktale that it can blend smoothly the fabulous and the modern, the fantastic and the realistic, and move its protagonists from one world into the other and back again, without disrupting the unity and natural flow of the narrative and without making self-conscious excuses for evident absurdities. If it had to be demonstrated that Arab storytelling abilities were still alive and well in the Israel of the 1980s, such proof is abundantly available in these folktales which effortlessly span two worlds and, in doing so, create a new world that has never before existed anywhere.[30]

Forest Hills, New York R. P.
February, 1995

Notes

1. Hans Schmidt and Paul Kahle, *Volkserzählungen aus Palästina* (Göttingen: Vandenhoeck und Ruprecht, 1918). For purposes of comparison, see Antti Aarne, *The Types of the Folk-Tale: A Classification and Bibliography,* trans. and enl. by Stith Thompson (New York: Burt Franklin, 1971), referred to hereafter as Aarne-Thompson.
2. Husain Haddawy, trans., *The Arabian Nights: Sinbad and Other Popular Stories* (New York and London: W. W. Norton, 1995), p. xxiii.

3. Inea Bushnaq, *Arab Folktales* (New York: Pantheon Books, 1986), p. 115. The original Arabic text in Schmidt and Kahle, pp. 216–23, given in my literal translation.
4. Bushnaq, p. 364; Schmidt and Kahle, pp. 100–102. My translation. Bushnaq, pp. xxv, 379–83, has a brief review of other sources.
5. Bruno Bettelheim, *The Uses of Enchantment: The Meaning and Importance of Fairy Tales* (New York: Vintage Books, 1989), pp. 65–66.
6. Fatima Mernissi, *Beyond the Veil: Male-Female Dynamics in a Modern Muslim Society* (New York: Schenkman, 1975).
7. Nawal El Saadawi, *The Hidden Face of Eve: Women in the Arab World* (Boston: Beacon Press, 1980).
8. See, e.g., story 23, "The Prince Who Turned into a Deer."
9. See Stith Thompson, *Motif-Index of Folk Literature: A Classification of Narrative Elements in Folktales, Ballads, Myths, Fables, Mediaeval Romances, Exempla, Fabliaux, Jest-Books, and Local Legends,* 6 vols. (Bloomington: Indiana University Press, 1955–58).
10. See, e.g., stories 7, "The Emir's Daughter," and 24, "Pomegranate Seed."
11. See story 26, "Seven Brides for Seven Brothers."
12. Hilma Granqvist, *Marriage Conditions in a Palestinian Village,* vol. 2, Helsingfors, 1935, p. 9. Reprint: New York: AMS Press, 1975.
13. Ibid., vol. 2, pp. 10–11.
14. Ibid., vol. 1, p. 152.
15. Ibid., vol. 1, p. 154.
16. Ibid., vol. 1, p. 48.
17. Ibid., vol. 1, p. 50.
18. Ermete Pierotti, *Customs and Traditions of Palestine Illustrating the Manners of the Ancient Hebrews* (Cambridge: Deighton, Bell, 1864), p. 181; as quoted by Grandqvist, vol. 1, p. 58.
19. See the writings of Leonhard Bauer, Elihu Grant, Antonin Jaussen, Edward Westermarck, and others, as quoted by Granqvist, vol. 1, p. 58.
20. Granqvist, vol. 1, p. 153.
21. Joseph Ginat, *Women in a Muslim Rural Society: Status and Role in Family and Community* (New Brunswick, N.J.: Transaction Books, 1982), p. 171.
22. Ibid.
23. Ibid., pp. 107–10, 179–83.
24. Antonin Jaussen, *Coutumes des Arabes au pays de Moab* (Paris: V. Lecoffre, 1908), p. 50; Granqvist, vol. 1, p. 111; and earlier literature quoted by Granqvist, vol. 1, pp. 117–18.
25. Ginat, pp. 89, 100.
26. Ibid., p. 100; see Granqvist, vol. 1, p. 117.
27. Granqvist, vol. 1, pp. 112–15.

28. E. M. Forster, *Aspects of the Novel* (New York: Harcourt, Brace and World, 1955), p. 38.
29. Hilma Granqvist, *Muslim Death and Burial* (Helsinki-Helsingfors, 1965), pp. 53–54.
30. Although it appeared too late for use in this introduction, mention should be made of Hasan M. El-Shamy, *Folk Traditions of the Arab World: A Guide to Motif Classification,* 2 vols. (Bloomington: Indiana University Press, 1995). Readers may also be interested in Ibrahim Muhawi and Sharif Kanaana, *Speak, Bird, Speak Again: Palestinian Arab Folktales* (Berkeley: University of California Press, 1989).

Part One

1910–11

1
The One-eyed Ghoul

Told by Abū Ibrāhīm, recorded by Hans Schmidt in Bi'r Zayt, 1910–11.

They tell about a Badawī, an urbanite, and a fellah that they got together and went to steal. They saw from a distance a shepherd, they said, "We want to steal an animal for slaughter."

When they came near him they saw that he was one-eyed, and his eye was like a rock-cup.[1] They said, "Better and better!"[2]

They went around him all day long, and he, with the one [eye] of his Noble One,[3] watched, and they could not outwit him. They walked in front of him and went away.

When it became evening, the shepherd led his sheep and went home to a cave. Those came to him. He welcomed them, and spread out a rug for them, and they sat down. He locked the cave behind them. And the kettle was taken off the fire, he began to stir under it[4] thoroughly. When the food was ready, he broke a trough[5]-full of bread into pieces, poured the dish over it, and said to them, "Please!"

They approached and began to eat. When he distributed the meat among them, one got the hand of a man, another his foot. When they saw this meat, they became nauseous, and stopped eating.

The shepherd was a ghoul. He fell over the trough until he licked it clean. After the evening meal he wanted something sweet. He seized the urbanite, slaughtered him, sat down, roasted him and ate, until he was finished with him. The others looked on, with their arms tied to their backs. Then he seized the fellah, he bent back also his neck,[6] sat down, cut it, roasted, and ate.[7]

The Badawī said, "Where do I want to go?"

Since he saw that the door was closed and he could not escape, he went in among the sheep, deep, deep. What did he see if not a woman hanging by the hair of her head from the ceiling of the cave.[8] He said to her, "Who are you?"

She said, "I am a grass-gatherer.[9] I came here in order to drink with those who dwell in the cave. This one-eyed seized us, and he slaughtered my woman companion and cooked her. Me he hung up until he slaughters me [too] and eats me."

They untied one another. He said to her, "What can be done?"[10]

She said, "Look, now after the evening meal he stretches out and begins to snore. Let him sleep, and then drive a burning stick of wood into his healthy eye, blind him!"

He said, "Succor is near, if Allāh wills."

He returned among the sheep, in order to watch him, and his snoring was like a wadi.

Then he went to the fireplace, and put a stick into it. When it caught fire, he took it and thrust it into his healthy eye, and it ran out.[11] That one cried aloud, and groped for him throughout the night, while threatening him. The Badawī was a brother of Shamma.[12] He slaughtered a young[13] animal, and skinned it, and put on the skin with its head and horns, and sat down. When the day came, he [the ghoul] opened the cave, and stood inside the door and called the sheep, and each time a head went out he touched it. That Badawī went by among them. The ghoul touched him but did not recognize him.

When he got out and was outside the door, he cried, "*Ya waw!*"[14] When that one heard the "*Ya waw*" he burst with anger,[15] fell down and died.

The Badawī returned, drove out the sheep, and married the girl who had been hanging by her hair. Then he returned home, peaceful and rich, and may Allāh give that all those who are away should return peaceful and rich.

Comments

This, of course, is but a modern version of the classical story of the cyclops Polyphemus, made famous by Homer (*Odyssey* ix, 105–542), and after him in the satyr play *Cyclops* by Euripides, written around 423 B.C.E. Its best summary can be found in Robert Graves, *The Greek Myths* (Baltimore: Penguin, 1971), vol. 2, 170 b–f. Sailing home from the Trojan War, Odysseus and his men take shelter in the cave of Polyphemus. When the one-eyed giant returns with his flock, he finds them and blocks the entrance with a huge rock. He devours several men until Odysseus gives him wine to drink and then blinds the intoxicated cyclops with a heated staff. When the sheep have to be let out to pasture, Polyphemus removes the rock, seats himself at the entrance, and strokes the backs of the animals to make sure none of the Greeks can escape by sitting on them. But Odysseus and his men tie themselves to the undersides of the sheep and escape.

Since ancient Greek days the story has spread far and wide. See Stith Thompson Motifs K1011 "Eye-remedy," K603 "Escape under ram's belly"; Aarne-Thompson Tale Type 1137 "The Ogre Blinded (Polyphemus)," and literature there. It appears in *The Arabian Nights: Sinbad and Other Popular Stories,* trans. Husain Haddawy (New York: Norton, 1995), pp. 17–25 in the third voyage of Sindbad the Sailor. Among the Arabs of Palestine, the story must have been indigenous for several generations. It was first recorded in 1910–11 by Hans Schmidt in Bi'r Zayt, Palestine; this is the story given here. A later version, recorded by Yoel Perez from the mouth of an Israeli Bedouin woman in 1984, appears below as tale 21.

The Bi'r Zayt version differs from the Homeric one in several significant respects. First of all, there is a difference in the original intentions of the men who enter the cave: Odysseus and his men enter the homestead of Polyphemus simply to rest and to eat; the three Arab protagonists enter the shepherd-ghoul's cave with the express purpose of stealing his animals. Instead of the homogeneous crew of Odysseus, we hear of three different types of Arabs—an urbanite, a fellah, and a Bedouin—and the story makes a point of emphasizing that it is the Bedouin who, by luck and cleverness, manages to survive. Secondly, Polyphemus, as soon as he notices the uninvited visitors in his cave, kills and eats two of them, while the ghoul, in typical Arab fashion, at first receives the three men with great hospitality, spreads a rug for them, and cooks them a meal, even though it turns out to be a dish of human flesh, the flesh of the women the ghoul had captured earlier. Polyphemus eats the humans raw; the ghoul, more delicate, roasts them before he devours them. Odysseus and his men remain free to move about in the cave; the three Arabs are tied up by the ghoul. Odysseus gives wine to Polyphemus to make sure he can blind the giant while in his stupor; in the Bi'r Zayt story, wine does not figure—in the Muslim Arab environment, wine is not available, nor could a Muslim ghoul be expected to drink wine, but he nevertheless falls asleep and snores no less powerfully than Polyphemus.

Entirely new in the Bi'r Zayt story is the appearance of a woman. Since the surviving Bedouin was tied up by the ghoul, he has to be untied by somebody in order to escape. The woman who unties him, and whom he in turn unties, hangs by her hair in the cave; women held in captivity by being hung by their hair figure frequently in the Arab folktale. Also frequent in Arab folktales is the turn of events that now takes place: it is the woman who advises the Bedouin what to do to the ghoul to enable them to escape from his clutches. The instrument of blinding is the same in both versions: a heated stick.

The Bedouin escapes, not by hanging on to the belly of an animal, as does Odysseus, but by slaughtering an animal and dressing in its skin. Not a word is said about how the woman escapes, but we know that she does, for the Bedouin marries her.

Once they manage to escape, both Odysseus and the Bedouin let out a triumphant shout. But the cyclops lives to throw rocks at the departing ship and to ask his father Poseidon's vengeance on Odysseus, while the ghoul, when he finds out that his victims have escaped, bursts with anger and dies. Odysseus continues his wanderings and troubles, while the Bedouin returns home with the sheep of the ghoul, becomes rich, and lives peacefully ever after.

Notes

1. Arabic *muqur,* a cup-shaped hollow in a rock, which is often found next to a well.
2. Meaning "So much the better." They thought that since the shepherd had only one eye, it would be easier for them to steal a sheep from him.
3. Meaning "He to whom the beneficent Allāh had given only one eye."
4. He stirred the bottom of the kettle.
5. The terms used to describe the utensils of the shepherd denote very large vessels (*kettle, trough*), as if to indicate, without saying so explicitly, that the ghoul was of superhuman dimensions.
6. The ghoul bends the neck of the fellah back, as one does with an animal when slaughtering it.
7. The huge amount of food the ghoul eats also shows that he was of gigantic size.
8. For women held in captivity by being hung by their hair, see tale 22.
9. One of the duties of women used to be to collect grass, primarily for making fire or feeding animals.

10. Typical scene in the Arab folktale: when a man and a woman are faced with a problem, the man asks the woman what to do, and she finds a way out of the difficulty.
11. The liquid contained in the single huge eyeball of the ghoul ran out when the Badawī thrust the fiery stick into it.
12. Shamma is a popular hero of the Palestinian Arab folktale.
13. In Arabic, *thinī* ("toothy"). The term designates a young animal whose eye-teeth have appeared, that is, a fully grown animal.
14. "*Ya waw*" is an outcry of triumph, something like "Hurray!"
15. That a ghoul or ghoulah bursts with anger and dies is a recurring motif in Palestinian Arab folktales. One version of the tale about Ḥidaydūn, recorded by Yoel Perez in 1980 from the mouth of Ibrāhīm ʿAlī Ibrāhīm of the ʿArab al-Ḥujayrāt tribe of northern Israel, ends with this scene: Ḥidaydūn tells the ghoulah that he had given her her daughter to eat, whereupon the ghoulah bursts with anger and dies.

2
Allāh's Dispensation

Told by Sh'hāde il-Khūrī, a Christian teacher in Rāmallāh, recorded by Hans Schmidt, 1910–11.

Do you pray for your friend? O my lord, there was neither here nor there,[1] except for an emir. He had—what a blessing!—seven sons, like fresh dates. When he rode out with them on the horses you would say, "Behold, they are his brothers."

The brothers grew up. Their father swore that he would marry them only to seven sisters[2] from one belly and one back[3]—as were his sons. He who wants to marry off his sons goes about and searches for brides for them.[4] He asked for somebody who had seven daughters from one mother and one father. They told him of a poor man of the Arabs among the Arabs.

He filled the saddle-bag of each of them with money. They rode their horses and went to the Gate of Allāh,[5] exalted be He. They traveled five, six days, came to the Arabs who were described to them. They asked for the man, the father of the girls. They said to him, "There he is, in the farthest of the houses."[6]

He took his sons, and they went to the tent.

The Badawī hastened to rise, helped them down, and hammered in the pegs for the horses,[7] and spread for them,[8] and they went in. The emir grasped the tent-pole[9] and said, "I shall not sit down until I have told you my request!"

The host said to him, "Ask, nothing will be denied to you, except the evil."

He said to him, "I am Emir So-and-so, and I want your seven daughters for my seven sons."

He said to him, "You will get them without capital and without interest!"[10]

All of them got up, took their saddle-bags, and threw them before the father of the girls.[11]

That one gathered the Arabs, and they began the festivities, and the fine nights, and fetched the *Khaṭīb*, and he gave them to them,[12] and they pitched a tent for each one of the bridegrooms. And the grooms went in to the brides—may those who wish it attain it, O you Father of beloved ones!—and the people withdrew, and slept.

When the day rose, the people sat and slaughtered for the emir and his children for breakfast, and waited for the bridegrooms. They did not come.

"Now they will come, now they will come out!"

But nobody came.

The world became bright. Their father went to look for them. A slavegirl[13] approached him, crying and sniffling with her nose, and her eyes were like meatballs[14] for much crying. He said to her, "O Protector![15] O girl, what happened?"

She said, "May no evil come upon you! May your head remain in peace concerning your children!"

He entered the tent of his eldest son—he was dead, and his wife was combing his tresses of hair[16] on her knees, and the other one, and the other one, and the other one. All of them were dead, and their brides were crying over them. He, when he saw this sight—help is with Allāh, may Allāh not let any of His creatures see such a thing, neither a friend nor an enemy! may Allāh protect us from the evil of their fire!—he rubbed together his hands,[17] went back, and sat down next to the Sheikh of the Arabs. The Arabs came to express their sympathy.

A day passed, two days, he called his relative[18] and said to him, "O my uncle, [it is] a gift. You gave, and I, there is no advice in my hand for you. What is from Allāh, O how sweet![19] The horses and the money, all is yours. And I, Allāh will recompense me!"

Then he took leave of his relative and rode and went.

"Where shall I go, where shall I turn?" He said, "By Allāh, I shall not go home to my Arabs, they may say about me, 'He went away full, and returned home empty.' I shall roam about and search. If I find somebody whose plight is like my plight, I shall then go home, otherwise I am in no hurry."

He went, let us say to Shām,[20] tied his horse at an inn, and sat down in the coffee-house. He filled the narghile,[21] knocked out the narghile, and spent what he had until his money gave out. He sold his horse and his saddle-bag, and then sold his *ʿiqāl*[22] and exchanged it for a rope. The silk headcloth[23] he exchanged for a rag. What was his condition? One had to lament it.

One day a lady saw him from the window. She sent her slavegirl to him, she called him, he went in. This lady commanded her servant-girl to provide him with everything he needed, with food and drink, with coffee and tobacco, for three days and one third.[24] Then she went down and greeted him, and sat down next to him, and asked him about his root and branch,[25] and about his situation. In brief, he told her from beginning to end.

She said, "I, my affliction is like your affliction, unless it is greater. Listen, I shall tell you about it."

He said, "Be so kind!"

She said, "My father and my uncle did not get children, and had property which the fire could not consume.[26] They went on the pilgrimage. When they arrived they prayed to Him—May He be praised and exalted!—and your Lord is beneficent. When they returned, their wives became pregnant. My uncle got a son, and my father got me. When they cut my umbilical cord, they cut it on the name of my uncle's son.[27] When our folk died, and we grew up, my uncle's son said to me, "O daughter of my uncle, you are for my name, and I am for you. Let us take one another, and let us put together our property."

I said to him, "Good."

He went, called the *Khatīb*. He gave me to him, and he married me, and stayed together with me four months, and he died, and left me pregnant. I became cut off, had nobody but Allāh and that which was in my belly, and all the money and the houses and the property that belonged to my father and my uncle, as His blessing. When I approached the birth I saw one day a sand-diviner.[28] I called him and gave him what was his due, and told him he should see what I was about to bring forth. He spread out the cloth, and strewed sand on it, and began to draw lines, and to make dots, to turn the hand, and to shake the head. I said to him, "What have you seen?" He heaped the sand together, and did again as at the first time. I said to him, "Tell me, what do you see?" He repeated it a third time. I said to him, "If Allāh wills, good?" He said, "This is the third time, and all the three are the same.[29] You will bring forth a son, and he will marry you." I said to him, "Say and change!"[30] He said, "What is fated cannot be changed."

The day came, the day went, and I gave birth, I brought forth a boy.

I took a knife and cut open his belly, wrapped him up, and threw him into the street.[31] There comes a fellah woman, picks him up, and takes care of him, and he became well. When he grew up, he became a brother of Shamma,[32] became famous, and became counted among the select people. His mother said to him, "I want to marry you off, my son, I want to ask for Lady So-and-so, she is abandoned and rich."

He said, "Good."

She asked for me. In brief, she took me in marriage.

Four months passed over us. One day, while I bathed him,[33] the apron fell off his body: behold, he was sewn up. I said to him, "Who are you?"

He said, "They call me the son of the fellah woman."

I said, "O your origin! You are my son!"

He said, "How is that?"

I told him, "The story is thus and thus and thus."

He went to his mother, asked her, and she told him about the event.

He came to me, and since he knew that I was his mother, and that he had married me, he took a knife and killed himself.[34] And I remained without father, and without uncle, and without husband, and without child. And now we are here, I and you, in equal affliction."

The *Badawī*[35] said, "Since this story is your story, I shall return to my country."

He came to his Arabs, approached the tent, and called the mistress of the house. His wife was in it. He said, "Open!"

She said, "Who are you?"

He said, "A guest."

She said, "The guest goes to the house of the Sheikh. What do you want here?"

He said, "Are you not the house of the Sheikh?"[36]

She said, "O the enmities![37] The Sheikh and the children are gone. O my uncle, don't remind me of the events!"

He went to the guest-tent of the Sheikh. It was full of guests. He entered, greeted, and sat down, covering his mouth and full of shame over his experiences, in fear, lest anybody recognize him. The Sheikh commanded, and they gave him coffee to drink. When he uncovered his mouth the Sheikh recognized him, that he was the father of the seven sons. He arose, kissed him on the head, greeted him and said, "This blessed hour! These are the children of your children who died on the night of their wedding, and you are their grandfather."[38]

He married them off to seven sisters from one belly and one back,[39] and all their properties and their herds remained in their possession, and he remained a Sheikh and the great one of his Arabs. And hail to him who waits for the dispensation of Allāh, praised and exalted be He!

Comments

This folktale combines two stories of woe: that of the emir who loses his seven sons on a single day and that of the woman who unwittingly marries her own son. Especially interesting is the second story, because the Oedipus motif of unwitting mother-son incest is unusual in Arab folklore. The closest parallel I could find is in the modern Egyptian story "The Falcon's Daughter," in which the sultan's son returns from Hijāz and his mother pretends to be his wife, sleeps with him, and becomes pregnant by him. That story ends with the son pouring gasoline over his mother and burning her. See Richard M. Dorson, *Folktales Told Around the World* (Chicago: University of Chicago Press, 1975), p. 161. On the Oedipus story in folk literature in general, see Tale Type 931 "Oedipus" and Motif T412 "mother-son incest." For comparative studies see Lowell Edmunds, *Oedipus: The Ancient Legend and Its Later Analogues* (Baltimore: Johns Hopkins University Press, 1985), pp. 69–79, and Lowell Edmunds and Alan Dundes, eds., *Oedipus: A Folklore Casebook* (New York: Garland, 1983).

Notes

1. "There was neither here nor there" is a stereotypical beginning of the Arab folktale.
2. A father's decision to marry his seven sons to seven sisters, or even his forty sons to forty sisters, occurs elsewhere, too, in Arab folktales. See the modern Israeli Arab folktale "Seven Brides for Seven Brothers," tale 26 below.
3. "From one belly and one back" means from the same mother and the same father. To specify the same mother is important in traditional Arab society where a man can have children by several co-wives.
4. An aside comment, to explain that setting out in search of brides conforms to the Arab custom.
5. See tale 4, "The Price of the Bride," note 5.
6. *House* in Bedouin context can mean either a house of masonry or a tent.
7. The host hammers pegs into the ground to tie the guests' horses to them.

8. Namely, the mats on which to sit.
9. A Bedouin gesture, underlining the importance and urgency of the guest's request.
10. That is, without paying any bride price for them. A polite exaggeration, not meant seriously. Even merchants used to pretend, as the opening statement in a bargaining exchange, that they offered the merchandise as a gift to the customer.
11. Another customary gesture. They throw their saddle-bags full of money before the father of the girls to indicate that they consider the amount they pay as the bride price to be of negligible value.
12. The formalities of the wedding are performed by the *Khaṭīb,* the religious functionary.
13. *ʿAbda* (literally "slavegirl") always means a Negro female slave.
14. Arabic *kubaybāt* ("meatballs"). That is, her eyes were as big as meatballs.
15. An epithet of Allāh.
16. Young Bedouin men used to wear long tresses of hair hanging down on both sides of their heads. The bride combs the tresses of her dead husband in preparation for the young man's funeral.
17. A gesture of helplessness or despair.
18. The father of the seven girls.
19. Imprecise expression of this thought: *You gave me your daughters, but I, since my sons died, have nothing to give to you.* The words "What is from Allāh, O how sweet!" are difficult to understand, unless they are intended to indicate a total submission to the will of Allāh, and the acceptance of his decree as if it were "sweet."
20. The exact place where the emir went is not important for the storyteller. He mentions Shām (Damascus) as an example of a city to which the emir may have gone.
21. The Arabic text has *ghalyūn,* a synonym of *nārajīla* ("narghile"). Once one finishes smoking (or, as the Arabic has it, "drinking") the narghile, one knocks it out, so as to remove the tobacco ashes from its top.
22. *ʿIqāl* is the crownlike headband, made of camel's hair, that holds the headcloth in place. Well-to-do people have *ʿiqāl*s into which gold and silver threads are woven, and they can be very costly.
23. In the Arabic, *al-ḥarīr* (literally "the silk"), but meaning a luxurious silk *kūfīya,* the square headcloth folded diagonally and worn under the *ʿiqāl.*
24. The traditional time period of hospitality, during which the host is not supposed to address any inquiries to his guest.
25. Figurative expression for origin and family.
26. Meaning a very large amount of property.
27. It was a traditional Arab custom for a father "to cut the umbilical cord" of

his newborn daughter "on the name of So-and-so," meaning to promise her in marriage to somebody (usually her paternal cousin) at the very time of her birth.

28. A "sand diviner" (Arabic *rammāl*) is a soothsayer who tells the future by observing and interpreting dots and lines in sand spread out before him. Among the Palestinian Arabs, these diviners used to be mostly from the Maghreb (Morocco, Algeria), or they were Negroes. The diviner makes four lines of dots in the sand. If the number of dots happens to be uneven in a line, he obtains from it a dot; if even, a dash. A group of four dots or dashes is called a *bayt* ("house"). In this manner he gets four houses. By calculations he derives another twelve houses from these first four. The last house is the most important, but each of the sixteen has its special relevance for the life of the person for whom the divination is being performed. In addition, each of the sixteen possible combinations of dots and dashes has its special meaning. Thus, a clever *rammāl* can interpret the sixteen houses in an infinite number of ways. See Hans Schmidt and Paul Kahle, *Volkserzählungen aus Palästina* (Göttingen: Vandenhoeck und Ruprecht, 1918), p. 176, n. 13.
29. If the divination yields the same answer three times in a row, it must be true. Similarly, if one sees the same dream three times, it is believed to come true unfailingly.
30. Meaning "Say it again, and change your interpretation! I cannot believe what you are saying!"
31. Believing that the horrible augury would come true, the mother decides to kill her newborn son. The motif, including the survival of the son, is familiar from the Oedipus story.
32. Shamma is a mythical hero to whom reference is occasionally made in Palestinian Arab folklore.
33. The loving wife serves her husband by washing him in the bath.
34. Oedipus only blinds himself, but in the more violent Palestinian Arab folktale, the son, who unwittingly becomes involved in an incestuous relationship with his own mother, kills himself.
35. From this point on, the hero of the story is no longer identified as an emir but as a simple *Badawī,* a Bedouin, whose tribe, to which he now returns, is headed by another person, a sheikh.
36. After the hero left his tribe, and the tragedy of the death of his seven sons became known, he was no longer considered head of his tribe.
37. That is, "O enmities of fate!"
38. The story motif of the man who loses his sons and then receives divine compensation by new children being born to him is as old as the book of Job (see Job 42: 13). In our story it is grandchildren who replace the seven dead sons. Since these grandsons are of marriageable age when the hero returns to

his tribe, his wanderings must have taken fifteen to twenty years. However, in typical folktale fashion, the passing of years is ignored.

39. The hero of the story considers his seven grandsons a replacement for his seven dead sons, and hence again insists that they marry seven sisters from the same father and the same mother.

3
The Jinn's Gratitude

Storyteller unknown, recorded by Hans Schmidt in Bi'r Zayt, 1910–11.

There was here an old man. He had a son. When it came for him to die, he commissioned his son and said to him, "Revive your property with property."

He said, "O father, how shall I do it?"

He said, "Either marry one who knows her seventh grandfather, or buy for yourself a piece of land which brings in its price in one year through its fruit." [1]

And he died.

That one [the son] sent his mother, she asked for him the daughter of the sultan. Say,[2] the sultan gave her to her. He said to her, "Do you know your grandfather and the grandfather of your grandfather until the seventh grandfather?"

She said, "I know nobody beside my father."

Thereupon he drove her away, and asked another one, and drove her away because she did not know her seventh grandfather. In this manner he took five, six women, and drove all of them away.

The relatives of the girls complained about him, and notified the *qāḍī* of his affair. The *qāḍī* called him. When he learned of his affair, he gave him his own daughter to wife. A few days after the wedding the *qāḍī* robbed the house of his daughter, and left him neither provisions nor furniture.[3] Thereupon that one [the youth] moved away from the town, until he came—let us say—to Achcha [Acre].[4]

His wife said to him, "What *dirhams*[5] do you have?"

He said, "Three *bishliks.*" [6]

She said to him, "Buy for us two loaves of bread for a *bishlik,* and a *raṭl*[7] of wool for two *bishliks.*

He did as she told him. She spun the wool and wove of it three belts. Next day she sold each belt for three *bishliks,* bought wool, wove belts, and sold them, until she had nine *qirshes.*[8]

One day merchants went to Shām.[9] They said they wanted to have a camel driver. They hired this one, and went. On the way they came to a well. They lowered him, so that he should give them to drink.[10] The *raṣad*[11] said to him, "What brought you from the land of the humans to the land of the jinn?"[12]

He said, "By Allāh, O my lord,[13] I am a stranger and ignorant."

The *raṣad* said, "Where are you going?"

He said, "To the land of Shām."

He said to him, "Will you bring me a basket of dates with you?"

He said, "Upon my head and my eye,[14] O my lord!"

The *raṣad* gave him three pomegranates, and went away.

That one [the man], when he came up from the well, met people who were going home.[15] He knew them, and said to one of them, "By Allāh, give these pomegranates to my wife!"

He took them, and when he arrived in the country, he gave them into her hands. She opened the first fruit, and behold, it was full of pearls. And the second and its sister were like it. She went to a person, entered into sisterly ties with him,[16] and gave him one pearl, so that he should ask about its price and sell it. He gave her more than twenty *liras.*[17] She sold all the pearls, and put the *liras* in the trunk,[18] line by line, and continued to work as was her wont.

After several weeks her husband returned from Shām. He passed by the well and gave the basket of dates to the jinns who were in the well. And they gave him in exchange a basket full of pomegranates. And he went home. When his wife saw the pomegranates, she took them and sold the pearls that were in them. And when the trunk became full of *dirhams* up to its lid, she said to him, "O, son of man, go to the mountain which faces the palace of the sultan, and build for me a palace exactly like his, and make around it fruit gardens and pleasure gardens. Here are the *dirhams.*"[19]

He did as his wife told him.

And when they built the house and the walls,[20] she said to him, "Go down and bring me rice and eggplant and seven, eight sheep and fat. I want to prepare a repast and invite my father and the whole retinue of the seraglio."[21]

When she prepared everything, she sent to invite the pasha and his people and all of them, and did not leave out even one. They came to her house, found the meal prepared and ate. Her father the sultan[22] said, "All my life I have never eaten a better meal since the day my daughter went away."

She said to him, "I am your daughter! You took away what I needed, in order to make me poor. But Allāh made me rich. And praised be He who makes rich and poor. Behold, all men are but beggars at the door of the Beneficent!"

Comments

This story was told by a storyteller of limited ability. Of the two pieces of advice the youth's father gives him on his deathbed, the second plays no role at all in the story, while the first—"marry one who knows her seventh grandfather"—is forgotten in the course of the narrative. The intention of this advice clearly was that the son should marry only a girl whose descent was known back seven generations. The son follows his father's advice, but in a rather peculiar way: he first marries the sultan's daughter and five or six other women in turn and then finds out that they don't know who their seventh grandfathers were, whereupon he "drives all of them away." After all this, we are not told whether the daughter of the *qāḍī* (pasha, sultan), who is the youth's seventh or eighth wife, knows her seventh grandfather. It seems that at this point the storyteller has forgotten this element of his story. The heroine's father is termed first *qāḍī,* then pasha, and finally sultan. Early in the story the *qāḍī* robs the house of his own daughter—a completely unmotivated act—but toward the end of the story he is a sultan who has a sumptuous palace, in which, nevertheless, his daughter used to cook for him.

Likewise inconsistent is the presentation of the wife's role in the marriage. In the beginning of the story, the wife (the *qāḍī*'s daughter) is the practical, efficient half of the couple: she tells her husband what to do and what to buy, spins the wool and weaves three belts, then sells the belts and thus obtains some money. All this is in keeping with the stereotype of the efficient wife and the inefficient husband often figuring in the Arab folktale. After telling that the wife sold the three belts she wove for three *bishliks* each and went on weaving belts and selling them until she had nine *qirshes,* we would expect the story to relate what she did with the money thus obtained. However, nothing more is said about the wife, and instead we hear that the husband goes to work for a caravan of merchants as a camel driver, encounters by pure chance some benevolent demons, who live in a well they are unable to leave, and gets from them pomegranates full of precious pearls. Only after she gets the pearls does the wife again come into the picture. She sells them, hoards the money she gets in her trunk, and instructs her husband to use it for building a palace precisely like that of her father and, to boot, on a mountain facing his palace. By the very next sentence the palace has been built, with fruit gardens and pleasure gardens around it and surrounded by a wall, whereupon the wife invites her father and his retinue. The father does not recognize her, but when he tastes her cooking, it reminds him of the cooking of his daughter. She makes herself known to him and closes the story with a reference to the power of Allāh, who makes people rich or poor—an idea that up to this point has not been broached by the story.

The intermingling of realistic and fantastic elements found in this story is characteristic of many Arab folktales. The realistic situation of poverty in which the married couple lives ends with the fantasy of the husband obtaining precious pearls from demons in exchange for a basketful of dates he brings them from Damascus. Why the demons cannot get out of the well is yet another of the fantastic features that remain unexplained in the story. Likewise unexplained are the relationship between the father and his daughter, both before and after he robs her of all her provisions and furniture, and the motivation of the daughter in going to all the trouble of cooking a meal for a large company of guests only to tell them of the power of Allāh to make men either rich or poor.

Notes

1. "The land which brings in its price in one year" is completely forgotten in the sequel of the story.
2. "Say" indicates the storyteller's awareness that it is unlikely that the sultan would give his daughter to the young man.
3. There is no motivation or explanation in the story for the *qāḍī*'s act in robbing the house of his newly married daughter.
4. The storyteller mentions Acre (ʿAkka in Arabic, which he pronounced *Achcha*) as an example of the kind of town to which the youth came.
5. *Dirhams* are drachmas, but here used in the sense of money in general.
6. *Bishlik* is a small coin.
7. A *raṭl* is a weight unit corresponding to about three kilograms.

8. A *qirsh* is a monetary unit, also called piaster; it is one hundredth of a *lira,* or pound.
9. Shām is the popular Arabic name of Damascus.
10. A folktale feature, at variance with the reality. To draw water from a well, people would lower a bucket, but in the folktale the hero had to go down into the well in order to encounter there the jinn.
11. A *raṣad* is a demon guarding hidden treasures. He dwells in wells or springs issuing from caves and has the shape of an animal or a human being. The *raṣad* of this tale seems to be unable to leave the well.
12. The underground realm of wells, cisterns, and caves is the world of the jinn.
13. The hero is afraid of the *raṣad* and addresses him respectfully as "my lord."
14. Meaning, "I swear upon my head and my eye."
15. That is, to the hometown of the hero.
16. This is an oft-encountered feature in Arab folktales. A young girl enters into a compact with a youth to the effect that he will regard her as his sister and protect her and will make no sexual advances.
17. See above, note 8.
18. The fellah woman kept her property—clothes, jewelry, money she earned, etc.—in a trunk of her own. She carried its key, and her husband had no knowledge of what it contained.
19. As in many Arab folktales, so here, too, it is the wife who takes the initiative to improve her husband's and her own situation. The husband follows the wife's instructions.
20. "Walls" (Arabic *duwar*) refers to the walls surrounding the courtyard and the gardens.
21. "Seraglio" (Arabic *sarāya,* also *sarāy*) actually means palace.
22. In the beginning of the story the girl's father was a *qāḍī.* Here he has become a sultan. This inconsistency, and several other features in the story, indicate that the storyteller was not a true master of his craft.

4
The Price of the Bride

Told by Sh'hāde il-Khūrī, a Christian teacher in Rāmallāh, recorded by Hans Schmidt, 1910–11.

There were two emirs, brothers, they had no children. They requested Allāh, and Allāh—praised be He and extolled—looked at them.[1] Their wives became pregnant. One brought forth a boy, and one brought a girl.

The father of the girl gave his daughter to the son of his brother,[2] when she should grow up. When they grew up the father of the boy died. After the death of his father the boy made a name among the Arabs. They knew him everywhere, and the name of his uncle was extinguished. This one, when he saw that the fame of the son of his brother flew about among the Arabs, felt hurt and slighted.

When the boy reached the age of youth he asked for the daughter of his uncle. But his uncle did not want to give her to him. He [the youth] sent intermediaries to him, but of no avail. Finally they said to the emir [the uncle], "The proverb says, 'If you don't want to marry off your daughter make her bride price high.' "

The youth again went to his uncle and asked for the girl. He said to him, "If you want my daughter, I shall give her to you on condition that you bring me the head of the emir Ibn is-Sʿūd[3]—that was a famous emir—and the horse of Ibn Ḥamdān[4]—another emir."

The youth told his mother of the demand of his uncle. She prepared for him provisions for the road. He mounted his horse, and went to the Gate of Allāh.[5]

He traveled five, six days. He arrived at the Arabs of Ibn is-Sʿūd, at the tent of the emir. He received him. He entered, and the tent glittered and sparkled with much gold and silver. The youth was amazed by the riches. As soon as he sat down, and the sun wanted to set,[6] the tent became full of guests. They fed their horses, and slaughtered the animals of slaughter, they cooked and poured out,[7] and the herald called and said, "The food, O you hungry!" The crowd pushed to the guest-tent of the emir. The people ate and were sated.

And this one [the youth] did not touch the food. They pressed him that he should eat, but he touched nothing, because he wanted to kill the emir, and had he tasted of the food, he could not have deceived him.[8]

After the evening meal the singer sat and beat the *rabāb.*[9] The people entertained each other, until the night took and gave.[10] Then they slept.

When the night reached the middle, this one [the youth] got up, slipped into the tent of the emir to kill him. He drew the sword, and stood over his head. Something said to him, "Strike!"[11] and something pulled at his hand and said to him, "You want to kill the emir who fed all these people for the sake of a girl who pisses [in her bed]?"[12] The Compassionate vanquished Satan. He slipped out, and went to sleep.

On the second night he did as on the first night, and went to sleep. Finally he said, "Go, get the horse of Ibn Ḥamdān.[13] If I bring it, I shall kill this one here, and if I don't bring it, then may Allāh smooth him the way!"[14] He took leave of the emir, and went off.

In a few days he reached the Arabs of Ibn Ḥamdān. He had a mare which had no sister.[15] He had made her a special tent, and the sister of Ibn Ḥamdān—her name was Ḥamde—stayed all the time in that tent, she slept next to the mare. When the youth came to the Arabs of Ibn Ḥamdān, he went after midnight to the tent of the emir's sister. The mare was tied by all fours, and a golden half-moon was hanging from her neck, and a star between her eyes.[16] He tried to untie her, all night long, but could not loosen the tether.[17] Toward morning he went and slept. In the second night he could not untie her either. He uncovered the face of the girl; she was—praise be to him who created her![18] He again went out and lay down to sleep.

On the fourth day he took his leave, as if he wanted to go his way. But he hid in a valley, near a brook.

The emir had a slave,[19] appointed over his house, by the name of Saʿīd. He loved Ḥamde, the sister of the emir, and wanted to have her. But he did not dare to talk to her about it. He said to his wife, "O, daughter of man![20] I want you to bring me Ḥamde so that I have my will on her, and if not, I shall kill you."[21]

The soul is dear.[22] She said to him, "Good. Where shall I bring her for you?"

He said to her, "Bring her tonight, to the valley, in the moonlight, to the water."

She went to Ḥamde, when no foot stirred any more, and said to her, "*Yallah* (let's go), O my mistress, let us go to take a bath in the moonlight in the valley."

She said to her, "In all my life I never went out at this time, and if my brother finds out, he will kill me."

She said to her, "Who could see us in this night?" And she pressed her.

She went with her to the valley, to the place where her husband was hiding. When they got there, Ḥamde took off her clothes, and wanted to enter the water. The wife of Saʿīd went off to a distance from her, as if she wanted to relieve nature. At that moment Saʿīd approached her, and threw himself on her, and she offered resistance. The woman, whoever she be, remains a short rib.[23] He overpowered her, and was about to take her, when she cried out, "Where is the noble man who protects my honor? He will get from me whatever he wants!"

That youth was hiding near her, and Saʿīd knew nothing about him. When he heard her crying for help, he drew his sword, rushed to Saʿīd, struck him with the sword, and cut off his head.

When Ḥamde saw him, she got dressed, and said to him, "You, Allāh sent you to protect my honor. Ask and wish!"

He told her about his intention.[24] She said to him, "Come, so that I give you the mare, then go in peace!"

She untied the tethers of the mare, put the saddle on her, gave him the reins in his hand, and said to him, "Be careful with the mare. For more than twenty days nobody has sat on her back. Be careful that she does not throw you!"

He said to her, "Don't worry about it!"

He mounted the horse, and said, "Earth, be smooth before me!"[25]

The mare raced the winds. For the duration of an hour he galloped ahead.

He reached a pit called the Well of Doves. A dove flew out of it, the mare got frightened and threw him into the pit. The noble mare knows her house, so she ran home. When Ḥamde saw her, she said, "Ah, he fell!" She mounted the mare and rode off. When she reached the Well of Doves, she called him. He answered her from the well. She tied up the mare, and let down a rope for him in order to pull him up. She brought him up. When he was at the edge of the pit, he grabbed her foot and wanted to swing himself up. She slipped, and fell down together with him. "What shall we do? What can be done?" [26]

After a while the son of her uncle, who was engaged to her, passed by there. When he saw the mare alone, he wondered. He went to the well, and asked, "Who is there?"

She said, "I, Ḥamde."

He said to her, "With whom were you talking?"

She said, "With nobody. It was the echo of my voice that you heard."

"What has brought you here?"

She said to him, "The mare threw me."

When he lowered the rope for her, she said to the son of the emir, "Take my clothes and put them on,[27] and go up before me, for if he finds you he will kill you." [28]

He put on her things. When the other pulled him up and he got out, he cut off his head, before he could notice him. Then he pulled up the girl, seated her behind him, and rode home to his Arabs. But he did not take the way that passed by Ibn is-Sʿūd in order to kill him, and said in his heart, "The daughter of my uncle will not be better than this one, why should I kill that generous man?"

Thus he reached home with the girl and the mare, and let nobody notice anything.

Let us return to the Emir Ibn Ḥamdān. When the day rose, the Arabs came to drink coffee, and they whispered among them. The emir said, "What is it?"

They said, "Masʿūd[29] was killed in the valley."

Shortly thereafter people came and said, "Ḥamde, the sister of the emir, and the mare cannot be found."

Shortly thereafter shepherds came and said, "The son of the emir's brother has been killed at the Well of Doves."

When the emir heard this he rose in order to see. The news was true. Instantly he let five hundred riders mount behind his son.[30] They went to search for Ḥamde. They came to the Emir Ibn is-Sʿūd, and asked him about the girl. He said, "Nobody knows about her."

He went on to ask, from Arabs to Arabs, until he reached the house of that emir. He asked about the girl. He said, "The girl is here with me, and the situation with her is this and this."

Then he sent for his father, and they gave her to him in marriage, and gave him also the daughter of his uncle.[31]

I have told my story, and placed it into your bosom.

Comments

All miraculous elements are absent from this story, which paints a quasi-realistic picture of Bedouin life and mentality. Each and every element in it is taken from actual life. The engagement at birth of the son of a man to the daughter of his brother, the jealousy of the brother over the greater reputation achieved by his nephew, and his consequent unwillingness to give his daughter to him—all these are features well attested from traditional Bedouin life. Likewise realistic is what the emir then does. He cannot openly refuse to honor the pledge he gave to his deceased brother, so, on the advice of people who quote him a proverb, he demands a bride price from his nephew, which he thinks the latter will be unable or unwilling to provide: the head of a famous emir and the famous horse of another emir.

Realistic, too, is the behavior of the youth. He is willing to kill the Emir Ibn is-Sʿud and, of course, to steal the other emir's horse. But there are traditional restraints in Bedouin behavior which the youth cannot ignore. He cannot kill a man of whose hospitality he has partaken, so he eats nothing in the emir's tent. But when it comes to carrying out the deed, the youth has compunctions. His internal struggle is externalized and objectified—Satan urges him to kill the emir, but Allāh vanquishes Satan, and the youth goes away without committing the killing.

The events that take place in the camp of the other emir all reflect traditional nomadic Arab conditions. He values his prize mare so highly that he has his sister, Ḥamde, sleep in the tent in which the horse is kept. The youth sneaks into the tent but has trouble in untying the horse. In the meantime, he sees the sleeping Ḥamde, and his reaction to her beauty is indicated by the pious outcry, "Praise be to him who created her!"

Ḥamde is desired by the emir's black slave (a recurrent motif since the frame story of the *Arabian Nights*), who forces his wife, by threatening her life, to arrange for the girl to go out of the camp at nighttime to a bathing place, where he can have his way with her. The youth happens to be there and saves the girl's honor by cutting off the slave's head. In gratitude, the girl gives him the mare, and he rides off happily on her back. However, the spirited animal gets frightened, throws the youth into a well, and then, on its own, trots back home to its mistress.

The girl guesses what has happened and rides back on the mare to the well. When she is about to pull the youth out of the well, he grabs her ankle, and both of them fall back into the well. At that crucial moment, the son of her father's brother, to whom the girl was engaged, comes riding by. Before he pulls the girl up, she has the youth put on her clothes, because she fears that if her cousin finds that he was in the well with her, he will kill him. Once the cousin pulls up the youth, who he thinks is the girl, the youth cuts off his head. This is the second killing, but the story passes over it in a single sentence, as it did in reporting the killing of the slave.

Now, of course, the youth and the girl cannot return to her camp, and instead he rides back with her to his own people. The end of the story is that the youth marries Ḥamde and also gets his cousin, to whom he was engaged since birth.

The laconic, casual references to killing a person are paralleled in the story by the likewise laconic and casual references to the changes in the identity of the persons whom the boy and the girl marry or are supposed to marry. The boy is engaged to his cousin, and in order to get her, he is ready to kill a famous emir, but when he sets eyes on Ḥamde he is willing to give up his fiancée and take her instead. Ḥamde is engaged to her cousin, but when the youth kills him, she is willing to take him instead and rides with him to his camp. Ultimately, the youth marries both Ḥamde and his cousin. On what the two girls feel when they find themselves as co-wives, the story wastes not a word.

Under the mask of fiction the story presents a slice of traditional Arab life, values, and attitudes. The engagement of cousins at birth, the uncle's jealousy of his nephew, his hesitancy to go back openly on his given word, the low valuation of human life, the high valuation of honor and of a prize mare, the ease with which one intended marriage partner is substituted for the other—all these are features that have informed traditional Bedouin life, and the story is built on them.

Notes

1. That is, Allāh fulfilled their request.
2. A frequently observed custom was for the father of a newborn girl to promise her to a boy, preferably to her paternal cousin. The promise would be made

at the moment the umbilical cord of the girl was cut; hence the saying, "He cut her umbilical cord on the name of So-and-so."

3. Ibn is-Sʿūd is the popular pronunciation of the name Ibn al-Saʿūd. The reference is either to ʿAbd al-ʿAzīz ibn Muḥammad ibn Saʿūd, ruler of the town al-Dirʿiyya in Arabia, who in the late eighteenth century made Wahhabism the dominant religion in the Najd and withstood several expeditions by the Ismāʿīlī Nakramids of Najrān, or else to his son, Saʿūd ibn ʿAbd al-ʿAzīz, who by the early nineteenth century had brought virtually the whole of the Arabian Peninsula under the authority of al-Dirʿiyya. The luxury with which Saʿūd ibn ʿAbd al-ʿAzīz surrounded himself, the thousands of Arab horses he owned, the largesse he dispensed to his subjects and guests, his hearing of petitions, and so on, have been vividly described by an eyewitness (Ibn Bishr) and became a part of the Arab folklore of the Syrian Desert.
4. The Banī Ḥamdān, a large Arab tribe of the Yamanī moiety, dominated a large territory of the north of Yemen. See R. Patai, *Society, Culture and Change in the Middle East* (Philadelphia: University of Pennsylvania Press, 1971), pp. 189–90, 199–200.
5. That is, asked for Allāh's help. A pious reference to setting out on a voyage.
6. "Wanted to" in Arab phraseology means "was about to" or "decided to."
7. "Poured out" means dished out. Since the food is cooked in a sauce, it is poured out from the pot into the dishes.
8. The traditional mores make it impossible to kill a person of whose food one has partaken.
9. A "singer" (Arabic *shāʿir* [poet]) is the Arab equivalent of the bard. He entertains his audience by singing *qaṣīdas* and other poems and accompanies himself on the *rabāb,* the one-stringed Arab violin. The plucking of the *rabāb* is termed in Arabic "beating."
10. That is, until a major part of the night had passed.
11. As in several Arab folktales, so here, too, the decision of whether or not to commit an evil deed is ascribed to powers outside the person himself. Two lines later we learn that it was Satan who tried to persuade the youth to kill the emir, and the Compassionate One, Allāh, vanquished Satan and kept the youth from committing the crime.
12. Here the cousin of the youth is referred to as if she were still an infant wetting her bed. The storyteller forgot that the girl was of the same age as the youth.
13. The youth, in his thoughts, addresses himself in second person.
14. Again the same approach as the one discussed in note 11. The youth lets an external event decide whether or not he will kill Ibn is-Sʿūd. "May Allāh smooth him the way" means "Let him live without worry."
15. That is, had no equal.
16. The half-moon and the star are for protection against the evil eye. People

who cannot afford such amulets of precious metal hang blue glass beads on their animals which are vulnerable to the evil eye.

17. "Tether" (Arabic *qēd,* in literary form *qayd*) means fetter, shackle, chain.
18. Typical, modest, indirect reference to the reaction a man has when seeing an exceedingly beautiful woman. Instead of saying, or even hinting, that she was beautiful, the story says that the youth uttered a praise to Allāh for having created such beauty.
19. The Arabic term, *ʿabd,* usually denotes a Negro slave.
20. A popular colloquial manner of addressing one's wife.
21. A situation of this kind—a man forces his own wife to help him violate another woman—could be imagined only in a polygynous society, such as the traditional Arab environment.
22. Meaning "life is dear." The wife of the slave holds her life too dear to sacrifice it by resisting the demand of her husband.
23. A philosophical observation: women are weak.
24. The youth is still so obsessed with his search that he disregards the enticing offer of the girl—even though he was struck by her beauty—and asks her to help him get the mare.
25. A horseman's wish, poetically expressed.
26. The motif of the hero and/or heroine falling into a pit and being unable to get out of it without outside help occurs frequently in the Arab folktale. Its basis in reality is the fact that in many places there are large cisterns, used for collecting rainwater, so that the possibility of falling into one is actually present.
27. Change of clothing whereby a man appears to be a woman or vice versa is yet another frequently encountered motif in Arab folklore.
28. Ḥamde's warning that her cousin is out to kill the youth serves as the reason (or excuse) for the youth to kill the cousin.
29. Until now he was called Saʿīd.
30. That is, a party of five hundred riders led by his son.
31. The hero's reward in the polygynous Arab society: he marries both girls.

5
The Virtuous Maiden

Recorded by Hans Schmidt in Bi'r Zayt, 1910–11.

There was a rich *Khawāja.*[1] It came to his mind to make the pilgrimage.[2] His wife said to him, "I too want to make the pilgrimage with you. With another than you it is not possible for me."

[He said, "Good."]

His son said, "I, O father, want to serve you, take me along!"

He said, "Good."

His daughter said, "And I?"

He said to her, "My daughter, you are delicate, and the road of pilgrimage is hard."

In brief, he did not let her go. He said to her, "My child, whatever you need for livelihood is with you. And meat, some lemons, a head of radish—the *Khaṭīb*[3] will bring you. I have recommended you into his care."

He went, he, and his son, and his wife.

But the *Khaṭīb* forgot to serve the girl. One day, when he went out to call for the midday prayer,[4] he looked at the house of the merchant and saw the girl as she was busy with her hair, and it was black like the night, and her arm shone like a sword.[5] He remembered her, he began to stammer, shortened the prayer call, rushed down, and went to her. He stood in the courtyard of the house, and called her. She answered him, but did not let him see her.

He said to her, "Let down a basket with the money, so that I can bring you what you need."

She lowered the basket on a rope, but did not let him see her. He took the money with the basket, shopped in the market for her, and returned. He called her, she lowered the rope, and pulled up the basket. He thought he would get to see her, but he did not see her. He went away, stayed away two or three days, came again and said to her, "What do you want, my daughter?" She told him what she wanted, and lowered the basket on the rope as at the first time. When he did not succeed in seeing her, he became angry. He went to a shrewd old woman, and said to her, "This and this is the matter, and how shall I tackle it?"

She said to him, "That's all? I myself shall take you to her."

She set out and went to the girl, knocked at the door, and said to her, "My daughter, no decent woman is without money. I too have bracelets of metal and glass, and many jewels, and since I would like to go on pilgrimage, I want to give the things to you for safekeeping. When I return, I shall fetch them; if I don't return, you can keep them for yourself."

She said, "Good."

She [the old woman] went to a carpenter and ordered from him a chest, as long and as wide as a man, with the lock on the inside. When she had it ready, she took it to her house, called the *Khaṭīb,* put him in the box, and he locked it from the inside over himself. Then she loaded it on a porter, and took it to the house of the *Sheikh* [i.e., the merchant]. There she knocked at the girl's. She opened, and let her in. She placed it in the room in which the girl slept, gave it into her care, and went away with the porter. And she [the girl] locked the door after them.

Then she ate the evening meal, and sat down to recite the Koran and to pray for her people. When midnight came, and there was nobody who could have paid attention, the chest suddenly began to rattle. He [the *Khaṭīb*] turned the key in the lock, creaking, lifted the lid, and sat up. The girl knew what was proper.[6] She said to him, "Welcome, I have for long been waiting for you, but you didn't come to me, even though my father placed me in your care. Be welcome a hundred times!"

Therewith she kissed his hand, stood up—O Owner of peace![7]—and made him, slowly and carefully, a cup of coffee. Then she sat down, to converse with him. But he was like one who sits on fire, and could not wait. Finally it was time to go to sleep. He said to her, "Spread out[8] so that we sleep!"

She refused. He said to her, "Nobody knows about us, and as soon as your father comes I shall request you from him."[9]

But she said, "We don't want to go to sleep until we play [chess], and become sated with it. But if I defeat you, I shall tie you up."[10]

They played, and she defeated him. Instantly she took a rope, like the one there on the wall,[11] and tied him from top to bottom. Then she brought a head of radish, and stuck it into his behind up to the leaves. Then she threw him out the window into the street.

He was bruised badly, and cursed her father.

He lay there tied up, and his tarbush rolled away from him. He feared that somebody could see him. Just then one came by with a load, one who traveled early in the morning, in order to get ahead and make exchanges.[12] He passed by him and said, "Who is this?"

He said, "It is your master the *Khaṭīb.*"

He said, "What is wrong with you?"

He said, "This fate overcame me. Cut me loose."

He untied him, and he went home. The *Khaṭīb* sat moaning at the door of [his] house. His wife said to him, "What hurts you?"

He said to her, "I kept night vigil, and fell into a pit. Come quick, rub my back with oil." She did it.

Next day a messenger came to the city and said that the pilgrims had arrived in Jaffa. That buffoon[13] [the *Khaṭīb*] wrote a letter to the Sheikh, and said in it, "Your daughter So-and-so turns your house into a factory.[14] One comes, the other goes."

He sent the letter with the grape sellers.[15] When her father read the letter, he became black like the pest. He said to his son, "Go to your sister, don't let her rejoice when she sees you, nor utter the trills of joy! Take her with you, and slaughter her, and bring me this [bottle] here filled with [her] blood!"

The son arrived late in the evening, and knocked at the door. She asked, "Who is there?"

He said, "Your brother."

She wanted to utter the trills of joy. He cut her off and said, "Be quiet!"

And when he entered he said to her, "*Yallah* [let's go], we want to receive my father!"

She got up, dressed, and followed him. He preceded her, deep into the copse. When she became tired she said to him, "I want to rest, O my brother!"

They sat down under a tree, and she put her head upon his knee and fell asleep. When she was asleep Satan came and said [to himself], "O people, shall I slaughter her? O people, shall I let her live?"

The Merciful [God] defeated Satan. He let her live and went away.

He [the brother] found a dog, slaughtered it and filled the bottle with its blood. He went to his father and gave it to him. And after a few days they came home.

Let us return the talk to the girl. The cold nipped her. She woke up and called her brother. But there was no word and no reply. She got up and went on and on. Behold, a spring, and above it a tree, like the one you saw yesterday.[16] She climbed up and sat down. That night raiders[17] passed by. When they approached to water their horses, the animals got frightened of her mirror image.[18] The emir of the raiders looked up. There she sat cowering. He said, "Are you a human or a jinn?"[19]

She said, "A human, as good as anyone!"

He said to her, "Come down! The protection of Allāh is over you!"[20]

She climbed down. He approached her and unveiled her face. There she was—praise be to her Creator![21]

He said to his companions: "Go and raid! As for me, this is my booty!"

Then he got on his horse and returned with her to his Arabs. But he spoke no improper word to her. When he arrived, he gave orders to his slaves. They set up a separate tent for her alone. And he gave her a slavegirl to serve her, and to give her to eat nothing but sheep's brain.[22] She stayed there about a month, and nobody was allowed to approach the tent in which she was in order to glance into it.

She sent her slavegirl and called the emir. He went to her. She said to him, "Why did you bring me here? Allāh commanded about getting married and taking in marriage. And you, only your honor keeps you from speaking to me about it. I want to get married."

He called his three sons who were already young men, and said to her, "Choose one of them, whomever you wish."

She said, "You are my preference."[23]

He married her according to the manner of the Arabs, and took her to wife according to the law of Allāh and His messenger. And she brought[24] three boys.

One day he came home from the hunt. She heard from afar the rattling of his stirrups and got up to go to receive him. But at first she wiped her tears. Then she went and held the reins of his horse. When he saw her tears he swore that he would not get off the horse until he knew the reason of her crying. She said to him, "Nobody came near me.[25] But my relatives came to my mind, and I had to cry."

He said to her, "Do you have parents? Whose daughter are you? And from where are you?"[26]

She told him about her situation. He instantly entered, and loaded everything that was light of weight and heavy of value on three camels, and seated her on a noble camel and set out for her relatives. Barely were they outside the village when a group of Arabs encountered them. They asked him, "Where to?"

He said, "I want to visit my parents-in-law."

They said, "We are standing here before your face, O emir, [and beg you] to turn aside from the road and reconcile us with each other." [27]

They begged him very much. He commissioned his uncle, entrusted him with his wife and children, and went with the Arabs. His uncle drove the camels and continued on the way.

When he was at some distance he said to the camelmen, "Drive on and go ahead to the place—let us say Lydda[28]—to the relatives of the woman!"

He himself turned aside from the road in the vicinity of a spring, and made the camel kneel down. And they sat down. Satan started to play in his head. He implored violently the virtuous woman, but she—there was no way for him. He said to her, "I shall slaughter your children!"

She answered him, "I am a woman who receives and gives in return; the children are your children!" [29]

He instantly killed the oldest upon her bosom, his brother upon her knee, and also the third one with them. After he slaughtered them he said to her, "Now comes your turn."

She said to him, "There is no escape from the decision of Allāh. But I am unclean." [30]

He said to her, "Take his jar, and wash yourself."

She wanted to go. He tied her arm to a rope.

When she moved away, she took off her bracelets, tied them to the rope, and tied the rope to a tree, and fled. He pulled at the rope time and again, in short intervals. The bracelets clanked, and he said, "She is still washing."

But when she stayed away long, he went there in order to check on her. She had escaped. Now, where could he search for her in the night? He arose, mounted the camel, fetched his companions, the camelmen, and went to her relatives.

That one [the woman] fled to the seashore. There a soldier was taking a bath. When he saw her he lost his mind over her, and addressed her in a foreign tongue, "*Pre orat! pre orat!*" [31] and he stuttered. She said to him, "Hush! I am yours. Where could I flee from your hand?"

He wanted to get dressed. But she said, "Wait! If somebody should see me now with you, he would kill you and take me. Give me your clothes, so that I put them on. You put on my clothes, and seat me on the horse, and *Yallah* [let's go]!"

He gave her his clothes, put on her clothes, and seated her on the horse, and they set out. When they were near Lydda, she beat the horse, and escaped. The soldier hit one hand against the other,[32] called upon Allāh's help, and went on toward Lydda.

The woman arrived in Lydda, tied the horse in the khān,[33] sat down in the coffee-house like a youth, and began to give away coffee. After a while a cake-seller passed by. She bought cake for them, and also distributed free food, one day, two, three. The bakers complained to the basha.[34]

One evening they said, "Sheikh So-and-so wants to marry off his son."

They said to the bridegroom, "Invite this foreign youth who gives away free food and drink." He went to him [i.e., her], and invited the youth. She went with him, to wit, to the house of her father.

When her father saw her, he said, "O youth, from where are you?"

He said, "I am a stranger, and my story is long. I am afraid that if I start telling it, one of you will go away."

They locked the door and gave him the key.

She let her eyes roam, and saw her father, her brother, the *Khaṭīb,* her husband, and her uncle. Then she told her story from beginning to end, and said, "See, here is my husband, by Allāh, let him overcome you [if you lie]! How did you find me when you took me to wife?"

He said, "A virgin."

When her father saw that this was how things were, he said, "He who loves me,[35] let him bring a little fire and a load of wood!"

The people quickly gathered the wood as high as the house, put the *Khaṭīb* and the uncle on it, and burned them. And everyone went home to his house.

The bird flew away. May you have a good evening!

Comments

The background of this story, like that of many Arab folktales, is the world of Arab sex mores. As in other Mediterranean cultures, the women are segregated to the extent that an unmarried girl is not supposed to go out of her house alone, and therefore it is necessary that a man should take care of her and bring her food. In traditional Muslim Arab society, it used to be the man of the house, not the woman, who went out daily to the market to shop for food.

A virtuous woman does not even let herself be seen by a man who is not her father, brother, or husband. On the other hand, the mere accidental sight of a woman's hair and arm (as happens in this story) is sufficient to create in a man an irresistible impulse to possess her, whether in or out of marriage. If a woman is confronted by a man, and the two are alone, she knows that he has only one thing in mind, and the only way for her to escape being violated is to use her brains and outwit the man. The wrath of the man thus rebuffed by a woman is limitless; he will do anything to avenge himself, including accusing her of immorality which would result in her being killed by her father or brothers—this being the only way to restore the family honor damaged by the woman's behavior.

Again, as in many Arab folktales, in a confrontation between a man and a woman, it is the woman who proves to be superior. She always finds a ruse to escape the man's attempts to violate her. She resorts to all kinds of tricks, which ultimately not only exonerate her but bring about the brutal man's downfall, usually his death.

Another feature of the tale is the traditional image of the noble, chivalrous Bedouin chieftain. In this story, the Bedouin emir, whose habitual occupation is to lead his people on raids (raiding is a morally impeccable, even desirable, activity), is the epitome of chivalry. He finds the girl hiding in a tree, takes her under his protection, does not say an untoward word to her, sets her up in a separate tent, does not even ask about her "story," and waits until she indicates that she wishes to marry him. Years later, when he finds that she yearns to see her parents, he immediately packs up and goes with her on a long journey.

A third feature is the moral duty of the chieftain to mediate in a disagreement between tribesmen not even related to him. This duty has precedence over the emir's consideration for his wife, and he goes with the tribesmen who appeal to him, leaving his wife and three sons in the care of his uncle.

This uncle turns out to be an even more evil character than was the *Khaṭīb*. In fact, he is a base murderer. In order to force the woman to submit to him, he kills her three sons as they vainly cling to her for protection. But even an evil monster like the uncle is subject to the commands of the traditional sex mores, which make it impossible for a man to have sex with a woman who suffers from menstrual impurity. Claiming to be impure, the woman manages to escape from the uncle. The incident on the seashore with the soldier is a repetition of the preceding two incidents; with her cleverness, the woman succeeds again in escaping humiliation.

The scene in the coffee-house is based on the high valuation accorded in traditional Arab mores to generosity, especially as expressed in lavishly providing food even to people whom the hero (or heroine) had not known up to that point. Her conspicuously generous behavior secures the girl (disguised as a young man) an invitation to the wedding feast arranged by her father.

The closing scene, the death penalty by burning suffered by both the *Khaṭīb* and the uncle, is a reflection of the seriousness with which seduction, even attempted and unsuccessful seduction, of a virtuous woman is considered in traditional Arab society. Even though the uncle killed the three sons of the woman, he is sentenced to death, or so it seems, not because of that crime but because of his attempted rape of the woman, for which the *Khaṭīb* also must suffer the death penalty.

Yet another characteristic feature is the objectification of the emotional struggle the brother undergoes in trying to decide whether or not to kill his sister, who trustingly sleeps with her head on his knee. In the story, it is not the brother who struggles with himself but Satan, and the brother's decision to let his sister live (and to give a bottle of dog's blood to their father instead of his sister's blood) is represented as Allāh's victory over Satan. Also, the uncle's desire to violate his nephew's wife is presented as having been planted in his head by Satan. Likewise, when the soldier wants to rape her, it is because "he lost his mind." In this manner evil acts are excused, or at least explained, as being the results of Satanic influences in the face of which man is powerless.

Notes

1. *Khawāja* is used in the sense of *Mr., Sir,* or the German *Herr.* Among the Palestinian fellahin, it had the connotation of urban merchant.
2. To perform the pilgrimage to Mecca once in a lifetime is one of the five "Pillars of Faith" in Islam.
3. *Khaṭīb* actually means a preacher, he who preaches the *khuṭba,* the sermon, in the mosque during the Friday morning prayers. Here it is used in the sense

of *mu'adhdhin* (*muezzin*), the prayer caller who calls the faithful to prayer from the *manāra*, the tower attached to many mosques.

4. The midday prayer is the third of the five obligatory daily prayers in Islam.
5. The sight of the girl's hair and arm was enough to arouse the *Khaṭīb*'s passion for her.
6. Although the girl evidently knew what was the intention of the *Khaṭīb* in having himself smuggled into her house, she behaved properly and tried to divert him by polite manners.
7. The inserted exclamation presents the reaction of the *Khaṭīb* when he sees the full stature of the girl standing up in front of him.
8. That is, spread out the mattresses. The storyteller has in mind the simple habitation of the fellahin, who spread out the mattresses rolled up for the day, to serve as beds for the night in the same room in which they take their meals.
9. The *Khaṭīb* tries to reassure the girl that as soon as her father returns, he will ask him for her hand.
10. To enter into a game of competition with the provision that the winner ties up the loser is a frequently recurring motif in Arab folktales.
11. The storyteller points to a rope hanging on the wall.
12. Much of the buying and selling by the Palestinian fellahin was done in the form of barter.
13. The storyteller expresses contempt for the *Khaṭīb* by calling him "buffoon" (in Arabic *sʿīd innaṣbe*).
14. In the Arabic *kirkhāne;* in literary Arabic *karakhāna* ("workshop," "factory"). In the Egyptian colloquial used with the meaning of "brothel." Here probably used as a euphemism for "whorehouse."
15. The grape sellers used to go regularly from the Bi'r Zayt area to Jaffa to sell their produce there.
16. The storyteller refers to a tree one of the listeners saw the day before.
17. In the Arabic *ghazzāye,* a group of riders taking part in a *ghazw* ("raid"). To undertake raids for the purpose of robbing another tribe of its animals was considered an honorable act and an opportunity for demonstrating bravery.
18. The girl's reflection in the water.
19. A frequently uttered question when encountering a person unexpectedly, especially in an unusual situation.
20. By pronouncing these words, the speaker guarantees the safety of the person he addresses.
21. "Praise be to her Creator!" expresses the reaction of the emir of the *ghazw* upon seeing the girl's beauty.
22. Sheep's brain represents the choicest food.
23. Literally, "You are for me the first of what there is." The girl's preference for the mature man over youths shows her fine character. See Ruth 3: 10.

24. In the popular idiom a woman does not "bear" children but "brings" (*jābat*) them.
25. The woman first of all reassures the emir that nobody has violated her in his absence.
26. The fact that up to that point the emir had not asked about the family and origin of the girl is intended to show his refinement.
27. If a tribe is involved in a blood feud or other dispute, the arbitration of a respected outsider is required to reconcile the opponents.
28. The storyteller, in an aside, mentions the name of a city known to the listeners, as an example of a place that could have been the destination of the riders.
29. Meaning that a woman is merely a vessel receiving the man's seed and returning to him the child. The child itself belongs to the father and, by extension, to his patrilineal male relatives, such as his paternal uncle.
30. See the similar scene in tale 7.
31. Actually *Bre avret,* Turkish for "Stop, woman!" The words show that the soldier was a Turk.
32. To clap the hands together is a gesture of despair.
33. In Arabic, *ash-sha*ʿʿ*ara* ("inn," "caravansary").
34. The bakers complain because the foreign youth buys from the itinerant peddlers and thus hurts their business.
35. Formulaic address by a ruler to his people, meaning something like "he who is loyal to me."

6
The Banished Prince

Recorded by Hans Schmidt in Bi'r Zayt, 1910–11.

There was a king. And when he was in a sweet sleep an angel called him and said, "When your wife reaches the age of seventy years she will become pregnant and bring[1] a son. And call him David, and he will become an opponent to you."

He called him once, and repeated the call three times, and said, "This is truth, not a dream!"[2]

When she completed seventy years she became pregnant, gave birth, brought a boy. He called him David. Then he said to her, "I have eaten my share of you, and you have eaten your share of me.[3] Get up, take your son. And here is a hundred and fifty *liras,* and may Allāh smooth [your road] for you."

She went with him to another house, a year, two years, three. When the boy grew, she said to him, "*Yallah* [up] to Jaffa, we should work!" (The *dirhams*[4] were finished.) And they remained there a year or a year and a half. And [then] they returned to the place. Then they arose and went to Beirut. And the boy's age was seventeen years.

In the vicinity of Beirut the evening descended on him. He was in a garden, and in it were all kinds of fruit. He said to her, "O mother, come, let us stay overnight in this garden." They turned aside [into the garden].

Behold, there was a palace in the middle of the garden. The boy looked into the room. Behold, there was a set table. And nobody was there. And on it were forty[5] plates, and on each plate was rice and on it meat. He entered through the window, ate a little from each plate, and a little of each meat, as much as a raisin. And he passed a plate to his mother. They ate and hid in a tree in the garden. He hid his mother in the tree, and returned to lie in wait at the door of the palace.

One came down to set the table. Behold, they were forty robbers of the jinn.[6] He entered, looked around, and noticed that the table had been touched. He went, let their eldest know.

The boy saw a camel's thighbone, took it and stood at the door of the palace. The table-waiter came. And as soon as he [the boy] saw him he cut off his head,[7] killed him, and threw him out of the palace. And the second and the third. Only one of the forty remained. The last one came down. The son of the king hit him. His neck remained hanging on a tendon. He thought he was dead, and remained in the palace with his mother.

His mother had the water of life[8] with her. She touched the robber, put some of the water of life on his wound. He recovered, loved her, threw himself on her, and had relations with her.[9] Each time her son came back from the hunt, she hid him in the sheepfold.

In time her son saw that she was pregnant. He saddled his horse as was his wont. When he went away she said to that one [the robber], "My son noticed it on me. What shall I do?"

He said to her, "When he asks you, 'What is the matter, O my mother?' say to him, 'I don't feel well, and the physician came and prescribed for me this-and-that medicine.' "

That one [the son] came back from the open. He said, "How are you, O mother?"

She said, "By Allāh, the physician came and said to me, 'You have no medicine except to eat of the ram of Shams eḍ-Ḍuḥā.' "[10]

He said, "Where is it?"

She said, "With the Arabs of the east, as you would say, beyond Karak."

And she thought that before he would get there he would be killed.[11]

He said, "Prepare for me provisions."

Then he mounted his horse, and hung his rifle on his shoulder, and went.

Wherever he saw Arabs he asked about Shams eḍ-Ḍuḥā. She was the daughter of the emir, very rich, very proud, and lived alone in the desert, lonely. She made a vow that she would marry only one who would come to her.[12]

Each time he asked about her, they said, "Before you!"[13] Until he reached her. Then he saw a black slave,[14] and said to him, "To whom belong these sheep?"

He said, "To Shams eḍ-Ḍuḥā."

Thereupon he went among the sheep, and seized the ram of Shams eḍ-Ḍuḥā.

When the slave saw him, he took off his headkerchief, tied it to his staff, and waved it about.

Shams eḍ-Ḍuḥā saw it and said, "The shepherd has been attacked!" And she said, "Where are the horsemen? Quick, catch for me whomever you find, and bring him!"

They went there, caught him, and said to him, "May Allāh's safety be upon you![15] Come to Shams eḍ-Ḍuḥā!"

He went there, entered, and received coffee.

She said to him, "Your mother sent you.[16] She wants to get rid of you. She is pregnant from a dwarf who is with her. When she sends you next time to the garden of the virgins, pass by here at my place!"

He stayed there overnight. Next day she gave him the ram, and he departed. He came to his mother, slaughtered the sheep, and gave it to his mother to eat. She said, "I am well, Allāh be thanked!"

After two, three days she said to the robber, "How shall I do it?"[17]

He said, "Ask him for the apple from the garden of virgins. Before he gets there he will be killed."

Good. On the third day she began to complain and said to her son, "The physician was here and prescribed for me apples from the garden of the virgins."

He said, "I shall bring them."[18]

She prepared provisions for him, and he departed. He came to Shams eḍ-Ḍuḥā, and stayed overnight with her.

Then she said to him, "The guards of the garden of virgins are a camel and a tiger. The straw is before the tiger, and the meat before the camel. Put the straw before the camel, and the meat before the tiger. Then each will be busy with his food."[19]

He went and did as she had told him. He went into the garden, filled the saddle-bag with apples, and went out, and returned the same evening. He went to Shams eḍ-Ḍuḥā. She said to him, "Take a kerchief-full to your mother, and leave the rest with me." Then she said to him, "See, I shall take nobody else but you.[20] This time your mother will ask you for the water of life. Don't answer her."

He took the apples, said farewell, and returned home to his mother. She began to complain. He gave her out of the bundle. She ate and said, "I have recovered."

On the third day she again pretended to be sick. He said, "What do you want, O my mother?"

She said, "The physician said, 'You must have the water of life.' "

He said, "Where is it?"

She said, "I don't know."

Then she prepared provisions for him, and he rode off.

He came to Shams eḍ-Ḍuḥā, and asked her about the water of life.

She said, "Behind the garden of the virgins, one day's travel, between two mountains. He who goes down, the two mountains snap closed over him.[21] Nobody who went down has ever come up again in his lifetime. But you draw [water] from above."

He reached the place. There was a tree, and a bird hovered over its top. He drew his sword and approached the tree. There was a snake there. It wanted to eat the chicks of the bird. It drew near him. He struck at it and killed it. Then he tied a bottle around the neck of the bird. It flew there, filled the bottle, and flew up again. While it flew, the two mountains snapped closed, and plucked its tail and wings. He took the bottle and went back to Shams eḍ-Ḍuḥā. She did not let him take all the water of life. She retained a small bottle of it. He stayed overnight, and in the morning he set out, and she gave him a dog to protect him.

He came to his mother. She greeted him. But it was not according to her wishes to see him safe and sound. She rubbed her body with the water, and pretended to be well. But Shams eḍ-Ḍuḥā had commanded him not to play cards (with his mother), or, if she should win, not to let his arms be tied by her,[22] except when he was sitting on his horse.

When her son rode off, the robber came out, and she said, "What now?"

He said to her, "Play a game of cards with him, with the condition that you can tie his arms, so that I can cut off his head for you."

When he came home she said to him, "My little son, come, we want to play a game of cards!"

He said, "Good."

She said, "With the condition, that he who loses, his arms will be tied."

They played, and she defeated him.

She said, "Play with me a second game!"

She defeated him.

But he jumped on his horse. She tied his arms while he was on the back of the horse. He set spurs to the horse, and rode off. The robber also mounted a horse and rode after him. The dog which was with the youth jumped in the way of the robber's horse, so that he should not overtake him. He went through a plain which was full of *durrēs* [thorny shrubs]. The robber overtook him, dealt him a blow, but it hit him only a little. Then the robber returned. He [the youth] went to Shams eḍ-Ḍuḥā. She put some of the water of life on the wound, and he was healed. He swore that he would kill his mother and her customer.[23]

He returned, bought a donkey, and transformed himself into a peddler. The wife of the robber[24] called him. He entered, and she bought [something] from him. It became evening.

He said, "I want to sleep in this and that village."

She said to him, "Stay here overnight! The safety of Allāh is over you!"

Good. He remained there. She had given birth to twins. When she was fast asleep, he got up, struck the robber, and cut off his head. The blood squirted on her. She got up and said, "I am under your protection, my son!"

He said, "Accursed gray one! By Allāh, I shall slaughter you!" And he slaughtered her and her children.[25] Then he returned to Shams eḍ-Ḍuḥā.

Thereafter she fetched the *Khaṭīb* [preacher], and gave herself to him [the youth] in marriage.

After three months he said, "I want to go home to my relatives!"

So they led the livestock and the slaves and moved. On the way they gathered warriors, and set up troops against his father. He camped near the city of his father, and his livestock was behind him. When the king woke up—behold: soldiers and armies were on the mountain. The king sent people to him as intermediaries, and invited him.[26] They came, he invited them and gave them to eat. The youth told his whole story, and greeted his father. He abdicated, and he set himself up in his place as king.

The bird flew away!

Comments

The central theme in this story—a mother's attempts to kill her son—is an unusual one in the folktale. Also unusual is the continued devotion of the son to his mother even though he knows that she intends to kill him.

The opening scene, in which an angel announces to the king that when his wife reaches the age of seventy she will give birth to a son, puts the story in the category of miraculous birth stories, of which an early example is found in Genesis 17 (the birth of Isaac to the ninety-year-old Sarah). The mother's age is subsequently forgotten by the storyteller, and he relates that more than seventeen years later—when she is eighty-seven years old or older—she becomes the lover of a jinn-robber, becomes pregnant, and gives birth to twins.

The owners of the palace that the mother and the son find in the vicinity of Beirut are identified as jinns, but they have no characteristics at all that would distinguish them from ordinary humans. The son manages to kill them one by one and mortally wounds the last one, the fortieth, who remains alive only thanks to the "water of life" which the woman has with her. When she sees that her son has noticed that she is pregnant, she and her jinn lover plan to kill him. However, he escapes thanks to the miraculous knowledge of the girl Shams eḍ-Ḍuḥā, an emir's daughter who lives alone in the desert of the east, in Transjordan, beyond the city of Karak. She knows what the evil mother plans and what she will next ask of her son in order to bring about his death. In the typical Arab folktale manner, the girl instantly falls in love with the youth and informs him that she will marry nobody else but him.

The third dangerous expedition on which the mother sends her son is to fetch the "water of life" for her. Here the storyteller seems to have forgotten that at the beginning of the story the mother had this elixir in her possession and that with it she healed the mortally wounded jinn who became her lover. Or, possibly, one is supposed to understand that the son did not know that she had the miraculous water in her possession or else that she had used up all the water she had in healing the wounded jinn.

The manner in which the youth obtains the "water of life" is surprisingly similar to an incident told in the Greek myth of the Argonauts. They manage to sail through between the clashing rocks by sending a dove (or a heron) to fly ahead of the *Argo.* The rocks close and nip off the tail feathers of the bird, then recoil, thus giving just enough time for the Argonauts to sail their ship through between them before they close again. In this story, likewise, the mountains snap closed and pluck the tail and wings of the bird, but it manages to fly through with the bottle of the "water of life" tied around its neck. The similarity of this detail in the two stories is much too specific to be attributable to coincidence. It must rather be the result of a familiarity of the Arab storyteller (or, rather, of the originators of the story) with the well-known motif of the clashing rocks; see Stith Thompson, *The Folktale* (New York: Holt, Rinehart and Winston, 1946), p. 244. The specific detail of the rocks clipping off the tail feathers of the bird is found in the Greek and Roman sources; see the sources listed in Robert Graves, *The Greek Myths* (Baltimore: Penguin, 1971), vol. 2, no. 151, n. 1.

When the son finally recognizes that his mother is definitely out to kill him, his filial devotion to her evaporates, and he kills first her lover, then her and her twin children. These killings are recounted with the casual brevity usual in the Arab folktale.

Now the prediction the youth's father had received before his birth comes true. Although he and his mother were expelled from the royal palace at the very time of his birth, the mother must have told him about his father and what he had done to them, and thus inculcated in him an enmity to his father whom he never knew.

In any case, having killed his mother, her lover, and his two half-siblings, and having married Shams eḍ-Ḍuḥā, the youth goes with an army to his father's city and besieges it. The father surrenders without a fight; he abdicates his throne, and the son becomes king in his place.

The miraculous element is underplayed in this story. Nor does it have many elements reflecting conditions in Arab society. All in all, it has much of the character of *Märchen.*

Notes

1. "To bring" (Arabic *jābat*) in popular idiom means to give birth.
2. If something is repeated three times in a dream, it is believed unfailingly to come true.
3. That is, "I have had enough of you."
4. *Dirhams* (in Arabic, *darāhīm*) actually means drachmas but is used in the general sense of money.
5. The number forty is a favorite of the Arab folktale, which tells of forty thieves, forty robbers, forty raiders, forty jinns or ghouls, etc.
6. The forty robbers were not human but of the race of the jinn.
7. To kill an adversary, or a person who in some way represents an obstacle for the hero, is a commonplace in Arab folklore.
8. "The water of life" is imagined as a kind of elixir. In the sequel of the story, the storyteller forgets that the mother already possesses the water of life and has her ask her son for it.
9. This is the first indication of the evil character of the mother. A decent woman would not have accepted a jinn as her lover.
10. Shams eḍ-Ḍuḥā ("Morning Sun") is a girl's name.

11. Here it is stated clearly that the mother wishes for the death of her son. This is an unusual motif in the folktale, which, as a rule, has the *stepmother* plot to kill her stepchild or stepchildren.
12. That is, she vowed to go against the Arab custom which requires that the marriage be arranged between the father of the girl and the father of the boy, and that following the wedding the bride should go to the bridegroom's house.
13. That is, "continue to go in the direction in which you are heading."
14. The Arabic word *ʿabd* has the meaning of both "slave" and "Negro," and in the folktale it usually denotes a black slave.
15. Although Shams eḍ-Ḍuḥā's troops overpowered the youth, they assure him that no harm will come to him.
16. These and the subsequent words show that Shams eḍ-Ḍuḥā is not an ordinary woman but one endowed with supernatural powers. Upon seeing the youth, she instantly knows that it was his mother who sent him, that she wants to kill him, and that she is pregnant. She refers to the jinn lover of the mother contemptuously as a dwarf. And she even knows in advance what the next request of the mother will be.
17. Now the evil mother not only wishes that her son should die but asks the jinn robber what to do to bring about his death.
18. Although the youth has been told by Shams eḍ-Ḍuḥā that his mother wants to kill him, he nevertheless continues to do her bidding with filial obedience. This detail underlines the sterling character of the youth.
19. While the two animal guards of the garden are busy eating, the youth will be able to slip into the garden.
20. By this time Shams eḍ-Ḍuḥā has decided that she wants to marry no one but the youth. Such a decision by a girl to marry a certain youth and nobody else is a frequent motif in the Arab folktale and is used to indicate that the girl is possessed of an exceptionally strong willpower, since in the actual situation it is the father of the girl who selects a husband for her.
21. This, of course, is the well-known motif of the clashing rocks; see comments above.
22. The motif of tying up the loser in a game appears several times in Arab folktales. See tale 5, "The Virtuous Maiden."
23. Now, finally, the youth has reached the point where he feels he must kill his mother and her paramour, referred to here as "her customer" (in Arabic *zbūn,* in literary Arabic *zabūn,* "client," "customer").
24. The woman is at this point called "the wife of the robber."
25. The youth kills not only the jinn and his own mother but also her half-jinn, half-human children. Killing with a sword is termed "slaughtering" (in Arabic, *dhabaḥ*). At this stage of the tale the storyteller feels that the mother and all the others deserve death.

26. The youth marries Shams eḍ-Ḍuḥā and returns with her to his father's city. But he is not reconciled with his father, who expelled him from his palace as soon as he was born. Hence he comes to his father's city with an army. The story hints, but does not say so explicitly, that the father surrenders ("invites him"). Once the son makes himself known to him, the father abdicates and lets the son become king in his stead.

7
The Emir's Daughter

Recorded by Hans Schmidt, 1910.

Allāh spoke and he spoke graciously![1] Neither here nor there,[2] but there was an emir of the Arabs. One year of the years the pasturage was very meager. So he sent seven or eight of his Arabs to search for pasture grounds. They rode their horses and traveled three, four days. They came to a well-watered wide wadi. They saw it and returned to inform their emir. During their absence raiders[3] came under their leader, whose name was Mḥammed, and went to the gate of the wadi, sat there and kneaded and baked flat loaves of bread.[4]

While they were sitting and baking those who had searched for the pasture brought their animals and appeared in the wadi. When they appeared, the raiders got frightened, fled, and left their flat loaves in the fire. Their leader said, "Who will go to fetch us the loaves we left in the fire?" When nobody arose, he himself went, and found them [the Arabs] having pitched their tents and camping. The dogs were completely still, and everything was quiet and dark.

He went straight to the place of the loaves, and behold, the tent of Ḥamde, the daughter of the emir, was pitched over the fire. Her bedstead was over a loaf, and the lamp was lit above her head. He crawled through the seams of the tent,[5] entered, and began to scrape away the ashes from the flat breads under the bedstead. Ḥamde woke up above him, grabbed him and threatened him. He begged her humbly, implored her by the name of her father, and said to her, "I did not come to seek women; my wish is to get the flat bread that we left here. And if you don't believe me, let me scrape off the ashes from it." And he pulled it out from beneath her bedstead.

When she saw that the matter was true, she took a leather bag with flour, kneaded and baked for him *shrākh*[6] bread, out of a small bag of clarified butter poured a little over it, and said to him, "Take it and go. But be careful when you go out that you fall not into the pit that is before you."

When he went out the dogs followed him. It was dark, and he fell into the pit. He called out for the daughter of the emir to help him, because her tent was at the edge [of the encampment]. She detached a cord from the tent ropes, let it down, and pulled him up. When he grabbed the ankle of her foot to pull himself up, and made an effort, the girl slipped and fell together with him into the pit. And she remained there all night.

Her father used to pray every day at the opening of that pit.[7] Early in the morning he came with a pitcher in his hand.[8] When he reached the opening of the pit, he heard talk from it. He looked down: there sat his daughter and the Bedouin in the middle of the pit. He instantly turned around, without having prayed, and called, "Start moving, O Arabs, start moving!" They said to him, "What is it, O emir? We arrived only yesterday, and already today we should move on?" He said, "Start moving, start moving!" And he went to his tent, pulled up the stakes, folded up the tent, put it on the she-camel, and started to ride away on her. When the Arabs saw that their emir started up, they became quite dismayed. They loaded up and followed him.

After they had traveled three days, the emir called his slave ʿAwwād and said to him, "Go to the pit in the wadi, next to which stood the tent of my daughter, slaughter whatever is in it, and bring me of the blood of both of them. Woe to you if you should disobey my order!"

He mounted, rode there, reached the pit, and looked into it. There sat the girl with the Bedouin. He [the slave] began to scold her and curse her for having a love affair, and said to her, "Why don't you take one of your relations?"[9]

She said to him, "O ʿAwwād, have you ever seen anything wrong from me? Have I not always done good to you? What will you have from slaughtering me? Pull me out! And by the life of my father, I shall take nobody else but you. What will my father give you if you kill me? Pull me out and take me to wife, and do not return to my father. I, my situation is this and this."[10]

He pulled her up, and brought her out, and went and brought thistles in heaps, and threw them into the pit, wanting to burn the Bedouin. When the pit was almost full, the girl stepped up to look into it, and she pushed ʿAwwād. He fell into the pit. Instantly the other one jumped at his throat and strangled him. She pulled the Bedouin up, he threw himself on the back of ʿAwwād's horse, seated her behind him, placed his sword between himself and her as a pledge of her safety,[11] and said, "O road, open up for me!"[12]

Two, three days passed. He reached his Arabs, his mother, entrusted the girl to her and commended her to his mother. He took care of her twenty-four karats.[13]

Thus passed one to two months. He said to his mother, "O my mother, ask her whether she wants to marry, and whom does she want to take." She said, "I take only him who brought me, on condition that he stamp forty camels with the tribal mark[14] of my father." And she described to him the mark. He went, made purchases for her, and married her, and slaughtered,[15] and went in to her, and loved her more than his first wife.

Time passed after time. His companions said to him, "Let us go out on a raid." He said, "After the Friday prayer." He was not used to going raiding without a prayer. Friday came. They prayed. He called his brother and said to him, "Take care of Ḥamde! What she wishes has to be, and what comes into her mind must be done!" He charged him, took with him fifty riders, and they set out.

When they were far away, his brother put a silken headcloth on his head, wound around it an *ʿaqāl*[16] woven with gold and silver wire, put on fine clothes, and went to her. They drank coffee. Then he began to make unseemly jokes, and demanded of her that which is not right. When he grabbed her, she said, "O shame on you! Are you not ashamed to grab the wife of your brother? Am I not called your flesh and blood?[17] Where is your honor?" She kept him away. He left off her. But as she bent down for the coffee pot, he tried to grab her. She hit him with her hand that was full of rings, and wounded him at his eye, so that his blood flowed. Now he desisted, wound about the headcloth, and went to his tent.

A few days later the raiders returned. The Arabs ran to receive them—the big and the small, even those who were in the cradle in swaddling clothes. But he [the emir's brother] did not go. They arrived. The emir looked for his brother but saw him not. He asked about him. They told him that he had bad eyes.[18] They slaughtered and ate. Two, three days passed, but he did not go to his brother.

Thereupon the emir went to him and greeted him. But he did not respond. "What is the matter?" He said, "This wife of yours does not refuse anybody, one goes out from her, the other goes in to her."

The emir said, "Quiet!" [19] The emir got up, had his wife sit behind him, and he rode, as if he wanted to enjoy the fresh air. They went a distance of one day's journey. They reached a wadi, and she lay down on his knee to sleep. He let her have the sweetest sleep, got up, removed her head from his knee, and rode back to his Arabs.

The woman awoke, and called for her husband, "So-and-so, O father of So-and-so!" But there was no word and no answer. She went after her face,[20] and into the distance. She found a way, and followed it. She found a spring, and over it there was a tree. She climbed up the tree, and sat among its branches.

In that neighborhood there was an emir, his name was Mḥimmid.[21] He watered his horse only at this spring. He came there early in the morning, to pray,[22] and to water his mare. He dismounted, and let her approach [the water]. The mare became frightened by the reflection of the woman. He looked up: behold, there she was sitting. He said to her, "A human or a jinn?" [23] She said, "A human, as good as any human. I am a thread of your *ʿabā*." [24] She got down. He mounted his mare, and said to her, "Your hand!" She extended her hand to him. He pulled her up, and in a moment she sat behind him. He placed the sword between himself and her, returned to his mother, and said to her, "I recommend to you this chaste woman. Protect her from the herdsmen." [25]

From here to there, two months passed. The old woman said to her, "O my child, will you not listen to me, and marry this boy?"—her son. She said, "O my lady, upon it and upon similar things[26] rests the whole world. I shall marry him, but on condition that he stamp forty camels with the tribal mark of my father, and that I write a document with him that he takes me along wherever he goes." He said, "Good." He stamped the camels, wrote the document, and took her according to the law of Allāh and his Messenger, and went in to her. She brought forth a boy, in the second year [again] a boy, and in the third year a daughter.

The Arabs came and said to him, "Come on, let us go raiding!" He said, "I ask to be excused." They said, "Without you we don't go." [27] He said, "If so, let us go fast!" He pitched a tent for his wife and children on the back of a riding camel, and seated them in it, and they set out.

They traveled four to five days, and met Bedouin who wanted to rob them. The emir said to his brother, "O my brother, stay here with the family until I return."

After he departed, that one [the brother] demanded of her that which was not right. She refused. He said, "If so, I shall slaughter your children." She said, "The children belong to their father and to you, you will slaughter from your own pocket." He slaughtered the oldest boy, and threw him in a pit. Then he slaughtered the second one, and then the daughter. But she did not surrender to him. Then he said to her, "What has been slaughtered will be one heap, and you will be the other." Life is dear.[28] She said, "I am unclean. I want to enter and wash myself." She took a pitcher, went to the pit, and threw herself upon her children. She tarried a long time, and did not return. He searched for her, but could not find her. Thereupon he slashed the two hind legs of his horse, until blood flowed like a gully, and chased after his brother and overtook them. The emir said to him, "What is it?" He said, "You wife is a *ghoulah,*[29] she ate your children, and wanted to eat my horse. Look, how she slashed it!" He said, "Allāh be thanked for your escape, O brother!"

When he went away from the pit, the woman put on an *ʿaqāl,* as if she were a man, and threw the headcloth across [her face]. A caravan passed. She called out to them. They pulled her up, and said to her, "What is your name?" She said, "Jalāl." They said, "Up, with us!" She went.

There was there a famous emir. All the Arabs sought justice from him. His name was Emir Ziadeh. Jalāl stayed with him. They gave him coffee and food. Thus he stayed for three days and a third as a guest. Then[30] they said to him, "What occupation do you have?" He said, "I am a plowman."[31] They said to him, "Serve with us!" He came to an agreement with them about the hire and remained with the Emir Ziadeh.

One month followed the other. The pastures became scarce for her father and for her first husband Mḥammed and for her second husband Mḥimmid. All three moved with their animals to a place rich in water—let us say to Biʾr Zayt—and stayed there for grazing. But none of them knew anything of the others. Each one camped on a different side. The black slaves of her father came and saw the same tribal marks on the camels as on his own camels. Camels of his had got lost. The slaves came and said to him, "Happy news for you! Your camels turned up with the Arabs of the Emir Mḥammed, who are encamped in this and this place." Next day the slaves went to another place to graze, and saw the camels of the Emir Mḥimmid marked with the tribal mark of their master. They returned and told him about it. He went there and demanded his camels from them, and they quarreled about it. He said, "These are my camels that were stolen from me." But they said, "This is our lawful property." Thereupon he summoned them to come to judgment to the Emir Ziadeh.

He and his children, and the Emir Mḥimmid and the Emir Mḥammed and her brothers went and came to him [to the Emir Ziadeh]. Each of them told his story, and proved the correctness of what he claimed. The Emir Ziadeh, who otherwise was never embarrassed in judgment, was this time completely baffled, and said, "Give me one hour's time, so that I can sleep a little." [32]

They said to him, "O Emir, our animals are far from here, we want to go home. Let us go betimes." He said, "If so, I can do nothing in this matter."

Then the servant Jalāl spoke up. "My lord, I want to adjudicate the thing before you." And the woman began to relate her story from beginning to end. She proved it, detailed it, and said, "I am So-and-so, this is my father, this is my first husband, and this my second. And this and this one persecuted me, and this is the one who slaughtered the children of his brother."

When they heard this extraordinary story, they were startled. The Emir Ziadeh instantly gave orders, and they burned the two brothers of the emirs who wanted to betray their brothers. But the honor of the woman was white before her parents and her husbands.

He who does not protect his honor nothing good is in him. And peace!

Comments

This long, complex, and repetitious folktale, of which several variants were current among the Arabs of Palestine in the years before World War I, provides a rare insight into the mores of the Bedouin, and especially into the position of women among them. It indicates that the sexual transgression of an unmarried daughter was considered a more heinous violation of the tribal mores than the unfaithfulness of a wife. At least it appears so from the unhesitant condemnation to death of Ḥamde by her father when he believes her to have committed immorality, while her husband, who believes that she was unfaithful to him during his absence, does not kill her but merely abandons her in the open terrain.

Another point shown by the tale is the credence the men give to the appearance of a woman's guilt, without as much as putting a single question to her about her guilt or innocence.

The contrast is interesting between, on the one hand, the two noble emirs who hold the woman inviolate until they enter into a lawful marriage with her and, on the other hand, their evil and lecherous brothers who try to seduce her or violate her as soon as she is left alone in the camp. The brother of the second emir is presented as a totally inhuman murderer of innocent children, his own brother's sons and daughter.

When an unmarried woman happens to arrive in their camp, the honorable men place her under the protection of their mother. In this story it is the mother of one of the emirs who takes the initiative on behalf of the woman to arrange a marriage between her and her son.

Another aspect of Bedouin mores illustrated by the tale is the lawful and honorable activity of the *ghazw,* the raid. To raid another tribe and drive off its camels is even more than honorable; it is a noble undertaking in which the men of the tribe can prove their valor and which results in augmenting the herds, that is, the assets of the tribe.

The purpose of the raid is purely economic. Care is taken not to kill a member of the other tribe, since that would trigger a blood feud which could be disastrous for both tribes involved in it.

An insight into the social organization and juridical institutions of the tribes is afforded by the scene in which Ḥamde's father and her two husbands submit their dispute concerning the camels stamped with the father's tribal mark to the arbitration of a "famous emir," whose superior qualifications as a judge they all recognize. The three tribal chiefs (emirs) do not try to settle the matter of the camels by force but are willing to accept the judgment of Emir Ziadeh. But he is baffled by the case since Ḥamde's two husbands argue that they themselves stamped their own camels with the tribal mark of her father, while her father argues that the camels stamped by his tribal mark are indisputably his. At this point Ḥamde solves the impasse by telling what actually happened.

Incidentally, the story does not explain why she demanded that each of her two husbands stamp forty of his camels with her father's tribal mark. However, in effect those camels took the place of the bride price her father would have received from her suitor had she still lived with her father and had the suitor asked him for her. In this sense the two groups of forty camels served as a legitimation of her marriage to her two husbands.

Most interesting, of course, is the central image of Ḥamde, the heroine of the story. She is brave and resourceful and survives apparently unscathed all kinds of horrible trials and tribulations, including the slaughter of her children by her brother-in-law. Although she marries a second husband while the first one is still alive, the story does not censure or reproach her, and the question of whose wife she is at the end of the story, when her honor is finally vindicated, is not raised at all. Nor do we hear a single word about her feelings, her pain over the murder of her children, her hatred of the two brothers-in-law who abused her, her loyalty to her father, her satisfaction at the punishment that ultimately overtakes the two villains. All this remains for the listeners to imagine.

Notes

1. By referring to Allāh, the storyteller places himself under his protection.
2. This stereotypical disclaimer indicates that the story to be told is not necessarily true.
3. Arabic *ghazzāye* [literary Arabic: *ghuzāt*], "raiders." To raid another tribe was considered, in certain conditions, a legitimate, even praiseworthy, undertaking among the Bedouin.
4. Arabic *aqrāṣ* (colloquially *qrāṣ,* singular *qurṣ*) are flat loaves of bread made of flour, salt, and water, without yeast. The dough was laid on a flat stone or any flat surface on the ground, then covered with glowing ashes until it was baked. The ashes were knocked off the bread with a stick, and the bread was eaten warm.
5. The typical Bedouin tent was constructed of several narrow, long strips of material woven of camel and/or goat hair. The strips were often not tightly sewn together, and thus it was possible to crawl through between them.
6. *Shrākh* or *shrāk* is the name of a round, somewhat globular iron plate. It was heated over fire, then a thin layer of dough was spread over it, which was removed as soon as it was baked. This type of bread was considered to be better than the *aqrāṣ* (see note 4). Since neither the *aqrāṣ* nor the *shrāk* required an oven, these were the types of bread generally eaten by the Bedouins.
7. The storyteller forgot that the father of the girl had arrived at that spot only the day before.
8. Water is required for washing before prayer.
9. The slave reproaches the girl for having an affair with a stranger and not a relative, which makes her transgression an even greater crime.
10. This is the typical summary statement by a storyteller meaning that a person tells what happened to him or her.
11. When a man spends the night next to a woman and wants to assure her that he will not touch her, he places a sword between them. On a horse, this does not make much sense. In this context it is rather a figure of speech, indicating that he assured her that he would not violate her.
12. This figure of speech means "May I get to my destination without problems!"

13. Since twenty-four karats is pure gold, the expression means "He took care of her completely."
14. The tribal mark, *wasm,* was a sign branded into the skin of a camel, on its neck or upper thigh, to indicate that it was the property of the tribe. Each tribe had a *wasm* of its own.
15. That is, he slaughtered animals for the feast given in honor of the wedding.
16. *ʿAqāl* is a rope crown that holds the *kūfiya,* the headcloth, in place. Wealthy people had luxurious *ʿaqāl*s, interwoven with gold and silver threads. The brother of the emir puts on fine clothes in order to make himself attractive to the woman.
17. By having married the emir, she has become a blood relative of his brother as well.
18. In Arabic *ramdān,* one who has *ramad,* "ophthalmia" or inflammation of the eyes.
19. The emir indicates that he does not want the disgrace brought upon him by his wife to become known in the tribe. On the other hand, neither does he want to kill her, which would be the traditional way of restoring his honor. Instead, he removes her from the camp in a clandestine manner and abandons her to her fate.
20. That is, she went in the direction in which she happened to have turned her face.
21. Mḥimmid, like Mḥammed earlier in the story, is a dialectal variant of the name Muḥammad.
22. Since ablution is required prior to praying, a spring was a favored location for prayer; one could wash at the spring and then pray.
23. Stereotypical question when encountering a stranger. It is based on the ancient belief that a person can at any moment encounter a jinn in a human shape.
24. This is a statement of utter self-effacement, meaning "I am as insignificant in relation to you as a thread in your cloak."
25. The emir knows his people; they would try to take advantage of the strange woman, unless she is protected by his own mother.
26. Meaning "It is upon marriage that the entire world is built." An indirect way of saying, "I am ready to marry the emir."
27. The tribe is dependent on its emir to lead them in a raid. The emir, for his part, feels it is his duty to respond to the demand of his men.
28. Generalization, to explain and excuse the act of the woman who does not immediately reject the demand of her brother-in-law when he threatens to kill her. After this statement we would expect the woman to give in to him. Instead, we are told that she manages to elude him. Compare the same scene in story 5.
29. The belief that a *ghoulah* can assume the shape of a flesh-and-blood woman lies just beneath the surface in Bedouin thinking. The emir instantly believes

that his wife, with whom he has lived for more than three years and who has borne him three children, is a *ghoulah* and has eaten her own children.

30. When a guest arrives in the camp, for the first three days he is not supposed to be asked any questions. Only on the fourth day can the host inquire about the guest's intentions. A variant of this custom, to start discussing the guest's plans on the third day, is indicated by the saying that the three days of hospitality are for *salām, ṭaʿām, kalām*—greeting (the first day), eating (the second day), talking (the third day).
31. Some of the Bedouin of Palestine used to practice part-time agriculture. They would sow a piece of land, then move on with their herds or flocks to greener pastures and return at harvest time. Since working the land was not their métier proper, they often employed fellahin on a temporary basis to work the land for them. At the beginning of the winter one could often see fellahin from west of the Jordan move over to Transjordan to work there as plowmen for the Bedouin.
32. This statement corresponds to our "Let me sleep on it."

8
The Unfaithful Wife

Told by Yūsuf Abū Jīrius, recorded by Hans Schmidt in Bi'r Zayt, 1910–11.

There is nothing here and nothing there,[1] except for an emir. One day he got up, took his wife—she was like Umm Yūsuf[2]—an emirah in her house, and had many boys, and her husband lived peacefully with her.

And he got up to let her breathe the air, you could say like from here to Nablus.[3] He rode with her on the camel, and said to his slave, "*Yallah,* drive behind us!"[4]

In the evening he arrived in Nablus, let the camel kneel, spread the rug at its gate,[5] and said to his slave, "Watch over your mistress, take care of her!"

He, the emir, entered Nablus to spend the evening with the great ones. He who is like him, will he spend the evening with Abū Ibrāhīm?[6]

When the night had taken and given,[7] he returned to his wife, and, behold, she had been abducted, and the slave was asleep with exhaustion and snored on the rug.

He woke him and said, "Where is your mistress?"

The slave was as if he had a halter in his mouth,[8] and once sought refuge with Allāh, and once cursed Satan.[9] In brief, the emir sent him back home, and he rode on the camel and went to search for her.

It happened to be the end of the moon, and if you held your finger before your eyes you could not see it. Whomever he encountered on the road he asked about his wife, but she—the earth split open and swallowed her!

He said, "Is she a granule of salt, and has she dissolved?"

He went in the land from country to country. One night darkness overcame him in the open. He let his camel kneel, fed her, and tied her knee, and slept on it.[10] While he was in the sweetest of dreams, behold a slave[11] with a cudgel—this big[12]—stood over his head, woke him and said, "O uncle![13] Never has as yet anybody slept on this spot. What is it with you? You are not here for nothing."

The emir said, "I am a human being.[14] My wife went away, and I roam about in search of her."

He said to him, "I have knowledge of her. Get up, see that light in the distance. It is lighted above her head."

This one [the emir] arose, mounted his camel, directed his eye to the light, and said, "O road, be smooth for me!"

He went on and on, until he reached a tent. It was pitched and pegged to the ground. A lamp was lit, and hung from the tent pole.

He looked through the holes—behold his wife was sleeping on the bosom of a slave[15]—help is with Allāh! Each of his lips was as big as the kidney of a cow. And she—like a mirror on his bosom.[16] Outside the tent was a horse that cannot be described,[17] tied by all fours.

The emir tried to enter, but could not.[18] He took a whip and began to dig up the soil with it,[19] until he made a place under the edge of the tent, and entered carefully, carefully, and crouched down above their heads. And that one [the slave] snored next to her, and was totally exhausted.

He [the emir] called her, but she did not wake up. He started to rub her nose, whereupon she opened her eyes. He said to her, "O Eshe! O Umm ʿAlī![20] O you mother of my children! O you builder of my house! What brought you here? Get up, come home with me!"

She said to him, "Hush! If he gets up, your beard is gone![21] You have no share in me, go home to your children!"

He began to cry and to beg her.

She said to him, "Give up all hope for me!"

He said, "I want to go. Give me one kiss!"

She said, "Good."

He instantly crept out, and she stuck her head out under the edge of the tent, and he came near to kiss her, and gave her two kisses. She turned the other cheek to him. And instead of kissing her he bit her and struck her. Because of the pain she came out, and wanted to cry out. He drew the sword and said to her, "By Allāh, if you make one sound I shall cut you into two!" She remained quiet. He seated her in front of him on the camel, and rode off, as Allāh helped him.

Let the story return to the slave. He awoke, groped about with his hand here and there, and found nobody. He said, "O my Lord, am I in awareness or in a dream?" [22]

He stepped out of the tent, got on the back of the horse, and flew after the traces of the camel. She looked back, and behold, his dust rose high. She said to her husband, "O Abū ʿAlī, consider your situation. The slave has reached you!"

A moment, and he was behind them, aiming his spear whose point sparkled like lightning, and he threw it at the emir. The Bedouins are fast. He slid down the haunches of the camel, grabbed a round stone, hurled it and hit him behind his ear. He lay there stretched out on the ground. He approached in order to give him the rest and to cut off his head. His wife threw a fistful of sand in his eyes. He stopped in his place and tried to open the eyes. And she went to the slave, squeezed milk into his mouth and nose, and took pains over him. He opened his eyes, stepped up to the emir, and tied him to a tree which was like the oak of Tibne,[23] and wound the rope ten, fifteen times around him. Then he milked the camel into a bowl. They drank as much as they wanted, left over the rest, and again lay down together. And he did before the eyes of her husband what he wanted.[24] Then they turned their heads to the side and fell asleep.

Now a snake slithered down from the tree, and slithered past the face of the emir. For fear one temple of his became white. It moved on to the remainder of the milk which was in the pot, slurped it and spit it out again.[25] Then it made its way and slithered up the oak.

After about as much time as one needs for smoking a cigarette,[26] they woke up, and sat down to drink the rest of the milk. At first she took a drop. Her husband, who was tied up, said to her, "Shame! You drink before the men?" [27]

She gave the pot to the slave. He, his throat was dry from exhaustion and from that which he had done. He lapped it all up. He drank it here, and fell back from here,[28] without having a drop in the eye.[29]

When she saw that this was the thing, she said to her tied-up husband, "I am considering what will save me from you, since you saw me doing what you saw. There is nothing else but that I cut off your head, so that I have peace from you."

She took the sword and struck him with it. What is the strike of a woman? She only cut the rope that was around his neck. He rebuked her, and shook himself, and freed himself. She crouched down as the mouse before the cat.[30] He said nothing to her, seated her [on the camel], and returned home with her to his Arabs.

He gathered the heads of the tribes, and told them his story from its beginning to its end. They said to him, "It has no root.[31] You must tell your story from the beginning at the gathering place."

The people of the village gathered together, and he recited his story. And each time he told something, he asked her, "Right?" And she said, "Right." He finished it. They said, "He who loves the emir, let him bring a load of wood!"

The friends and the enemies gathered wood, until it became a heap—as high as this house and even higher. They set her on it, and lighted the fire under her. She was burned, and a smoke rose up, like the one yesterday at your evening meal. This is the due of each one who deceives her husband, and even more.

Comments

This is a rather simple and realistic story, without any supernatural or miraculous elements in it. The behavior of the unfaithful wife is similar to, but even worse than, that of the queen in the frame story of the *Arabian Nights.* In both stories the woman becomes enamored of a negro slave with a powerful body and engages in passionate sex with him. In this story the huge size of the black slave is indicated only by a reference to a physical feature the Arabs found repulsive: he had lips as big as the kidneys of a cow. The two queens in the frame story of the *Arabian Nights* carry on their amorous adventures with black male slaves in the absence of their husbands, while the woman of this tale flaunts her adultery in front of her husband. Moreover, when her paramour is killed by the poisonous drink he imbibes, she tries to kill her husband as well. He is saved only by the fact that she is inept at wielding the sword properly: "What is the strike of a woman?"

The emir, the hero of our story, is a rather meek and mild character, who, when he finds his wife in the arms of the black slave, begs her to return to him. She rejects him, whereupon he begins to cry. When he reaches his camp with her, he gathers the "heads of the tribes," meaning the heads of the families in his tribe, and tells them what happened. The woman brazenly confirms all the details. Only then does the emir reach the point where, apparently unwillingly and only indirectly, he indicates to his men that she should have the punishment she deserves. All he tells them is to gather wood, and when "friend and foe" alike do so, it is they, without his having passed sentence over her or having instructed them, who set the woman on top of the heap of wood and light the fire under her.

The story takes place in a traditional environment, in which there were still black slaves owned by the well-to-do of the Arab tribes. It is a narrative expression of the image of the black slave as a sexual superman as it lived in the Arab imagination and the anxiety Arab men felt about what they believed was an irresistible sexual attraction black slaves represented for their own "white" women.

Notes

1. This is one of the several stereotyped beginnings of the Arab folktale.
2. The storyteller refers to his daughter-in-law, called Umm Yūsuf, "Mother of Joseph," since her eldest son is called Yūsuf, after Yūsuf Abū Jīrius. The purpose of this aside is to illustrate the honored position the emirah of the story had in her house.
3. The emir took his wife on a ride to a distance such as that from Biʾr Zayt, where the story is being told, to Nablus.
4. The emir has his slave ride behind him on another animal.
5. Visitors arriving at a city used to leave their mounts before the gate of the city, where there was a suitable open area. Even in 1933 and in later years, I still saw large numbers of camels before the Damascus Gate leading into the Old City of Jerusalem.
6. Abū Ibrāhīm is one of those who listens to the story. The remark is a teasing aside; its intention is to indicate that an important man like the emir would, of course, spend the evening with other important people, and not with simple ones like Abū Ibrāhīm.
7. Meaning "when the night was well advanced."
8. Fright made the slave unable to speak, like an animal that has a halter in its mouth.
9. The slave alternately appealed to Allāh and cursed Satan. By cursing Satan, the slave shifts onto him the responsibility for having fallen asleep. See notes 11 and 14 to story 4.
10. One of the common ways of tying up camels. A rope is wound around the bent knees of the crouching camel, so that it cannot stand up. The animal becomes so immobilized that one can sleep by resting one's head on its knees.
11. Everywhere in this story, as in popular Arabic usage in general, the word *ʿabd* ("slave") is used in the sense of either negro or negro slave.
12. The storyteller shows with his hands the size of the cudgel carried by the slave.

13. This is how a person addresses somebody of a respected social status or of an older age group.
14. The emir answers the stereotypical, but in this case unrecorded, question "Are you a human being or a ghoul?" asked of somebody encountered unexpectedly.
15. The scene described here—the husband finding his wife in the arms of a negro slave—is familiar from the opening of the *Arabian Nights.*
16. In contrast to the black skin of the negro slave, the white skin of the wife appears like a shining mirror. White skin of a woman is considered among the Arabs a most desirable and beautiful feature and increases considerably the bride price of a girl.
17. The beauty of the horse defies description.
18. The flap of the tent that serves as its entrance was fastened from within.
19. Having no other implement at hand, the emir digs under the tent with the handle of his whip.
20. Eshe is the wife's name. The emir also calls her Umm ʿAlī, "Mother of ʿAlī," the usual way of addressing a woman who has a son. Later in the story the wife calls her husband Abū ʿAlī, "Father of ʿAlī."
21. Meaning "your life is lost."
22. That is, "am I awake, or am I dreaming?"
23. A sacred tree under which the storyteller had sat only the day before.
24. For the slave and the wife to make love before the eyes of her husband is the epitome of shamelessness.
25. By doing this, the snake turns the milk into poison.
26. A frequently used description of a short stretch of time.
27. The Arab woman only drinks and eats after the menfolk. The emir, even at this point, still wants to save the life of his wife.
28. That is, he died on the spot.
29. That is, before he was able to shed a tear.
30. Seeing that her husband, whom she had tried to kill, was unhurt and free, the wife collapsed.
31. Meaning "it is incomprehensible."

9
The Two Blind Women

Told by Umm Manṣūr, recorded by Hans Schmidt in Biʾr Zayt, 1910–11.

There was here one who married three women. Two became pregnant, and one, whom he loved in particular, did not become pregnant. Those pregnant went out to gather wood. While they were away, this one cooked for them a goose, and filled it with salt. When they returned, she called them and said to them, "Come, eat!"

They said, "What is it with her? It is not her custom to invite us and to cook for us!"

They sat down to the evening meal. They had come from the field and were hungry, and they ate the whole goose, also the crumbs,[1] everything together. After they had eaten they became thirsty. They said to her, "Give us to drink."

She said, "By Allāh, I give you to drink only if I can tear out your eyes for it. Otherwise you can die of thirst."

Life is dear![2] They demanded water again. She said, "Good. I give you to drink, but, of course, I tear out an eye from each of you!"

They knew no way out, and let her tear out their eyes. She gave them to drink, but purposely did not sate them.

In the time one smokes a cigarette they became thirsty again, and said to her, "Give us to drink!"

She said, "I shall give you to drink, [but] I shall tear out for it the other one of your eyes!"

At the end they found no way out for themselves, and so she tore them out, and they drank.

When their husband returned, he said, "What is it with the women that they became blind?"

She said, "Ah, if only I could bury you and bury your marriage![3]

They went out for wood, and while they gathered wood they pierced their eyes and became blind."

He said, "What do I want [to do] with them now?[4] Arise, get them away from my face, into some cave!"

She got hold of their sleeves, and seized them, and took them to a cave, and returned.

That night one of them gave birth, she brought a boy, wrapped him in rags. And they sat. Nobody gave them to eat, and nobody brought them anything, and they did not know where to go. When they became hungry, one said to her sister, "Give the child, let us eat it. And when I give birth, we shall eat my child."

This one arose, tore her son, and gave one half to her co-wife, and ate one half. Her co-wife hid her half of the child under her knee.

Next day she gave birth. Her co-wife said to her, "Give your son, let us eat him!"

She said, "O my sister, take half of your own son. I won't slaughter my son. I want to let him live. Perhaps he will help us, me and you."

By and by the boy grew up, and began to provide for his mother and the wife of his father.

One day he went to the *Khaṭīb*[5] and asked him for medicine for their eyes. The *Khaṭīb* prescribed for him the gall of a blue camel in the deep sea. This one mounted his horse and rode off. He passed a ghoul who had his hair hanging down across his face, and his nails were so long,[6] and his condition was pitiful. He greeted him. He [the ghoul] said, "Had your greeting not gone before your talk, I would have let all those here on the slope hear the crushing of your bones."[7]

This one approached, cut his hair and his nails. His [the ghoul's] face lighted up. He said to him, "May Allāh make it bright over you![8] Demand and wish!"

He said, "I want the gall of the blue camel in the depth of the sea."

He said, "Go on, you will find before you my brother, he will take care of you."

He went, and behold, that one was twice as big as his brother, and more horrifying than he—a hundred times. He greeted him.

He said, "Had your greeting not gone before your talk, I would have let all those in this valley hear the crushing of your bones."

That one stepped up to him and cut his hair and his nails. He said, "May Allāh make it bright over you, as you have made it bright over me. Demand and wish!"

He told him his wish.

He said, "Go on, there is my sister before you, she will take care of you. When her eyes are yellow, don't approach her; when her eyes are red like burning coals, approach her and suck at her breasts."

He went there, and behold, she was sitting and grinding [corn],[9] and her eyes were red like burning coals, and her breast hung behind her above her shoulders at her back.[10] He approached her and began to suck at one of her breasts.

She said to him, "He who sucks at my little breasts is dearer than my little children. Demand and wish!"

He said to her, "My mother is blind, and the *Khaṭīb* prescribed for her the gall of the blue camel which is in the deep sea."

She said to him, "Wait here, I shall fetch it for you."

She got up from the mill, went behind the seven seas, dived into the sea, and fetched the gall of the camel, and returned with it.

She gave it to the boy, he took it to his mother, rubbed it on her eyes. They became well, and they returned to her husband.[11]

Comments

This story is a rare compilation of illogical and extreme cruelties, quite unusual even in the rather rough, often murderous atmosphere of the Arab folktale.

That a wife should hate her co-wives and should plot against them is in itself nothing exceptional in Arab folklore. But that the evil wife should blind her two co-wives as the price of giving them water is rather far-fetched. That the two thirsty co-wives should agree to being blinded for a draught of water is outright absurd, especially in the situation described, in which the two co-wives have just returned from the field with their loads of wood. What prevents them from going and getting water for themselves?

Next, their husband, seeing that his wives became blind, expels them and leaves them in a cave, even though both are pregnant and close to giving birth. Why a man should want to condemn his wives to a practically certain death, and with them also his two unborn children, remains unexplained and unmotivated in the story.

Finally, when one of the two blinded wives bears a son, she agrees at the suggestion of her co-wife to tear the newborn in two and to eat it.

Again, this inhumanity is not motivated, and that a person isolated in a cave needs first water, and only then food, is not taken into consideration.

After this act of cannibalism we are not told how the two blind women and the second child, born the next day, manage to stay alive in the cave and not die of thirst and hunger until the boy grows up and is able to provide for them. What we next hear is that the son even has a horse and rides about at will, but still his mother and, presumably, the other blind wife remain in the cave.

The second half of the story is a run-of-the-mill fairy tale with the usual details about encounters between a human and a ghoul. However, in contrast to the evil humans, all three ghoul siblings behave most decently and are willing to help the boy in his quest for a medicine to heal his mother's blindness.

The end of the story is again impossible, according to the inner logic of the folktale: after the women regain their eyesight, they peacefully return to their cruel husband, and neither they nor their husband nor his favorite wife, all of whom committed unspeakable cruelties, suffer any punishment.

An interesting characteristic of this story, which it has in common with many other Arab folktales, is that many of the pronouncements of its protagonists rhyme. For example, in the response of the ghoul to the greeting of the boy, the words "your greeting," "your talk," and "your bones" all rhyme in Arabic (*salāmak, chalāmak, ʿaẓāmak*).

Notes

1. In Arabic dialect *il-fatt* or *il-fatta* ("the crumbs"). It also means a kind of bread soup, made by pouring gravy over bread. The scene described here—the two women coming home from the field hungry and then becoming so thirsty that they are willing to give everything for a drink of water—is, to some extent at least, reminiscent of Genesis 25: 29–34, where Esau comes home "faint" from the field and is willing to sell his birthright for "bread and pottage of lentils."
2. A statement often inserted in the Arab folktale in explanation of an act a person is ready to perform in order to save his life.
3. An emphatic exclamation of despair.
4. The expression "I want to do" something or other is in the Arabic colloquial the equivalent of "I intend" or "I shall do" this or that. What the husband intends to say is "What shall I do with them now?"
5. The *Khaṭīb* figures often in the Arab folktale. See tale 5.

6. The ghouls are often described as having long hair and nails that have grown into the ground, and being unable to cut them.
7. Many folktales all over the world attribute such words to a demon, giant, ghoul, etc.: "Had you not greeted me in such-and-such a way" or "Had you not addressed me as So-and-so, I would have killed you," or "I would have eaten you." See story 17.
8. The ghoul is, of course, a good Muslim and invokes Allāh.
9. The she-ghoul (*ghoulah*) is imagined to be like a fellah woman, who spends hours daily grinding corn.
10. Long, pendulous breasts are a characteristic feature of the *ghoulah.*
11. At the end of the story a certain impatience is evident on the part of the storyteller. She rushes to conclude it and omits all details.

10
Each Man Suffers Disasters

Recorded by Hans Schmidt, 1910–11.

In matters of disasters that overtake every man they said:

Once there was an Arab shekh [sheikh] who lived in the Balqa.[1] A group of Arabs from Gaza, to whom the shekh who died was dear, took for him a *qawad* [sheep][2] and went to show their sympathy to his people.[3] They went four, five days, and saw nothing but a *kharbūshe* [tent][4] pitched on top of a hill. It was eventide, so they turned aside from the road toward that tent.

When its master saw them approaching, he spread for them,[5] and received them with a thousand *ahla wa-sahla* [welcome][6] and a joyous face that was dripping with honey. They went to him, greeted him, and sat down. They looked around: camels, horses, cows, goats, donkeys—things that cannot be counted or calculated. The host arose, slaughtered a fattened camel, and set before them an evening meal *ʿa-lifrēnka* [European style],[7] and offered them coffee. They entertained themselves until they became sleepy.

The host spread beds for them, and each of them lay down on his separate bed.[8] He himself went behind the curtain that was between his family and the guests.[9] As the guests were about to go to sleep some of them said to the others, "By the Prophet, this Bedouin is in favor! This one has all his life never seen a misfortune!" The word penetrated his [the host's] ear like a nail. He raised the curtain and went over to them and said, "You say that I have never in my life seen a misfortune. Listen to me so that I relate to you the misfortune that struck me. Each one knows best his own fate.

"I had two brothers and one sister. One day of the days, while we were sitting about, what did we see but a Maghrebite [10] who was driving his donkey and approached the tent of the women. I got up to see what he wanted. Barely did I stand up, when he came out again and went on and away from us. Hah! Before you could smoke a cigarette [11] my sister was walking behind him. She stayed away a long time. I said to one of my brothers, 'See where did your sister go!' He arose, went after her, and stayed away about half an hour. When he stayed away too long, I said to my other brother, 'See what it is with your brother!' He got up and went and stayed away a long time.

"I felt like one sitting on burning coals. I got up, mounted my mare and rode after them. I did not ride more than a quarter of an hour, and I found my first brother slaughtered and his head thrown aside. I went on to look for my second brother. A little farther—there he lay murdered. I threw my horse forward, after the Maghrebite. Behold, my sister was walking after him, saying nothing and not complaining. When he saw me, he turned around toward me, grabbed the bridle of my horse, and wanted to throw me down and kill me. I spurred on my horse with the stirrup,[12] and it threw him over there.[13] He fell, and I jumped off the horse, got to the ground, and began throwing stones at him until I killed him.

"Then I went back to my sister. Behold, she was like a mute person. When I got near her I saw that there was something tied to her arm—it was a *siḥir.*[14] I cut off the string, and threw away the charm. Thereupon she began to cry over her brothers, and tore her dress, and began to mourn for them.[15] Then we both went back to the tent. But see: the tent and the property were robbed, and only my mother, this old woman, remained.

"I went after the raiders following their spoor. On the way I encountered people who robbed me and left me nothing but my jacket. Then I reached a tribe of Arabs over whom once in my good days I had attained mastery.[16] When their emir saw me, he recognized me, but doubted whether I was he. I remained with them as a Sharārī,[17] as a servant. I made coffee for them,[18] for several days. They prepared to go out on a raid. When they went, only the women stayed behind.

"In their absence Arabs came, they robbed the property and drove it away with them.[19] The women cried out for me and sought my help, and the sister of the emir brought me a sword and armor. I went after the Arabs and brought back all the property, and the emir's sister was looking at me from the distance.

"Several hours later the emir returned with a countless booty. When he learned what had happened during his absence, he called me and acquainted himself with me, and now he knew that I was his [erstwhile] enemy.[20] He made peace with me, and gave me this sister of his, and all the property that you have seen. And this is my mother who experienced all these blows of fate, and this is my bride—she has been with me only four days. And you say that all my life no disaster has hit me?"

When they heard his story, they said, "Every disaster is light compared to your disaster." Then they slept.

And be your morning pleasant!

Comments

The intention of this folktale is to demonstrate that every man, even one who seems to be the happiest, richest, and most fortunate, has to suffer his share of blows from the hand of fate. A man blessed with all worldly goods, who celebrates his wedding and is able to indulge in lavish hospitality, nevertheless turns out to have undergone enormous sufferings.

The precariousness of Bedouin life is illustrated by the repeated raids described in the story. As a consequence of a raid, a man can lose all his property and be reduced to utter poverty, but, on the other hand, by undertaking a successful raid he can just as suddenly gain uncounted riches.

The figure of the Maghrebite sorcerer in the story is interesting. The people of the Maghreb (Morocco or northwest Africa in general) had the reputation of being adepts at sorcery. By tying a charm to the arm of the hero's sister, the Maghrebite sorcerer renders her unable to speak, deprives her of all willpower of her own, makes her indifferent to everything that happens around her, and forces her to follow him like an automaton. The charms used were mostly written on paper or parchment, sewn in a cloth or leather bag, and tied around the upper arm. By removing the charm, its power is broken, and the person becomes again his former self. Charms used in the Maghreb are described by Edmond Doutté, *Magie et religion dans l'Afrique du Nord* (Alger: A. Jourdan, 1909), pp. 143–306; and Edward Westermarck, *Ritual and Belief in Morocco* (London: Macmillan, 1926), index, s.v. "Charms"; "Witchcraft."

Notes

1. The territory east of the Jordan between the Zerqa (Yabbok) and the al-Mawjib (Arnon) rivers.
2. A gift, and especially a gift of a sheep given to mourners. See I. G. Wetzstein, "Sprachliches aus den Zeltlagern der syrischen Wüste," *Zeitschrift der deutschen morgenländischen Gesellschaft* 22 (1868): 142; Schmidt and Kahle, *Volkserzählungen aus Palästina* (Göttingen: Vandenhoeck und Ruprecht, 1918), pp. 247, 250.
3. In honor of the deceased, those who respected him while he was alive bring a sheep to the bereaved family and prepare a meal of which also friends and poor people partake.
4. Term used in the Balqa to designate a wedding tent. See Wetzstein, 22: 105. n. 44.
5. The host spread out mats for the guests to sit on.
6. Colloquial pronunciation by the villagers of the literary *ahlan wa-sahlan.*
7. From the colloquial term *frenk* or *ifrenk,* meaning "European." In literary Arabic *ifranjī.*
8. That each guest was given a separate bed indicates the great wealth of the host.
9. A large Bedouin tent was usually divided in the middle by a vertical curtain that separated the part where guests were received from the part that was the family's living quarters.
10. Arabic Maghribī. In the folktales Maghrebites—people from Morocco, Tunisia, and Algeria—often appear as powerful sorcerers.
11. Popular expression meaning "within less time than you need to finish smoking a cigarette."
12. The Arab stirrup was not a flat-based ring like the European stirrup but a metal plate on which the entire sole of the shoe could rest. The inside corners of this plate served for spurring on the horse.
13. It is the custom of Arab storytellers to indicate or illustrate by hand movements what they are relating. We must imagine that at this point in his story, the storyteller pointed to some distance from where he was sitting.
14. In literary Arabic *siḥr* ("charm, amulet").
15. The Arab women's mourning for a close relative had a ritualized style and consisted of a series of traditional movements and utterances.
16. A delicate way of saying that he succeeded in conducting a raid against them.
17. The Shararāt were a weak tribe, which had placed itself under the protection of the powerful Banī Ṣakhr tribe; this, of course, meant considerable loss of face. Many individual members of the Shararāt hired themselves out to powerful tribes as menial workers, servants, or herdsmen, and hence the Shararāt were in general looked down upon with contempt, and the noble tribes did not intermarry with them. See Raphael Patai, *Golden River to Golden Road:*

Society, Culture and Change in the Middle East, 3rd ed. (Philadelphia: University of Pennsylvania Press, 1969), index, s.v. "Shararāt."

18. Well-to-do Bedouin families had special slaves whose only task was to prepare coffee for the family and the frequent guests.
19. In a typical raid the raiders were satisfied with driving off the camels of the tribe they attacked. They took care not to kill anybody and not to touch the women.
20. The emir recognizes his former enemy by his heroism.

Part Two

1946–47

11

The Lightest of the Light, the Heaviest of the Heavy, and the Fattest of the Fat

Read over Jerusalem Radio by its author, Ilyās Shiḥādah, February 11, 1947.

An emir of the emirs of the Bedouin got acquainted with a *qāḍī,* who lived in the town, became his friend, and the bonds of friendship and love developed between them. Before long the emir asked to be the *qāḍī*'s son-in-law, and the *qāḍī* gave him his daughter in marriage.

The emir brought her to his tribe, and she bore him three sons. The sons grew up among the children of the tribe as their equal, and the youngest, called Aḥmad, was the smartest and most clever of them.

However, they were not spared insults by the children of the neighborhood because they were the children of a city woman, and their maternal uncles were neither known nor famous. The Bedouin are very proud of their maternal uncles. And even had their uncles been known, they would still not have been worthy of respect, since they lacked bravery and generosity.[1] Even the emir himself was not exempt from mocking by the heads and the men of the tribe. They insulted him, saying he sat at home and yielded to idleness and sloth, and avoided raids and scenes of bravery for the sake of trivial things to which they had not been accustomed from before.

The emir knew that his city wife was the reason for this, and he wanted to get rid of her, and thus be free of the insults of the elders and of their mockery and disdain. He intended to resort to a well-knit trick by which he would be free of his father-in-law, and no longer be in a marriage relation with him. Thus he would save his reputation and fame from being blunted.

One day he went to his wife and said to her, "O daughter of my paternal uncle,[2] it has been a long time since you have visited your family, and soon it will be the blessed Feast of Sacrifice. I think that it is meet and good that you, the daughter of generous people, should go and visit your parents, and stay there about a month, and then return."

The wife became very happy and started to prepare for the trip. When the day of her departure arrived, her husband and sons went out, together with all the men and women of the tribe, to bid her farewell.[3] Then the emir remained alone with her for a short while, and gave her a message to his father-in-law, the judge.

He said to her, "See, O daughter of [noble] people, take this message and give it to my father-in-law, your father, and ask him to let me have his answer. If his answer will be correct, you will remain my legal wife, and the mother of my children. If his answer is not good, you will be divorced by the triple."[4]

Her son Aḥmad was listening to the conversation that was going on between the two of them.

She took the message from her husband and hid it among her clothes.

Thereafter the emir returned with the men of the tribe to their tents. As for her three sons, they went with her for some distance, and before their return Aḥmad said to her, "O my mother, by Allāh, show me the message that my father gave you to give to my grandfather."

She handed him the message. After he read it, and understood its meaning, he gave it back to his mother. Then her sons bade her farewell, and returned to the place from which they came.

As for her, she continued her travel until she arrived at her father's house. After the customary greetings she gave him the message, and he opened it and read the following:

"My dear father-in-law!! May Allāh protect you! After asking for peace upon you, and the mercy and blessing of Allāh, now, three difficult questions have come to my mind. And since I know that you are a *qāḍī* of the *Sharīʿa,*[5] understanding and clever, and you read and write,[6] and the noble people benefit from you, I come to put them to you, and ask you to answer them for me. These are the questions: What is the lightest of the light, and the heaviest of the heavy, and the fattest of the fat? Be well and be safe to your friend and son-in-law, So-and-so."[7]

After the judge folded up the message, he turned to his daughter and asked her what did the emir tell her. She informed him that the emir had told her, "If the answer of your father will be good, I shall like it, and you will be my wife and the mother of my children. But if, Allāh forbid, it will not be good, you will be divorced with the triple."

And the judge laughed until he fell on his back, and he said, "What a poor man is my son-in-law, the emir! How ignorant is he! These questions are difficult for him! Then why is he an emir? The lightest of the light is bran residue left in the sieve and the sawdust of wood, the heaviest of the heavy is lead, and the fattest of the fat is the fat spring lamb." [8]

Then he wrote down most of this in a letter, and entrusted her with the preceding answers. He folded up the letter and gave it to his daughter to keep it and deliver it to the emir upon her return.

The emirah spent a few months with her parents, then she bade them farewell and returned to her husband's tribe. When she was not too far from her home, her three sons came out to meet her in the early morning. They met at a distance from their large tents, and when she met them and greeted them, all of a sudden her youngest son approached her and asked her, "Where is the message that my grandfather sent to our father?"

She handed him the letter. He opened it with a trick, and learned what was in it. Instantly he was stunned, and the light in his eyes became darkness, because of the ignorance of his grandfather, and the smallness of his comprehension.

He said, "O mother, woe to me! You are divorced, because my grandfather is not good and has no understanding. His answer is not good."

Thereupon he gave his mother another message which contained the answers his father wanted, and replaced with it the message of his grandfather. He sealed it, handed it to his mother, and tore up the first letter.

And these were his answers: "The lightest of the light is judgment in a claim between two good people. The heaviest of the heavy is judgment between two spongers. The fattest of the fat is the water of the two *Kānūn* [months], namely the rain that falls in the months of *Kānūn al-awwal* [First *Kānūn*], and *Kānūn al-thānī* [Second *Kānūn*]."

Then he bid his mother farewell, and after warning her not to tell their father anything of their meeting, he and his brothers went on their way.

When the emirah arrived, she greeted the emir and all the members of the tribe, every single person of the tribe, and then she handed the letter to the emir. When the emir opened it and read what was in it, he knew instantly that the answers were not those of his father-in-law.

He said, "This is not the wisdom of my father-in-law. It has to be the understanding of one of my loins (*ṣulb*), namely the wisdom of one of my sons."

He asked her whether she had met by chance one of her sons. She denied it completely.

The emir decided to play a trick to know the truth. He summoned one of his slaves,[9] and said to him, "O kind slave, mount your mare and disappear for a while, and then come back screaming and saying, 'Woe to you, O Arabs! The emir's sons were killed! The emir's sons were murdered!' Be careful not to say anything to anybody, nor to reveal the secret."

The slave did as his master ordered him, and he returned screaming, "Fire is better than shame! Shame, O Arabs! The emir's sons were slaughtered! The three were struck in the ventricle!"

As soon as his voice was heard the Arabs became enraged, and they vehemently and violently rolled, and mounted their horses and girded on their weapons. When the emir heard this uproar of calamity, he went out to inquire about it. "O Arabs, I hope there is good news. Has something good happened? What is this misfortune?"

He heard the answer, "Woe to us, O emir! Your sons were slaughtered! Woe to us, O emir!"

This was said within earshot of the emirah, and she went out screaming, "Don't believe it, O emir! They have seen me two hours ago, and they are well. Don't worry! They have courage!"

When the emir thus learned the truth, he shouted, "Nothing bad has happened!"

As for the emir, he was seized with a great fury, mounted his horse, put on his weapons, and rode out from among the big tents to meet his sons and to mete out punishment to them for having deceived him. He did not ride long until he met them, and he shouted at them from afar, "Woe to you from my anger, O sons of the treacherous one, what did you do? And what is this treachery?"

The two older sons shouted back and said, "We did not deceive you, O our father, it is our brother Aḥmad who deceived you."

He left the two of them alone, and shouted at his son Aḥmad, saying, "Woe to you, Aḥmad, what is the matter with you? I shall not let go of you until I kill you!"

When Aḥmad saw the intention of his father, and knowing the sharpness of his temper, when he heard this he pulled the neck of his horse around and fled. His father pursued him, but could not overtake him, because the horse of Aḥmad was a superior charger, of the best breed, and its rider was a light boy, and the trainer who had trained Aḥmad was a skillful horseman.

When the father got tired, he called out to his son saying, "Stop, O Aḥmad! Be assured, fear not, you have my word that I shall not kill you."

Aḥmad stopped. His father reached him, and Aḥmad dismounted from his horse. The first part of the night had passed already. The father also dismounted, and said to his son, "O my son! I feel cold. Gather for us a few pieces of wood, and start a little fire."

The boy immediately gathered all the wood he could find. He set a fire, and when its flames reached high, his father took him by surprise, and held him fast by his feet, determined to cast him into the fire.

Aḥmad screamed at him and said, "Why, O father, do you wish to cast me into this victor and vanquished?"

Thereupon his father set him free and said, "Why is it a victor and a vanquished, O Aḥmad?"

Aḥmad replied, "It is a victor, O father, because it devours the whole of the universe, and it is vanquished because water can overcome it."

His father asked him, "What overcomes the water, O my son?"

Aḥmad said, "The mountain can overcome the water, because water cannot go up the mountain."

He said, "What overcomes the mountain?"

Aḥmad said, "The blooded horse overcomes the mountain."

He asked him what overcomes the blooded horse, and he said, "The horseman overcomes the blooded horse."

He said, "What overcomes the horseman?"

He said, "The woman, O father, overcomes the horseman."

He said, "What overcomes the woman?"

He said, "Women overcome women. Subdue the women by women."

Thereupon his father was gladdened by the cleverness and understanding of his son, and wanted to examine him more. He asked him, "Explain three words to me, O my son!"

Aḥmad said to him, "What are they, O my father?"

He said to him, "*Not, not, not.* Three *nots.*"

Thereupon the son answered, "The first *not*—Allāh be praised, who makes hair grow on the back of the hand but not on the palm. The second *not*—the son of your son is yours, but the son of your daughter is not. The third *not*—with your men you can instill fear, but with the men of other people not."

The father rejoiced a great rejoicing with his son's answers, and wanted to learn more of his cleverness and broad knowledge. He said to him, "O my son, three things lengthen life. What are they?"

The son answered him, "One: Your walking on the plants. Two: Your uprooting of plants. Three: The riding on horses. These make life longer."

Then the father asked, "Three things shorten life, O my son. What are they?"

The son answered him, "Taking [in marriage] widows; passing through deserts [disgraces]; walking behind biers [at funerals]."

The father said, "Good, O Aḥmad, good. And the last question is this, O my son, O Aḥmad: If two good people come to you seeking your judgment, how would you judge between them?"

He said, "The two good people will not come to me. One of them will settle with the other before they come to me."

He said to him, "If a sponger [*ʿawīl*] and a good person should come to you, how will you judge between them?"

He said, "I would take from the property of the good man and give it to the sponger, and will thus satisfy both of them."

He said, "If two spongers should come to you, how would you judge between them?"

He said, "I would pay from my own property and make them satisfied, O my father."

The father was very satisfied with the cleverness of his son and his broad knowledge. He took the seal of the emirate from his finger and said, "Listen to me, O my son, O Aḥmad! I have become an old man, O my son, and my mind is not firm. I think that you are more worthy of the emirate than I. Therefore take my seal, and from now on you will be the emir to rule over the Arabs, not I, because you are clever and understanding and fair."

Thereupon he bestowed on him the seal of the emirate, and returned with him to the tribe to proclaim him the emir of the Arabs. His fame became widespread, and he became famous among the tribes of that time for his cleverness, understanding, fairness, and generosity. And may peace be upon you!

Comments

The story, evidently originating in a Bedouin environment, holds the Bedouin superior to the townspeople. If a Bedouin marries a town girl, as does the emir in our story, the children of this "mixed" marriage are looked down upon and insulted by the other children of the tribe who are of Bedouin descent on both the father's and their mother's side. The Bedouin conviction is that townspeople "lack bravery and generosity" and that they are less sharp-witted than the Bedouin. Even the emir of the tribe has to suffer because of his marriage to the townsman's (the *qāḍī*'s) daughter, until things reach such a state that he wants to get rid of his wife, even though she bore him three sons. It is at this point that the narrative sets off.

The intention of the story is to depict the cleverness of the emir's youngest son, Aḥmad, but incidentally it throws light on the personality and position of the Bedouin chief. The emir is the autocratic ruler of his tribe, but the respect he commands in the tribe depends on his ability and willingness to lead the men of the tribe in raids and to be prominent in "scenes of bravery." Also, the emir is powerless to counteract the censure with which the tribe reacts to his marrying a city girl; that is, he can do nothing to change the traditional tribal mores. In fact, the pressure of tribal opinion is so strong that after almost two decades of marriage, the emir decides to divorce his wife, the mother of his three sons. He is depicted as not being honest: he gives his word that he will not harm Aḥmad but then grabs him by surprise and is about to cast him into the fire. He is also shown to be shrewd, and what impresses him most is superior mental capacity, which he recognizes in his youngest son.

The absence of all miraculous features, as well as of supernatural beings such as ghouls, places this story in the type of quasi-realistic folktales, to which also belong tales 2, 4, 5, 7, 8, and 10.

Notes

1. The storyteller finds it necessary to explain the Bedouin pride in maternal relations, and in bravery and generosity.
2. In Arabic *bint ʿammī*. Since the most favored marriage is between a man and his paternal uncle's daughter, the custom is for a man to address his wife, even if she is not his cousin, in this complimentary manner.
3. The Bedouin custom calls for the relatives and others to accompany a departing member of the tribe to some distance.

4. That is, by the triple divorce, which cannot be annulled.
5. The *qāḍī* administers the *Sharīʿa,* the traditional Islamic law.
6. Most Bedouin were illiterate; hence the emir's reference to the *qāḍī*'s ability to read and write is intended as a compliment.
7. The storyteller does not bother to invent a name for the emir. Instead, he refers to him as "So-and-so."
8. The foolishness of the *qāḍī* is indicated by the fact that he takes the questions of the emir literally and does not suspect that they have a hidden or symbolic meaning.
9. That the Bedouin have slaves is taken for granted by the storyteller even in 1946.

12
Ṭalāja of the Twenty and the Chicken

Recorded and read over Jerusalem Radio by Dr. Isḥāq Mūsā al-Ḥusaynī, December 3, 1946.

In times of old there lived a boy, his mother's only son. When he reached the age of learning his mother sent him to school.[1] He was clever, and obeyed his mother.

One day the teacher asked him to bring along money for the price of a book which the teacher would give him. Ṭalāja went to his mother and asked for the money. His mother was poor, and she gave him twenty *dirhams* and one chicken. She said to him, "Go to the market, and sell the chicken and exchange it for *dirhams.* Then bring them to the teacher as the price of the book."

While he was in the market, looking for a buyer, the chief of the thieves noticed him, took from him the *dirhams* and the chicken by force, and sent him to his mother.

However, as we have said, Ṭalāja was clever. Therefore he did not go to his mother, but rather followed the wicked thief secretly, from one place to another. The thief was not aware of this. He went and bought thirty-nine chickens, and carried them to a certain cook in the city. He handed them over to him, together with the hen that he had taken by force from Ṭalāja. He ordered him to cook them and to do it well with salt and pepper. He said to him, "I shall send somebody at noon to fetch them."

The cook said to him, "As you wish. At your service. I heard and obey."

He did whatever the chief of the thieves told him to do, saying that the chickens would be ready at the appointed time.

A few minutes before the appointed time Ṭalāja went to the cook, having heard before what the chief of the thieves had told him. He asked the cook to give him the chickens that his master had left with the cook. The latter gave him the chickens thinking that he was the person mentioned by the chief of the thieves. The cook asked him what was his name, and he said to him, "My name is Ṭalāja of the Twenty and the Chicken."

Ṭalāja took the chickens with him and gave them to his mother. Then he hurried back to the store of the cook to see what would happen. Exactly at twelve o'clock the messenger of the chief of the thieves came, asking for the chickens. The cook told him that a messenger from his master, by the name of Ṭalāja of the Twenty and the Chicken, had preceded him and taken the chickens.

That young man returned and told the chief of the thieves. He became angry and said, "By Allāh! How cunning he is! We took from him one hen, and he took from us forty!"

He threatened to do him harm.

Then the chief of the thieves went to market accompanied by members of his gang, and Ṭalāja followed them cautiously. He observed their moves and their talk. They decided to go next day to the bath house in order to wash and change from their old clothes into new ones, and so to prepare themselves to look for the cunning Ṭalāja.

The bath house which they had chosen was in a deserted place where almost nobody passed. Ṭalāja went there and offered to serve the owner in exchange for his food. The owner agreed.

Next day the forty thieves came and entered the bath house. They took off their clothes. Ṭalāja went to the place where they put their [new] clothes and carried them away saying to the owner of the bath house, "These people requested that I remove their clothes from such-and-such a place."

He went directly to his mother and put the clothes in front of her. They took out whatever *dirhams,* pistols, knives, and jewelry were in the clothes.

When the thieves finished bathing they asked for their clothes and the owner of the bath house told them that the servant had taken them away to change them in accordance with their wishes. They denied the matter, and put on their old clothes. Then they went out, furiously. Ṭalāja was watching their moves from afar. They went to a coffee house and sat there, and decided to work in some business. Each of them would open a store, so that when Ṭalāja passed near them they could seize him and kill him.

Ṭalāja knew about their conspiracy, because he was listening to their conversation while in disguise.

The thieves went to the market, and each of them rented a store. They waited for Ṭalāja to come by in order to attack him.

As for Ṭalāja, he went to a wood gatherer to whom he gave five *līras,*[2] and asked him to prepare for him forty pieces of firewood. Ṭalāja took them to his house, removing and cutting off their leaves. Then he smoothed them and cut them to the height of a boy. He wrote on top of each of them, "Ṭalāja of the Twenty and the Chicken." Then he wrapped around each of them [the skin of] a young sheep, and asked for his mother's help. He dressed them in children's clothes, so that each piece of wood seemed to be a child.

He brought his mother very nice new clothes, and said to her, "Go to the market and carry with you one of these pieces of wood, and go straight to the store of So-and-so."

He showed her the thieves' stores. Then he continued, "And buy from each store merchandise worth a large amount of money, starting with fifty *līras* and up, until you have covered all the forty stores. Make the owner of each store believe that you forgot your *dirhams* at home, and that you are leaving with him a young child[3] from your forty children[4] as a pledge until the time of your return with the *dirhams.*"

His mother carried out everything as he said, and collected a lot of clothes, and headed for her house.

In the evening the merchant-thieves gathered and started to discuss business matters. Their leader mentioned that he had sold merchandise worth fifty *līras* but had not collected the money. Instead, he had received something that had been deposited with him by the woman.[5] The second one said the same thing as the first. Thus the whole group knew that a woman had left with each of them a child as a security for a certain amount of money. They were puzzled by the matter. They went to their stores and opened them, and they rushed to the children—and found them bundled up. They removed whatever was covering them, until they reached the pieces of wood, and there, on each piece of wood, were written the words, "Ṭalāja of the Twenty and the Chicken." They were seized with a great rage, and realized that young Ṭalāja had mocked them and played a trick on them, and they swore to take revenge.

However, young Ṭalāja took action ahead of them. He went in a hurry to the king's palace and told him everything that had happened to him with these thieves who acted wickedly, causing corruption in the land. Ṭalāja led the king to their stores. The king sent his soldiers, who took them by surprise, apprehended them, and threw them into prison.

The king thanked Ṭalāja for the service he rendered the city by putting an end to their thievery. He praised his cleverness and his courage, and let him enter school at the king's expense.

Ṭalāja entered school, and demonstrated excellent capability and sharp wits. After he had finished his studies the king assigned him to a position on his official staff,[6] the *diwan* [council], and he demonstrated ability and loyalty. He lived under the protection of the king, in the care of his mother,[7] and enjoyed the best conditions with an easier and more composed mind.

So his story reached the ears of the inhabitants for everyone to hear, and they started talking about it. It remained long in circulation, until it reached the descendants in our own time.

Comments

This story is a variant of the widespread Arab folktale about a youth or a clever man who is able to outwit—or kill—forty thieves. Its hero, Ṭalāja, is the son of a poor woman, who lives in a quasi-modern environment. He is a pupil in a school and has to give money to the teacher for a schoolbook. His mother does not have enough money to cover the price of the book and therefore gives him the twenty *dirhams* she has and a chicken to sell in the marketplace and add its price to the money for the book. The money and the chicken are stolen from Ṭalāja by a thief, one of a gang of forty. However, Ṭalāja is much too clever for them and with various tricks succeeds not only in getting even with them but also in having them arrested by the king's soldiers. As a reward, the king lets Ṭalāja finish his studies at school, after which he appoints him member of the royal council.

The story exhibits a certain ineptness on the part of the storyteller. In general, it does not have the charm, the interest, the tension, or the fantasy that make the classical Arab folktale a jewel of folkloristic creativity. Even the conclusion ("He lived under the protection of the king, in the care of his mother") is inept and unsatisfactory. If indeed this story was, as was claimed, "a folktale" recorded by Dr. Ḥusaynī, it was a tale of low quality or else one that, while "it remained long in circulation," has lost much of the color it originally possessed.

Notes

1. Attendance at school figures in the story as an important factor in the boy's life. At the end of the story the reward of Ṭalāja is that the king pays his tuition fee at school. The importance attributed to going to school is a clear indication of the transitional situation between traditional and modern conditions in which the Arabs of Palestine found themselves in the British mandatory period.
2. *Līra* was the Arabic (and Hebrew) term for the Palestinian pound, the official currency during the British mandatory period. In this story the terms *līra* and *dirham* (drachma) are used interchangeably.
3. The stupidity of the thieves is shown by the fact that they did not recognize that the piece of wood wrapped in sheepskin was not a child.
4. The mention of the forty children at this point shows the ineptness of the storyteller. The mother was certainly not supposed to tell each of the merchants that she had forty children.
5. Again, a certain ineptness on the part of the storyteller. A merchant who received a child as a pledge from a customer would not have left the child overnight unattended in his locked-up store.
6. There is a hidden lesson in this conclusion of the story: go to school, and if you are good at your studies, you will get a fine position with the government. This again reflects the transitional situation under the British mandate.
7. An unusual feature of this story is that the existence of Ṭalāja's father is not mentioned at all. One would have expected at least a statement at the beginning of the story to the effect that Ṭalāja's mother was a widow.

13
Cunning . . . and Cunning

Written and read over Jerusalem Radio by Fāyiz al-Ghūl, December 5, 1946.

One of the greatest merchants—and he had already reached old age—started to proceed toward the Hereafter,[1] and wanted to make sure that his young son should obtain thorough knowledge about life in order to be able to safeguard, after him, the property which he had amassed by exhausting his body. He had spent the best years of his life acquiring and investing this property, and he wanted that his son should not underestimate the value of that property, nor that anybody should disregard his achievement. Therefore he gave him a large amount of money and advised him to travel around in the wide world of Allāh. He commanded him to be watchful and aware of all that surrounded him, and of all matters that went on around him, no matter how small they were, because small matters cause the large ones, and most fires are started from small sparks.

The youth went off and spent a month traveling around the country. Then he came back to his father and found him in a weak condition for which no remedy could be found. Neither a cure nor survival was anticipated. After only a few days his father passed away. They escorted him to his final resting place with solemn ceremony. His son was very sad.

After some days, the young merchant's desires were awakened. His childhood friends tried to persuade him to rush after pleasures, and to seize the opportunity of joys and delights. But he dismissed them with kindness, and explained to them gently that he did not wish to follow their ways, that they should not hope to be his companions, because he had made up his mind that those companions were only covetous of his property. They desired his friendship only for the sake of his wealth. He knew this in his soul due to the experiences he had acquired while traveling around the country. He had great self-confidence. In a prominent place in his store he put up a sign which read, "The cunning of men exceeds the cunning of women."[2] He wrote these words in large *thuluth* script.[3]

It happened one day that the daughter of the chief of blacksmiths[4] passed near the door of his store. She saw a good-looking young man with beautiful features and broad shoulders, and she liked him. However, when she saw the sign it made her angry, because she believed that the cunning of women was sharper, and their deception greater. Allāh has mentioned in the Holy Book the cunning of women, and described it as great,[5] but He did not mention the cunning of men.

In the afternoon she went back to her house, agitated by this young man who challenged and belittled the cunning of women. She lingered on this situation of confusion, until she decided to try a trick, which she worked out after much thinking. She then slept calmly, and when she woke up she applied much makeup, and chose her most attractive clothes, the most seductive ones, and put them on. She observed her reflection, thus dressed, in the mirror in her room, and primped for quite a while until she was pleased with herself. Then she headed in the direction of the young merchant.

She passed in front of his door twice or three times, driven by her determination, but prevented by shyness from entering. However, she returned and approached him. She drew his attention to herself, and said, "Good morning, O uncle!"[6]

He heard a charming voice, emitted from a beautiful throat, overflowing with life. It reached into his soul like water reaching a thirsty being. He answered her with the best greeting, and wanted her to continue speaking. But she did not do so.

He said, "Is there anything I can do for you? Can I get you something, O my lady?"

The young woman remained silent, and when he repeated the same question she started to cry. The youth was touched, and his sense of honor moved him, since there is no greater hurt to a man's heart than that inflicted by beauty in distress. He asked her what caused her to cry. She did not answer. Rather, her weeping increased. Her sobs rose, and the youth felt that his heart broke because of her pain and weeping.

Finally he said to her, "Listen, O my girl, this weeping is of no use. Be gentle to yourself and explain to me what bothers you. I promise to get you justice. I shall bring you release from your grief. I shall offer everything to cheer you up, and to remove distress and sorrow from you, even if it will require all my property."

When she was sure that she had affected him and had aroused his gracious emotions, she took off her veil.[7] From behind it emerged a face that put the clear morning to shame.

She said, "How do you find my face?"

The youth said, "Allāh be blessed, be praised! The best of creatures!"

She said, "How do you find my eyes?" and she closed her eyes out of shyness. Thus she became more tempting.

He said, "They are arrows in the hearts of men."

With a move, as if it was unintended, her veil fell down, and underneath it appeared pitch-black hair. The youth saw that night and day were united in her hair and her face. She took the veil and fixed it in its place. There appeared her forearm and a wrist that a flower would envy. Thus she revealed to him some other beauties, until he fell in love with her. Then she [again] wept bitterly, and showed both her legs, and they were like two pillars of silver.

Embarrassment overcame him, and he lost his mind from her beauty, and he said, "Cover these beauties, and inform me what has caused you to cry, because I shall vouch for your safety with my soul and my property."

While with both his eyes he saw her magic she poured out her heart to him, and said, "I am the daughter of the *qāḍī,* and because of his love for me and his jealousy about me he wants to prevent me from marrying. If a youth were to come to ask him for my hand, he would say, 'My daughter is ugly, my daughter is one-eyed, my daughter is crippled.' He would describe me as having many repulsive qualities in order to turn him away. The youth proposing would give up, and I would remain in confusion, drink the cup of sorrow, and be filled with bitterness. If a young woman, enjoying the richness of her parents and the strength of their love, were in no need of a husband, I would be the most happy human being. But women were created for the sake of men, and men for the sake of women.[8] I am afraid that in a short while my body will fade, my youthfulness will dry up, and the dew of my beauty will diminish from my face. I shall spend the rest of my life—may it be long—in deadly despair. Do you think I am wrong in seeking relief from this distress, and asking for deliverance from this predicament, O gracious and righteous one?"

When the youth heard her he said to her, "Be good to your soul, and be delighted. Be in good spirits. The stubbornness of your father is my luck. Tomorrow I shall not be deceived by this ruse.[9] Now go, may safety accompany you."

She was about to kiss the hem of his garment, but he stopped her from doing so, and she bade him farewell, thanking him.

In the evening the merchant went to his house, and his eyes were not refreshed with slumber. The shadow of the girl remained like stakes in his heart. She had accomplished her trick. Then when he woke up, he hurried to the *qāḍī*'s house, and asked permission to enter. When he was brought in to him, he greeted him. The *qāḍī* had coffee brought to him, and after the merchant had drunk he said, "O your honor, the *qāḍī,* I am requesting the hand of your daughter."

The *qāḍī* said, "She is ugly."

The youth said, "I know it, and I agree."

Then the *qāḍī* said, "She is one-eyed."

The youth said, "I know it, and I agree."

Then the *qāḍī* said, "She is baldheaded, and has crippled fingers."

Then the youth interrupted him saying, "Be brief, O my Master, because I agree to marry her regardless of the defects she has. Name the bride price so that I can pay it to you."

The *qāḍī,* overtaken by greed, said, "Her bride price is ten thousand denars,[10] to be paid in advance, and the same amount to be due as the deferred portion of the bride price."[11]

The merchant agreed, and he paid the advance bride price in cash, and brought witnesses who wrote the marriage contract and fixed a date for the wedding ceremony. The young merchant was waiting with impatience, wishing himself lasting happiness.

When the appointed day arrived, the young man invited his friends and important people of the city. He prepared for them a sumptuous banquet, and it was decorated with delightful colors and with whatever the soul could desire. All eyes were delighted. He sat with the invited guests, waiting for the arrival of the procession of the bride with her family, so they could go to meet them and greet them.

While they were waiting, all of a sudden there came a porter who was barely able to carry a big trunk, and he asked for the young man. He was directed to him. He said, "This is a trunk from the *qāḍī.*"

The young man commanded him to bring it to the room which was designated for the bride, because he thought it was the trunk of her clothing. Then his heart urged him to go up so as to gratify his eyes with the clothing of the bride. He fumbled around, and turned the handle of the trunk. He opened it and looked inside it. It was, O how terrible was the sight he saw! [12]

Next day the youth went down and opened his store. He sat there, overwhelmed by strong confusion, and seized with wonder about the cunning trick which she had played on him. He raked his memory to see what caused this misfortune, and could not figure it out. His thoughts swam, and nothing could hold his attention except the voice of the daughter of the chief of the blacksmiths which kept ringing in his ears.

[Suddenly she came to his store and said to him,] [13] "Good morning, O uncle, may you have well-being and good living and continuance, and sons and daughters . . ." [14]

He said to her, "May you never have happiness in the morning, and may the Merciful One not bless the hour in which I saw you. How did I deserve this from you? Woe unto you for all this! What did you have against me?"

She said, "Because of your bragging. Are you not the one who hung on the door of your store 'The cunning of men exceeds the cunning of women'? I wanted to test your cleverness, to expose your deception. How do you now find the cunning of women, and how does it compare with the cunning of men?"

He said, "It is for that reason that you did whatever you did last night? Indeed, I was deceived. Now what is your opinion as to how to save me from the situation I am in?" [15]

She said, "What is your opinion, O smart fellow?" And she said, "Then will you remove this writing from its place, since you have no good claim for it? I shall pass by your store tomorrow. If I see that you desisted from your deception, I shall find a way out for you from this difficult situation. It will be a relief for you, Allāh willing."

He said, "I have already seen the light. Indicate to me your opinion."

She said, "Wait until you do what I am telling you, and tomorrow I shall pass by your store, and tomorrow is near."

She left him and went her way. He immediately arose and erased the old writing, and instead wrote in gold, "The cunning of women exceeds the cunning of men."

When the young woman returned in the morning of the following day, she saw the youth sitting there, and saw the paleness of his face, and

[knew] by the expression of his eyes what anguish he was having. They bore witness that he did not taste the taste of sleep all night.

She looked around and saw that he had changed the written sign, and put instead of it the following, "The cunning of women exceeds all other cunnings." She smiled at this with a full smile. She said, "We are the daughters of Eve. We know this fact for ourselves, and we do not need anybody else to tell us."

He burned the sign. Then she said to him, "Go to the gypsies, and carry a gift with you for their elderly head and for that band of people. I have already explained to him the plan." [16]

He went immediately, and he brought a very expensive gift to their elderly leader, and other gifts to each individual in the group.

He told them, "I am your cousin, my origin is from the gypsies, and whoever denies his race denies his identity. I have married the daughter of the *qāḍī,* and he, as you know, is among the noble people. I want him to know my importance and the multitude of my relatives, and I shall go to him now. You too come there, and greet him with peace, and give a blessing to me and to him. Arrange for me a big wedding ceremony in the courtyard of his house, with your drummers and flutists, and the rest of your entertainment, so that he should know that he became the father-in-law of a respected man."

They said, "As you wish, with the greatest pleasure, O our cousin!"

He bade them farewell and left. He sat next to the *qāḍī* in his courtyard. The prominent people of the city were present.[17] Those who were present heard all kinds of sounds of music playing, twitterings of women, whinnying of horses, and the braying of donkeys. All the sounds were mixed together, so they formed an abominable music.

Then the group, including drummers and pipers, came to the *qāḍī.* Monkeys [18] and dancers frolicked. They greeted him and blessed him and their cousin, and trod underfoot his comfortable cushions, and sat down cross-legged on his velvety carpets and couches, and some of them gathered in a circle on the ground.

The *qāḍī* was wondering about what he saw. He asked his son-in-law about it, and the latter said to him, "O my uncle! Whoever denies his race denies his personal identity. Indeed, yes, my origin is gypsy, and I married your daughter so as to obtain the honor of being close to you. I think that this, my origin, should not offend you."

The *qāḍī* became angry and said, "Are these your relatives? O, what a disgrace! Did I become father-in-law to a man from this people? Divorce my daughter! You are not suitable for my lineage. Why did you not inform me about your origin?" [19]

He said, "I shall not divorce my wife. It is not an easy thing what you want to impose on me to do. If there was any mistake, it is yours. You did not ask me about my roots. Had you asked me, I would not have hidden my origin from you."

The *qāḍī* said, "I shall not deprive you of any of your property. I shall return to you the bride price you paid, and shall hand over to you the gifts you gave, or their equivalent, and shall forward the remainder of whatever you have spent. I shall forgo the bride price to be paid later, and you divorce my daughter for me."

The young man pretended to decline the offer, and expressed non-acceptance. However, the people in attendance continued to persuade him, until he agreed. He recovered the bride price and the gifts of the bride, and divorced her. The *qāḍī* at once sent a porter who brought his daughter back to his house.[20]

The young man went back to his home, and worldly goods became too small for him, and there was no room for his joy. That night he slept a deep and peaceful sleep.

In the morning he went to his store, opened it, and sat in it as usual. The daughter of the chief of blacksmiths came. She asked him what he had done. He told her that he did as she recommended, and that everything was achieved according to what she had foreseen.

Then he said, "And now, how is the achievement for you?"

She said, "Ask for my hand from my father, the chief of the blacksmiths, and he will let you marry me." [21]

When evening came, he went to the chief of blacksmiths. He bid him welcome, and greeted him. After he sat down comfortably, he said, "O uncle! I come to you to ask the hand of your daughter in marriage."

He said, "You are an appropriate match."

The young man said, "But I have one condition, that I see her before the marriage contract."

The chief of the blacksmiths said, "That is impossible. It cannot be done. I am of those who respect tradition. Our daughters are confined to the women's quarters. They will not be exposed to men."

He said, "O uncle! I only want to look at her face. Pretend, O uncle, that she was walking on an empty road, and lifted her veil. I shall come out from the bend of the road, and see her. I don't want more than this accidental glance."

He said, "I shall ask her advice in this matter, because she is smart."

She was listening from the other room. When her father asked her, she said, "I heard, O my father, that you said he was suitable. Then his condition should not prevent me from marrying him. It is a sound condition, since the *Sharīʿa*[22] permits the engaged person to see the young woman he desires in marriage. It is a matter the experts of *Fiqh*[23] have already dealt with in detail. The engaged person may see the face of whomever he has chosen as partner in his life. It is a matter which is tolerated. This is not a departure from the ideal of manly honor. Islamic law even imposes it!"

He agreed with her. When the merchant saw her, he knew that this time she had told him the truth. Then he said, "I agree to marry your daughter."

He was about to go out and bring the *maʾdhūn sharʿī*.[24] The chief of the blacksmiths sent somebody from among his people, who brought him and the witnesses. He wrote a marriage contract between the lawful man and the lawful woman.[25] Then the youth arranged a wedding ceremony of which there was no equal.

When the bride and groom were alone, the young woman smiled and said, "Why did you insist on seeing me before the marriage contract?"

He said to her, while overflowing with happiness, "I was afraid that you would set me up in a trap, and that you would cause me more trouble, bigger than my previous trouble."

Comments

This story, which takes place in urban Arab society, is exceptional among Arab folktales inasmuch as it ridicules several traditionally entrenched values of that society. First of all, it lampoons the generally upheld opinion that men are more clever and intelligent than women and that women are foolish or weak-minded. In this sense, it is a distinctly feminist story. Second, it ridicules the strictly maintained class distinctions, which hold that blacksmiths and gypsies are low-class people with whom noble Arabs, such as a *qāḍī,* simply cannot enter into marriage relations, because it would be a disgrace they could not live down. In a less outspoken manner, the story also decries the way marriages are concluded in traditional Arab society: the *qāḍī,* the representative of that society, marries off his daughter without asking her opinion or telling her about it, and, to boot, he ships her off to the house of the bridegroom in a big trunk, as if she were a piece of merchandise. Along the same lines, the story ridicules the Arab custom that prohibits the bridegroom from seeing his bride before the wedding ceremony.

Nor does the story exempt women from its mockery. It tells in suggestive detail how the girl, when first visiting the store of the young merchant, manages to let him catch a glimpse of all the most enticing parts of her body, which Muslim tradition requires to be kept carefully covered: her face, her hair, her wrist and forearm, and even her legs.

Finally, the story demonstrates that the woman is the dominant partner in a marriage. The young merchant follows slavishly the advice and instructions of the girl, who—even though she is the daughter of a low-class blacksmith—is learned, thoroughly at home in traditional Muslim law, shrewd, and definitely more intelligent than he.

All in all, this is a remarkable story with its subversive attitude toward the prevalent values of traditional Muslim Arab society.

Notes

1. A religious, and at the same time poetic, phrasing of the idea that he felt that his death was near.
2. This conclusion was reached by the young merchant on the basis of his bad experience with his covetous friends.
3. An elegant script used in medieval times for inscriptions and mosque decorations.
4. Blacksmiths (*ḥaddādīn* in this story; also *ṣunnʿ,* singular *ṣāniʿ*) among the nomadic Arabs are as a rule, but not in every case, gypsies. Even if they are not gypsies, they constitute low-class and despised groups, with whom the noble tribes do not intermarry. See R. Patai, *Society, Culture, and Change in the Middle East* (Philadelphia: University of Pennsylvania Pres, 1971), pp. 18, 90, 252, 254, 258–62, 265. The fact that the heroine of our story is the daughter of a blacksmith lends her character a special piquancy.
5. The reference is to Koran 12: 28, where the husband of the woman who tried to seduce Joseph says to her, "Lo! This is of the guile of you women. Lo! Your guile is very great."

6. "O uncle!" is the address directed to a person who is older or has a more respected status than the speaker.
7. The provocative behavior of the woman, unimaginable in the daughter of a high-status Arab group, indicates to the listeners that she is of low-class background. However, the young merchant, smitten with her beauty, disregards this.
8. Meaning that the normal way of the world is for a woman to get married.
9. In the Arab folktale, typically, a youth sees a girl for the first time, immediately falls in love with her, and decides to marry her, often without as much as having exchanged a single word with her. The same sequence of events also can happen in reverse.
10. An impossibly high, fantastic amount.
11. In the traditional Arab marriage, the bridegroom makes a legal undertaking to pay a certain amount to his wife in case he divorces her. Since in Muslim law a man can divorce his wife at will, this financial obligation serves as a safeguard for her.
12. The story leaves unsaid what everybody understands: what the young man found in the trunk was the *qāḍī*'s real daughter, with all her deformities.
13. The story omits these words, without which the sequel cannot be understood.
14. The girl teases the merchant with these sarcastic words.
15. By saying this, the youth explicitly recognizes the superior cleverness of the girl: he asks her what he should do now.
16. Here the story indicates, but does not say explicitly, that the girl was a member of a gypsy group or, in any case, had some special connection with it.
17. The story is not logical here. The celebration of the wedding of the *qāḍī*'s daughter would have taken place before, and not after, she was delivered to the bridegroom's house.
18. The gypsies frequently engage in entertaining performances with monkeys, music, and dances.
19. The *qāḍī* cannot countenance the disgrace of having married his daughter to a member of the gypsy tribe. He takes her back and returns the bride-price paid by the youth.
20. Not a word is said about the feelings of the *qāḍī*'s daughter. She is a totally passive object of the men's dealings and the manipulations of the heroine.
21. In the Arab folktale, the girl often takes the initiative and advises her suitor to ask her father for her hand.
22. In quoting the *Sharīʿa,* the traditional Islamic law, the girl shows herself to be not only exceedingly beautiful and clever but also learned—a highly unusual accomplishment in the traditional Arab world.
23. *Fiqh* is the science of religious law in Islam. For a girl to be familiar with the *Fiqh* is unheard of in the traditional Muslim world.

24. Registrar, the official who is authorized by the *qāḍī* to perform marriages.
25. In the Arabic *ibn al-ḥalāl* (son of *ḥalāl*) and *bint al-ḥalāl* (daughter of *ḥalāl*). *Ḥalāl* is that which, according to traditional Muslim law, is legally permissible, lawful. The statement indicates that it was legally permissible for the merchant to marry the blacksmith's daughter.

14
The Locust and the Sparrow

Written and read over Jerusalem Radio by Dr. Isḥāq Mūsā al-Ḥusaynī, December 17, 1946.

In olden times and a bygone age there lived a man and his wife. The man's name was ʿUṣfūr ("Sparrow"), and the woman's name was Jarādah ("Locust"). And the man knocked on the gates of work,[1] but was not successful. And he continued with his wife to suffer from a life of hardship. The man worked all day long,[2] but earned only a few *dirhams,* which were not sufficient for buying bread, and the world straitened in their faces.[3]

One day the wife said to her husband, "We have no choice but to move from this city to another one.[4] May Allāh provide us with the means of subsistence from his many favors!"

And her husband answered her, "With affection and in your honor, let it be as you wish."[5]

And the two of them loaded their bag and baggage on their backs, and turned toward the gate of Allāh the gracious.[6]

And they arrived at a distant city, and settled there and started to beg for alms on the open road. However, the city's inhabitants did not give them what would have eased their precarious situation. Finally they found that their position today was not better than it had been yesterday. Thereupon the wife, Locust, suggested[7] to her husband, Sparrow, that he dress up in the garb of dervishes, put sand in front of him,[8] and work in disclosing the fortunes of people and their secrets.

And the man accepted the suggestion of his wife, and put on the garb of dervishes, and collected white sand, and decorated it with a little red sand, and squatted as squat the poor and the miserable people who thoroughly know that which is hidden.[9]

And the people began to come to the man, seeking their fortunes, and gave him payment which at the end of the day he took back to his wife, and she bought with it her necessities, and they spent their days in a condition between comfort and destitution.

And the king of that city had a wife who had been barren for a long time, until Allāh decided to provide a child for her. And she became pregnant, and wanted to know whether the child would be male or female. And it so happened that she heard about the dervish who could reveal secrets, and she summoned him to her palace and put to him the question.

And the man was afraid that his deceit would become known, and he sat on the ground, with the sand in front of him, and started to rave[10] in a low voice, "A boy! A girl! A boy! A girl!" without adding a word to it.

And when the king's wife heard his words she thought he was giving her the answer, and she rewarded him with a lot of money, and promised him more of it, and dismissed him.

And the man, worried, returned to his wife, and recounted to her what had happened, and began to describe to her the calamity that would befall them from this act that led him to rave in front of the queen. And his wife calmed his fears, and told him to resign himself to the will of Allāh, and wait and see what would transpire.

Now it so happened that the queen gave birth to a boy and a girl, so that the prophecy of the raving dervish came true. And the queen was very happy, and informed her husband the king of everything. The king summoned the dervish, and showered him with many gifts.

And days passed, and the man and his wife enjoyed the best of wealth, and grief was removed from them, and the world turned toward them.[11] People started to come to the prophesying[12] dervish with their affairs and secrets, and would seek his guidance, his advice, and his blessings.

And on a day of the days a group of thieves broke into the king's palace and stole his treasures. And the king became furious with a great fury, and sent for the dervish to get from him the names of the thieves. And the dervish was bewildered and knew that his true identity would be revealed. He went lamenting to his wife about his misfortune and about the misery and punishment that were in store for him. He suggested to his wife that they leave the city and thus escape from disaster.

The woman thought about the problem for a long time, and said,

"Since we are going to be found out, let us spend our time eating the best food. Then we can leave the city in secret, without being regretful."

And the husband said to her, "And how can we do that?"

She said, "Ask the king to grant you forty days [13] to spend in solitude, secluded from all the people, and ask him that he send you every day a lamb."

And the man accepted the suggestion, and sent to the king asking for the solitude and the lambs. The king granted his request.

And the people got to know about the affair. And the thieves were afraid that the dervish would reveal their secrets, and they sent one from among them to the dervish's house to find out about his affairs.

The thief arrived at night, after the king had sent the lamb for the first day. And the man eavesdropped on the conversation of the couple, and heard the dervish say to his wife, "Behold, one of the forty has already arrived"—he meant the lamb—"and it is certain that the others will also arrive." [14]

And the words of the dervish fell on the thief like live coals. And he went and quickly told the gang what he had heard. The thieves were frightened by the power of the dervish, [went to him] and offered that they would return to him the treasure if only he would keep their identity secret. The dervish agreed, received the treasure, and kept it in his home until the end of the appointed period. Then he sent to the king to inform him of the safe return of the treasure. And the king took it, and bestowed upon the dervish many robes of honor,[15] and gave him plenty of property. He brought him close to him, and started to ask his advice in the affairs of his kingdom.

And the viziers were angry about the ascendance of the dervish over them. They conspired to get him in trouble, and to put him down by making a fool of him at a celebration of the king. They agreed to pose a question to him to which he could not successfully give an answer. As they were speaking to the king about the matter, behold a sparrow and a locust came into the room. They picked up both of them and covered them. They called the dervish and asked him to tell them what was under the cover, to see whether he really knew about hidden things.

And the dervish was bewildered, and knew that his death was near, and that it was inevitable that he should be covered with shame. And the man sat down thinking about the matter, and looked at the cover. And since he was incapable of answering, he started saying in a trembling voice, "If not for the Locust, the Sparrow would not have fallen! If not for the Locust, the Sparrow would not have fallen!" meaning that if it was not for his wife, Locust, who advised him about fortune telling in the sand, he, Sparrow, would not have fallen into the calamity.

And the king and the viziers thought that he was revealing what was under the cover, and honored him with many gifts.

And he went to his wife to tell her what had happened, and to urge her to leave the city in a hurry, before he would fall again and disaster was brought down upon him. And his wife agreed with him and said to him, "There is no choice but that before you leave the city you commit one act which will make the king angry with you and expel you from his city."

He said, "What shall I do?"

She said, "Go to the bath house of the king and steal his clothes and bring them out with you. When the king finds out about your theft, he will order you to be expelled."

And the man did as his wife had said. The king got angry with him, and commanded that he be driven out because of his insolence and perfidy. And in his great anger the king left the bath house before he had finished washing. As soon as he stepped out of the bath house, it collapsed. The king looked around at his men, and said to them, "The dervish knew that the bath house would collapse, and he did what he did for the sake of my safety. So set him free, and grant him the freedom of life."

And thereafter the man was in no need of any further work, because of the huge amount of the king's gifts with which he was rewarded. And he stopped working, and lived with his wife in happiness and comfort.

And he spoke about the gracious favors of Allāh that were granted to him without his knowing it. And he desisted from playing the dervish, and worked in agriculture,[16] and Allāh provided him with children. The people have talked about his miracles from those days until this very day.

Comments

This story, written in an authentic folktale style but without introducing any miraculous element, is actually a satire holding up to ridicule the foolish belief people have in the sagacity and vatic capability of the dervishes. The fake dervish himself is a bumbling bumpkin, but he has incredible luck with his muttered and confused utterances, which the people around him take for miraculous insights and the foretelling of events to come.

A typical Arab folktale element is the superior intelligence of the man's wife, to whom the man turns in every predicament as a child would to his mother, and who always has a solution to the problem her husband faces.

Notes

1. A figure of speech meaning he tried to find work.
2. The storyteller does not notice that this statement contradicts the one just made about the man not being able to find work.
3. A figure of speech meaning they suffered from straitened circumstances.
4. As in many Arab folktales, it is the wife who takes the initiative in a situation that concerns both her and her husband. See, e.g., tale 18. In the present tale the only suggestion the man makes is a repetition of an earlier one made by the wife: that they leave the city.
5. A polite, formalized expression of consent.
6. A figure of speech meaning they set out on the road.
7. Again, it is the wife who comes up with the suggestion for how to improve their lot.
8. Divination by means of sand used to be practiced in many parts of the Arab world, where it had a history of many centuries.
9. The dervishes, although they were believed to know hidden things and to be holy men, lived a life of utter poverty. The very name *darwīsh* has the primary meaning of "poor man."
10. He pretended that he was crazed. Madness has been associated with vatic and prophetic powers ever since biblical times. See Hosea 9: 7; Jeremiah 29: 26.
11. A figure of speech meaning their lot improved.
12. In the Arabic *mutanabbī,* a person who pretends to be a prophet. Also the name of Arabic literatures's most famous poet (915–965).
13. The concept of forty days in seclusion for the purpose of obtaining divine guidance is, again, as old as the Bible. See Exodus 24: 18, 34: 28, etc.
14. Forty is the standard number of a band of thieves in Arab and other folktales. Its classical example is the tale of ʿAlī Bābā and the forty thieves in the *Arabian Nights,* and it recurs in several tales in this volume. See also Tale Type 954 "The Forty Thieves."
15. An old Turkish form of the expression of royal gratitude.
16. Again, the storyteller forgot that only a moment earlier he had stated that the man was in no need of any further work and stopped working.

15
Tambar Tītī

Written and read over Jerusalem Radio by Dr. Isḥāq Mūsā al-Ḥusaynī, January 14, 1947.

In olden times and bygone days there lived two brothers. One of them was poor, the other was rich. As for the rich one, he was a greedy merchant, who bragged a lot and was haughty. He did not respect the rights of brotherhood, nor attach importance to blood relationship. He would not visit his brother, nor stretch out a helping hand to him.

And as for the poor brother, he was a wood gatherer. He would get up and leave his house early in the morning, and go to the broad hills and soft ground around the city. There he would collect whatever wood he found, load it on his donkey, and bring it to the city market. He would sell it for a few *piasters,*[1] which he would use to buy whatever would barely keep him and his wife alive.

And one night of the nights the wood gatherer woke up very early in the morning, contrary to his custom. The moon was full, and sent its silver light to the earth, filling it with such a glow that the wood gatherer thought that he had been overcome with sleep that night and that he was late going out. He mistook it for sunlight. He rushed to get his donkey and its halter, and faced the Gate of Allāh the gracious,[2] beside whom there is none more gracious.

When he arrived outside the city, and went up to the hills, it became clear to him that the sun was still hidden behind its veil, and that the moon had misled him with its shining glittering light. He tied his donkey to a nearby tree, and climbed up to a big branch of it. There he threw himself into the bosom of sleep.

As soon as he closed his eye to enjoy a morning nap, he heard a voice approaching. He looked through the branches, and all of a sudden saw forty black[3] thieves coming near from far away, and repeating in one voice, "*Tambar tītī! Tambar tītī!*"[4] The worried, restless wood gatherer was very frightened, but was able to get hold of himself and control his breathing. With caution and fear he watched what was going on. The slaves went near a large rock, and shouted in one voice, "Open, O *Fulayfilah!*"[5]

The rock cracked open. There appeared a big opening, through which they entered. They dropped the loads they carried on their backs, and went out one by one. Then they said, "Close up, O *Fulayfilah!*" The rock was joined, and the opening became smooth. Thus happened that which could never happen: it had indeed happened. And the slaves went off in the direction from which they had come.

The wood gatherer arose, looked right and left, and the sun was still hidden behind the veil. When he saw that nobody was around, he approached the big rock, and commanded it with the same command as the slaves had done with their chant. The rock broke open. He went inside, and found the gold which the slaves had stolen from houses and shops. He filled his bag with it, and carried it to his donkey. He turned his face toward his house in a hurry, fearing that somebody would see him.

His wife was still asleep. He woke her, put the gold before her, and told her about the wonderful treasure and the story of the slaves. The wife rejoiced a great rejoicing and praised Allāh who saved her husband from his hard work. And she said to her husband, "Come to the market. We shall buy whatever our souls desire, of food, drink, and clothing."[6] They went out in a hurry, and bought whatever they liked. Then they returned home to enjoy the comforts of life.

And days went by, and the wood gatherer and his wife lived the life of luxury and ease, and nobody knew what had happened to them. And one day the wife went to the bath house, and carried with her clothing of silk and raw silk, like the king's clothing.

And in the bath house there were several women, unveiled and bathing, and among them was the wife of her husband's rich brother. She saw that the poor wood gatherer's wife was dressed in the finest clothes. She was surprised. Fierce anger arose in her, and envy filled her. She hurried to her husband, and told him in detail what she had seen of the superb clothes: their kinds, colors, decorations, and many-colored ornamentations. She started to incite her husband, saying, "You say that your brother is poor, and here his wife has clothing which even the king's wife does not have. There can be no doubt that there is a secret to his sudden wealth."

And she persuaded her husband to visit his brother and to investigate his situation in the evening of that very day.

And they came to the wood gatherer's house, and found that his situation was not what they had known before. Behold, there were velvety carpets, and couches with precious cushions. There were expensive cloths on which food was served. There were flowing robes, rare ornaments, and luxurious food. They both were surprised, and tried to discover the source of the simple wood gatherer's riches. They used such sweet words until he revealed to them the secret, and told them in detail what had happened.

At this point the rich brother said to him, "I am your brother, from your mother and father, and I have the right of brotherhood with you. With this right I request that you take me with you tomorrow to the rock, so that I may carry away with me from the blessings of the buried treasure."

And his brother answered, "With love and honor, O my brother." [7]

In the morning of the following day they both went together, and they carried away a lot of gold. Each of them returned happily to his house. The wood gatherer was happy with what he got, and stayed at home, spending great amounts. As for the rich merchant, he was greedy to have more riches.

He no longer needed his brother to accompany him. He persuaded himself that he should be the only one to get the gold. He took along a donkey, and hurried in the early morning to the rock. He gave the command, and it cracked open. He entered, and started to collect the gold greedily. He was about to leave, but could not believe that he was to be the sole owner of this property, that nobody was to share it with him.

After he filled the bag, and was anxious to get out, he forgot the name of the rock, because of his intense happiness and confusion. He started to mention various names, and said, "Pepper, Spice, Cumin, Safflower," without finding the name.

And while he was shouting and repeating the names, the slaves came, as was their wont, in the morning. They entered the cave of the earth, and found the merchant crouching on top of the gold, with his bag beside him. And they took him and killed him, and put him on the back of his donkey. And they assigned one of them to stay near him and to watch him, to find out whether anyone came there who knew the place and was looking for him. Then they would follow that one to his house and kill him with all the members of his family. Thus the secret would remain hidden.

And the rich merchant was absent a long time, and his wife became afraid that some mishap had overtaken him. And she hurried to his brother the wood gatherer, and told him that her husband had gone alone to the rock and had not yet returned. And the wood gatherer set her soul at rest, and mounted his donkey, and went to look for his brother. And he found him killed, and carried him to his house. And the slave followed him without his knowledge.

The slave informed the rest of the members of the gang, and they plotted to kill the wood gatherer and whoever lived with him in the house. And they hired a camel driver and twenty camels, and told him that he should take them to a place which they specified: that he should take forty jars filled with oil to the wood gatherer's house. And the camel driver went carrying the forty jars to the house of the wood gatherer and told him that the owner of the jars would come to him after a short while. The man took them to his house, and waited for whoever had sent them.

And when the night became very dark the slaves started to whisper together inside the jars. And it so happened that the maidservant of the wood gatherer came to relieve herself, and heard the mutterings. And she pretended that she did not hear anything, and went on her way. Then she returned, went to the wood gatherer, and secretly whispered in his ear the matter of the slaves. And the man woke up, and asked her advice in the matter, and she reassured him. She was clever, with a capacity for tricks, and she hurried to the hallway of the residence, and collected wood and ignited it, and put upon it a big vessel which she filled with petroleum[8] and tar. And after the liquid was heated, she carried it in the vessel and started to put a little of it into each of the forty jars, until she destroyed the forty slaves.

And in the morning the slaves were removed outside the city, and the inhabitants were saved from their evil and their burglaries of their property.

And the wood gatherer went and brought all the gold into his house, and gave some of it to his clever maid, and lived with his wife in comfort and joy, thanking Allāh for his favors which are countless.

Comments

This story is actually a retelling of the classic tale of ʿAlī Bābā and the forty thieves, one of the best-known stories of the *Arabian Nights.*

The story itself is widespread all over the world (see Tale Type 676 "Open Sesame," and the list of motifs there). Combined with it is another folktale motif, that of the competition between the poor brother and the rich brother, which ends when "the rich brother tries to do the same thing but is killed" (see Motif N471 "Foolish attempt of second man to overhear secrets."

In this story, the rich brother and his wife are depicted as evil and selfish, the poor brother and his wife as good. The rich brother neglects one of the most important duties of an Arab man: to maintain close ties with his brother. The poor brother, to the contrary, is willing to share the riches he found with his rich brother. Even at that point, the rich brother wants to secure all the treasures for himself and goes alone to the rock, which proves his downfall.

Only a few items of local color are found in the story. Once the poor brother finds the treasure, the first things he buys for his wife and himself are food, drink, and clothes. He stops working and enjoys a life of idle luxury. His wife goes to the bath house, where the wife of the rich brother meets her. They also employ a maid, whose vigilance saves their lives.

The relationship between each of the two brothers and his wife is the typical one of the Arab folktale. In each of the two married couples, it is the wife who suggests to the husband what to do. When the poor brother returns home with the first haul of treasures, it is his wife who tells him to go with her to the market and buy the things they were lacking up to that point. When the wife of the rich brother finds that her sister-in-law has become rich, it is she who urges her husband to visit his poor brother in order to find out the source of his sudden wealth. When the forty thieves are hiding in the jars, it is his servant girl to whom the poor brother turns for advice, and it is she who heats up a mixture of petroleum and tar and pours the hot liquid into the jars, killing the thieves.

The forty thieves hidden in the forty jars, who enter the house of the poor brother in order to kill him but instead of acting sit in their jars and conduct a mumbling conversation, are a folktale motif whose improbability is questioned neither by the storyteller nor by his audience. Only at the end of the story do we find out that the thieves caused great hardship to the whole city with their robberies. The story ends on a religious note: everything that happened to the poor man was a manifestation of Allāh's favor, and the nouveau riche man duly thanks him.

Notes

1. During the British mandatory regime in Palestine, which ended in 1948, the official currency was the Palestinian pound, called *līra* in both Arabic and Hebrew. It equalled a British pound sterling but was divided into 1,000 *mils.* In poplar usage, ten *mils* were termed a *piaster.* The one-*piaster* coin was the most generally used piece of currency.
2. To face the Gate of Allāh meant in popular usage to set out on a journey.
3. In Arabic *ʿabd,* colloquially pronounced *ʿabed,* means "slave," and in particular a black slave.
4. I was not able to establish the meaning or derivation of these two words.
5. *Fulayfilah* is the diminutive of *fulful* or *filfil* ("pepper"). "Open, O little pepper!" is the tale's version of *iftaḥ yā simsim* ("Open, sesame!"), the magic words made famous by the *Arabian Nights* story of ʿAlī Bābā and the forty thieves.
6. As discussed earlier, the leading advisory role assigned to women is a characteristic feature of the Arab folktale.
7. Polite expression of consent.
8. In the Arabic *naftָ* ("naphtha"). The use of this term points to the influence of the modern (1946) Palestinian environment, where *naftָ* was the generally used fuel for both cooking and heating.

16
The Return of the Light

Read over Jerusalem Radio by Fāyiz al-Ghūl, January 28, 1947.

In days of old there lived a king who treated his people justly, regarding the rules and the orders. He raised the banner of justice, and offered protection, comfort, and easy livelihood, so that all the people of his kingdom loved him, and were faithful to him with affection and advice. But the lives of both the king and the people were most seriously troubled by the lack of an heir to the throne, because they feared that after the death of the king there would be a rivalry among contenders for the throne.

This matter weighed on the mind of every individual in the kingdom, until a day came on which a fortune-teller arrived at the capital city, and prescribed a medicine for the queen. And he advised her to take it on the first Friday of the lunar month. Shortly after this advice of the fortune-teller the queen became pregnant, and gave birth to a beautiful baby boy. Both parents hoped he would be the delight of their eyes.

The people greatly rejoiced over the successor to the throne. All parts of the kingdom were decorated, and much money and gifts were distributed among the poor, the orphans, and the widows. Time passed quickly, and all of a sudden the heir to the throne had become a hot-tempered young man. He was frivolous and reckless, and joined the company of bad people. Many complained about him to his father, and few were grateful to him. Even fewer excused him. Some were anxious that the king should punish him.

His father became greatly saddened by this. He would frequently offer his advice to the son, but, to his grief, the son did not listen to him. Rather, he turned his face away, as if he did not hear. When the king saw this, his eyes overflowed with sadness. This happened time after time, until the king's eyes became white,[1] because of this vain, mischievous boy.

The king's subjects grew worried because of what had happened to their king, and summoned physicians. But the physicians could not cure him. They brought fortune-tellers, but they too failed. Finally, they heard about a great physician whom they brought to the king, and promised him a huge reward. The physician told them that the remedy for the king was found in two golden hairs from the head of a famous fish in the sea. Those two hairs should be ground up, and the powder put in the king's eyes. This would restore his sight.

In their great love of the king all the seamen volunteered to throw their nets into the sea. After two days, when the sun had almost set, one of the old seamen was pulling in his net, and it seemed to be surprisingly heavy. He asked the seamen around him to help. They helped, and—there was the fish described by the physician! There were afraid lest they not be able to seize it when they took it out of the net. They started to strike at the two hairs with swords, but to no avail. The swords broke because the hairs were so strong. Then the son of the king came, and he too struck at the hairs with his sword, but it too broke before he could accomplish anything. He grew enraged, took a polished sword whose handle was made of iron, and struck blindly at the two hairs. This tore the net, and enabled the fish to swim away to the depths of the sea. Thus he frustrated the hope of the people and the hope of healing his father.

For a full month the seamen again searched for the fish, but all their efforts were in vain. They stopped searching, and gave up all hope. The people turned in wrath against the son of the king, and threatened to rebel unless he left the country. The emir obeyed, giving in to their demands.

The mother of the emir became saddened because of the departure of her only son. She begged the king, who was as sad as she, to intervene, but the king was forced to comply with the people's wishes. Then she accepted the accomplished fact. She prepared provisions for her son for his trip, and went to bid him farewell. She admonished him to learn a lesson from what had happened, and from then on not to keep company with impudent people, even if he liked their appearance. She advised him to associate with eminent and virtuous men, even if they were negroes.

The emir left the city, afraid and apprehensive, buffeted hither and thither by the winds of the road. He stumbled along mountain paths. The voices of animals frightened him at night, and he tasted enough of the bitterness of life to make him despair of life and love death. He reminded himself of the many comforts he had lost, and the great prosperity that had vanished with his fecklessness and recklessness. He regretted this, but it was too late for repentance.

After he had wandered for several days he came to a city on the seashore. A fine-looking young man, cheerful and talkative, approached him from the direction of the city. The emir thought that he was a fun-loving and impudent person, and was determined to be cautious with him. However, he preferred to test him. He greeted him with peace, and accompanied him on his way until they both arrived at a tree on the seashore. They sat down in its shade, and the emir said to his companion:

"I have met a hard life on this journey of mine. Would you give water to my horse, tie it under the shade of the tree, and prepare lunch for both of us from whatever is in the saddle-bag? After you do that, wake me up, for I feel exhausted, and slumber is upon me. I shall be thankful to you for whatever you do."

Then he pretended to fall asleep. The young man left the horse in the glare of the sun, got up, and approached the saddle-bag. He took whatever food was in it, and ate until he was full. Unbeknownst to him the emir was watching him from his place, and grumbled in his [pretended] sleep. The young man pulled the horse, pretending he wanted to take it to the water.

Thereupon the emir [made as if he] woke up, and stopped him, saying, "Do not bother, O my friend. I shall take care of it myself."

He gave the horse water to drink. Then he took a little food and said to his companion, "This is where I depart from you." Soon each of them went on his way.

The emir entered the city. The young man followed him, and gathered around him impudent people, who pretended to be faithful to the emir. They let him remain with them for a while. During that time they caused him to lose most of his money, and left him with only a little. His money was supposed to last him a long time. When he realized that this was their fault, he left that city, stealing away under the cover of the night, and fled from their company and the likes of their company.

He walked for several days. While he was walking, on a scorchingly hot day, when the scale of the daytime was equal in the center of heaven, the road brought him a negro, black as if he were a piece of leather cut from the night. He was wearing a sword, and carrying a bow upon his shoulder. He greeted the emir with peace, and said to him, "Do you permit me to be your companion on your way during the day?"

The emir remembered what his mother had commanded him when she bade him farewell, saying, "Associate with the eminent virtuous man, even if he is a negro." He hoped that this black man was of eminent good people. He answered him saying, "Welcome to you, welcome!"

Then both of them hurried along, keeping quiet until it became evening. They saw a sand dune, and took shelter there. They relaxed for a while, and ate some food. They slept in the place. When the emir fell asleep, the black man rose, drawing his sword on top of his head, and from his eyes beamed a glitter of strength and determination. He started listening, with his ears open to every sound or movement, until it was almost midnight. Then, all of a sudden, he heard a disturbing noise. He thought it was the gasping of a man, exhausted by running. He turned around, and there, all of a sudden, was the hissing of a poisonous viper. Its chest was as broad as a ram, its head was the size of a watermelon, and out of it protruded two fangs like arrows. It was approaching the emir. The negro came down upon it with his sword, and hit its head, cutting it in two halves. The negro remained awake until the dawn came, when he was confident. He removed the traces of blood from his sword, and pretended that he was asleep.

When the emir woke up, he was frightened by the sight of the slain snake. He awakened his companion, and asked him about the matter before their eyes, but the black man did not say anything. The emir asked him to show him his sword, and he handed it to him. The emir found no trace of the blood, and he was reassured.

They went on for days, until they saw a green field in a spacious plain. The shepherds and the cattlemen kept their animals away from that field. The travelers asked them about the reason: why did they not graze their sheep and cattle there? The shepherds sighed and told them that it was the domain of a giant. There was none more frightening in appearance than he, none more wicked or more vicious. None was quicker than he to strike. He had ten greyhounds of the size of Cypriote donkeys, and more vicious than hungry wolves. The giant had imposed a tax upon the inhabitants of the neighboring villages. They were paying it from their properties and cattle. Sometimes he would force them to work his lands, and if anybody disobeyed his command, he set his dogs on him. In the twinkling of an eye the disobedient would be torn to pieces, each piece in a dog's mouth or in its belly.

The emir and his companion were shocked and dismayed by what they heard. As for the emir, he wanted to change his way [so as to avoid meeting the giant]. As for the companion, he was anxiously determined to encounter the giant. The emir warned him of the outcome, and the shepherds frightened him with the dangers, but he would not listen.

He asked the shepherds to supply him with five sheep. They did this, and sent their prayers with him. When the emir saw his determination, he followed him, and said, "Agreement is the condition of companionship. I would not prefer my life to your life. I have already left my father's palace, having been evicted. I don't expect to return to it."

The negro welcomed him with a nod, and did not speak to him. When the green field was directly in front of them, the negro slaughtered the sheep, cutting each of them in two parts. When he finished, he took from his pocket a cane which had white paste [in it], and smeared it on the flesh. All of a sudden, the dogs came to them, barking in a disgusting manner. He threw them slices of the meat, and they swallowed them quickly. Just as the dogs were about to reach them they fell down on the ground, twisting in pain and groaning miserably. The negro left them suffering the agony of death, and got ready to meet the giant. He attached a string to his bow, and took an arrow out of his quiver and mounted it on top of the string.

The giant drew near like a huge mountain. If a tree blocked his way he jumped on it from above with the agility of a rabbit. When he had come close, the negro shot an arrow which did not miss his heart. The giant screamed and fell to the ground which was soaked in his blood. Thus they left him, in a generous amount of blood, he who had been stingy. Once they were safe from all resistance, they hurried to the giant's palace. There they found tremendous amounts of gold and jewelry, which they carried off on the backs of the giant's camels and mules.

They were ready to continue their travel when all of a sudden they heard a soft voice from the roof. They hurried toward it. There was a young woman. Nobody had ever seen a woman more beautiful than she was. The emir became enamored of her, and she too became enamored of him.[2] He asked her about her story, and she summed it up saying that she had been traveling with her father in a great caravan. Her father was the head of the merchants, and the richest among them. The giant came forth against them, and wiped them out. He seized their properties, but spared her.

The emir asked her name, and she said, "Nūr" [Light]. He regarded this as good news.

Then all of them went on, until they came to the shepherds, and the negro told them about the killing of the giant. He distributed among them whatever property he had seized, and said, "I am leaving you even better things than I have given you—it is the land. Build it up, and keep it well guarded, and you will be granted great profit."

Then he turned the caravan in the direction of the emir's kingdom, and after having encountered terrible dangers on the way, which the negro overcame with his courage and power, they reached the gate of the city from the direction of the sea. The negro arose and said:

"Know, O my master, that I have brought you to your city after having profited from the long experience. I have spent in your company six months, during which I tasted no sleep, and spent sleepless nights for you. Now I miss my homeland, and I long for my people. The time has come that I bid you farewell."

But the emir held on to him, and begged him to stay with him, in the choicest palace of his kingdom. The negro said, "There is no way I can do that. And even if I were a king's son. In fact, I am a king. Now I request of you that you accept this gift of me, because you were so gracious to me, even though you did not intend to get it from me. But let us look at the good side of every action."

And therewith he stretched forth his hand and held in it two golden hairs, and gave them to the emir saying, "Wipe the eyes of your father with these, but don't pound the two hairs as the physician prescribed, and your father will again be endowed with eyesight, Allāh willing."

Then he turned in the direction of the sea, and dived into it.[3]

The emir greatly regretted the departure of his friend. He sent to inform his father of his return, and asked his permission to enter. He was granted permission. He wiped his father's eyes with the two hairs, and the king was able to see.[4]

The people of the city heard about the story, and rejoiced at the healing of their righteous king, and at the repentance of the successor. They set up decorations in great gladness, and lavishly celebrated his marriage to the young woman, Nūr, who had been brought with him. And all the people lived happily and in good health, until the Destroyer of Pleasures and Separator of Groups reached them.[5]

Comments

The main interest in this story is in the person and character of its black hero. It is only at the very end of the story that we learn that he is the king of an undersea realm to which he returns after he has accomplished the task of reforming the profligate emir and providing the remedy for the blind king. All in all, the story reads like a didactic treatise on the antiracist theme of "look at the character of a man, not at his skin color." Considering the low status of negroes in traditional Arab society, this story presents a truly exceptional point of view.

Notes

1. Meaning he became blind because of constant crying.
2. This mutual love at first sight is a frequently figuring motif in the Arab folktale.
3. Only now, at the end of the story, do we find out that the noble negro hero was the king of an undersea realm.
4. There is here a brief trace of the well-known folktale about the sons on a quest for a wonderful remedy for their father (see Tale Type 551 "Search for the Golden Bird"). The ailment of the king is often blindness (see Tale Type 550/I[b] "Object of the Quest").
5. A poetic reference to death.

17
The Bird of Power

Recorded and broadcast on Jerusalem Radio by Dr. Isḥāq Mūsā al-Ḥusaynī, February 25, 1947.

In times of old there lived a king among the great kings, who enjoyed leisure and confidence. He had two wives. One of them was neglected, the other esteemed and loved.[1] The neglected wife had one son who lived with her. The second wife had two sons who were the center of the king's concern and attention.

One day the king built a lofty palace, and he summoned his vizier to see it. The vizier liked the lofty palace, and he said to the king, "Indeed, it is a magnificent palace, O my Master. However, it lacks one thing in order to reach the pinnacle of magnificence."

The king said, "And what does it lack, O vizier?"

The vizier answered, "It is a bird, O my lord, known as the Bird of Power."[2]

At once the king summoned his three sons, and told them what the vizier had said. He commanded them to search for the bird and to bring it to him.

The boys went and provided themselves with provisions for their voyage, and departed from the city, setting out toward the north.

While they were on their way, three roads opened up in front of them: a road of fire, a road of flood, and a road which takes but does not bring back. The youths were perplexed as to which road to take. Finally the two sons of the respected wife took the roads of fire and flood. The son of the neglected wife followed the road which takes but does not bring back.

Each one of them went on his way. As for the son of the neglected wife, as he was about to make good progress on his way, he saw a frightening ghoul whose fingernails were so long that they were implanted in the ground. When the youth came close to him, he cut the ghoul's nails, and also trimmed his long eyelashes. The ghoul was very pleased,[3] and he said to the youth, "May Allāh make your way bright as you brightened my way. What is your wish, O young man?"

The youth answered, "My wish is to find the Bird of Power."

The ghoul said to him, "Follow this road. You will find my sister who dwells in a forest, and she will guide you to it. However, be careful, and if you find that she is sprinkling her face with ashes, don't approach her. But if you find her grinding sugar, go and take a little bit of the sugar, then approach her, and nurse at her breast."[4]

The youth answered, "I hear and obey!"

The young man, the son of the neglected wife, continued on the road, and all of a sudden he saw from afar a woman resembling the ghoul whom he had met, and she was sprinkling her face with ashes. He remembered the advice of the ghoul, and hid himself behind a tree. After a while the woman quieted down, and took a grinder with which she ground sugar. At that the youth approached her quickly, and did whatever the ghoul had advised him to do. He nursed at both her breasts, and thereupon she accepted him with affection, and said to him, "I am afraid, O my son, that my children will harm you.[5] Therefore I must hide you until I see what to do."

He said to her, "As you wish. I hear and obey, O my mother!"

After a while her children came, and sat down beside her. They at once recognized that there was an unusual smell, which was the odor of a human being. They asked their mother about it, but she denied it, saying, "The odor of a human being is from you and in you."

Then they said to her, "Tell us about his nature, O mother, and he will be safe, first, second, and third."

She arose, went to where he was hiding, and brought him out. Her children greeted him, and asked him what it was he wished. He told them. Then the mother turned to her sons and said to them, "Who amongst you will help him to obtain his wish?"

The oldest one answered, "I will, O my mother! I will bring him to it before you get up from your place."

The youngest one said, "I will bring him to it in the twinkling of an eye!"[6]

So the youth rode on the back of the youngest son, bade the mother and her children farewell, and they flew off.[7]

In the twinkling of an eye the youth found himself in the midst of the Birds of Power, which were guarded by forty guards.[8] The youngest son put him down from his back, and said to him, "Here you are! Here are the birds. Take one of them. But be sure not to let your soul be tempted to take more than one."

However, when all of a sudden the youth saw the birds, their charming forms and their beautiful colors, greed overcame him, and he seized two of them. As soon as he did that, the guards woke up from their sleep, captured him, and brought him to the king.

When the youth was presented to him, the king asked him to tell him his story.[9] The youth told him. Then the king said to him, "Very well. I shall give you the bird on condition that you get me the horse called 'The Vaulter of the Two Seas.' "

The youth agreed readily, and praised Allāh for his safety. He went to the young ghoul, and told him what the king had asked. The ghoul said to him, "As you wish, for your sake, and in your honor." [10]

He took him on his back, and flew with him to wherever the horse dwelt. He said to him, "Here you are, take the horse. But you will see that he is bare. There is no saddle on him, and no bridle in his mouth. When you mount his bare back, be careful not to put anything else on his back."

Our youth approached the horse, and found next to it a perfect colored saddle and a golden bridle. He let himself be seduced to use both of them. He put on the bridle, and carried the saddle to put it on the back of the horse.[11] As soon as he did that, the horse neighed a neigh that shook the horizon. Immediately the guards woke up, and pounced on the youth. They led him to the king, so that he might give him the punishment he deserved.

The king was amazed at the situation of the youth, and asked him about his story.[12] The youth told him everything. The king said, "Very well, I offer you the horse. However, I request that first you bring me the daughter of the king of China. She is the object of my desire. When you bring her, I shall hand my horse over to you."

The youth consented, thanked Allāh for his safety, and returned to his companion, the young ghoul. He told him what had happened. The ghoul said to him, "You will have whatever you wish."

And he carried him on his back, and brought him to the country of China.

As soon as he arrived at the city, he found the daughter of the king strolling about. The youth seized her and abducted her. He brought her to the ghoul and they both rode on his back together. However, when he saw her beauty and her delicate bearing and the perfection of her mind, it was hard for him to deliver her to the king. He was perplexed, and did not know what to do. Should he take her for himself and relinquish the horse? Or should he deliver her to the king in exchange for the horse, and deprive himself of the young woman, perfect in beauty and mind?

He decided to consult the ghoul, who might show him a way out. The ghoul said to him, "Very well, my friend, I shall find a way to do it, if you really want to keep the young woman for yourself." [13]

The youth said, "But how will I get the horse?"

The ghoul said, "I shall change my appearance to that of a young woman [14] like this young woman of yours. After you deliver me to the king I shall change myself back and catch up with you."

The youth was very happy with this advice, and did as the ghoul told him to do, with all concern and attention.

The king received the young woman happily, thinking that she was the daughter of the king of China, and delivered the horse to the youth. The youth took the horse and left. After a short while the ghoul escaped as he had said, and caught up with the young man. They all went to the king who wanted to have the horse. The ghoul repeated what he had done previously, and changed himself into a horse, which the youth presented to the king. The king took him, rejoicing, and delivered instead the Bird of Power to the youth. Then the ghoul escaped, and joined his friend. All of them went toward the city, which also his two brothers, the sons of the respected wife, had reached. They set out to return to their father. The son of the neglected wife and the ghoul were traveling together, and with them was the bird which the father wanted to have.

His happiness upon meeting his brothers and his triumph in achieving his desire at the same time [were great]. The youth felt happy because he had fulfilled the wish of his father, even though he had endured pain and dangers in his troubles. These were lightened for him by his remarkable success in obtaining the daughter of the king of China and the wonderful horse.

When they reached the city the youth found that one of his brothers was working as a street sweeper, and the other as a baker, in order to survive, to make a living, and to escape perdition. The youth approached them, hugged them, and promised them a safe return. When they were on their way back to their father, they became thirsty. The youth volunteered to go down to the nearby well. When he reached the bottom of the well, he found there two beautiful young women who had been thrown into the well. He saved both of them and brought them out with the rope he had used to go down to the well. When both young women were safely out of the well, he grabbed the rope to climb up. When he was halfway up, and was holding on to the loop of the rope, it was cut,[15] and he fell back to the bottom of the well. He almost perished from the intensity of the fall and his grief about the action of his brothers.

Now one of the young women in her gratitude had given him, as a present, some of her bracelets. In a remote section of the well the youth found a horse which had been thrown there. In front of it was a stone. He went to the horse and put barley before it instead of the stone. The horse approached it and devoured it in the intensity of its hunger. After the horse had eaten, and its vitality had returned to its breast, it turned to the youth, thanked him for his favor,[16] and offered him three hairs, saying, "If you feel in distress, rub these hairs and you will see me in front of you."

The youth took the hairs happily, and sat thinking about his situation, about the horrors he was able to overcome, one after the other, and how his two brothers repaid him for rescuing them from miserable jobs and from bachelorhood, and for curing them. They gave him the worst reward, and were not concerned with brotherhood which imposes cooperation and mutual aid, not to mention nobility.

While he was thinking, Allāh was working on His plans. A caravan passed by and stopped to draw water from the well. The youth could cling to their rope, and he got out. When the people saw him they were happy to have rescued him, because of what he had done in noble deeds. He thanked them for having saved him, and turned his face toward the city which was not far off. When he reached it, he was afraid because of the ruthlessness and violence of his two brothers, should his situation be revealed. He went to a goldsmith's shop and offered him his services. The goldsmith accepted him, and took him on as a temporary worker.

It so happened that the two brothers and the three young girls and the Bird of Power arrived in the city. The king received them with open arms, and married the daughter of the king of China,[17] and gave the two girls in marriage to the two sons. Festivities were celebrated, and the lights shone. The huge palace was lighted up, and both old and young went to see it.

However, a humiliated woman with a broken heart appeared in the midst of the celebration, as if suffering from a bleeding wound in her body.[18] She felt in the depth of her soul that her son would not fail, and that he, with his boldness, was the ideal of manhood among his two brothers. What then was the reason that prevented him from reaching his city?

Before the wedding one of the sisters said to her fiancé, "I cannot marry you unless you make for me a bracelet like my bracelets."

She gave him the bracelets which were similar to the bracelets which she had given as gifts to the young brother when he saved her from the well. The middleman started to announce in the markets the request of the king's son.

The young brother, while sitting in the goldsmith's shop, heard the announcement. He said to his master, "I can make bracelets, and perfectly like them."

He gave them to him, and granted him time until the next day. The youth took them, came back on the second day, and handed over two bracelets to him.

When the young woman saw her two bracelets she realized that the youth who had saved her was in the city. She requested to see the goldsmith who had so skillfully handcrafted the bracelets in order to thank him. The youth was brought, and when she saw him she knew him. She told him of the marriage, and asked him to rescue her from the one to whom she was to be married by force. He requested that she grant him another day, and that was the day on which the marriage was to be celebrated.

On the morning of the following day the city was full of joy and festivities, and the markets were decorated. The people went out to the squares, the horsemen hastened to their horses, and they were roaming and roving. The two sons of the king were among the riders.

The youth rubbed the three hairs. Thereupon the horse which he had saved from death in the well came to him. He mounted the horse, took a sword, and entered into the fight of the horsemen in the square. No one was able to win the fight with him. Finally he attacked the two brothers, and struck them violently. The people were frightened.

The king heard what had happened, called for the horseman and asked him about his situation. The latter rushed to his father, kissing his hand, and telling him what had happened to him since his departure and until his return. Thereupon his father embraced him, and arranged for him to be engaged to the young woman who was the cause of his appearance.[19]

The youth lived for a while with his father. Then he asked permission from his father to build a private palace for himself. The king granted him permission, and he brought his mother and gave her the best dwelling place in it. He lived with his wife and children in wealth and comfort. He ruled after his father, and did good for his subjects, seeking justice among them. Ease and comfort were spread abroad, and prosperity became universal. He became the topic of conversation, then and until these days.

Comments

The frame of this story is yet another variant of the widespread Arab folktale motif of the evil sons of the favored wife and the good son of the neglected wife, but its actual content is concentrated on the adventures of the good son. These adventures are given in a chainlike sequence. Several times, in order to get what he wants, the youth has to obtain something else first: to get the Bird of Power, he must first get the miraculous horse; to get that, he must first get the princess of China.

The ghouls whom the good son encounters in his search for the Bird of Power are dangerous but good-natured demonic creatures who are willing to help in his quest. Once the youth nurses at the breast of the *ghoulah,* she conceives an affection for him and protects him from her own dangerous ghoul-children. In this motif there is perhaps a reflection of the motherly feeling an Arab woman has for a child for whom she acted as a wetnurse.

That the ghouls (and demons in general) can smell the odor of a human being is likewise a widespread folktale motif. The ghouls also can change appearance at will: the young ghoul who serves as the winged mount of the youth takes the shape of the Chinese princess and then of a horse.

The youth is brave but reckless and greedy: twice he does not heed the warnings of the ghoul, which almost causes his downfall.

The evil character of the two sons of the favored wife is revealed only after the good son meets up with them on his way back to his father's palace. They did not fare well, and after he rescues two girls from a well, in their jealousy they try to kill him by throwing him back into it. But he finds a miraculous horse in the well, which offers him three of its hairs to rub in case he should be in dire need and thereby summon it. The men of a caravan that passes by rescue him (see Genesis 37: 28), he goes to his city, and after summoning the miraculous horse he defeats his two evil brothers in a tournament. The father embraces him, he marries one of the girls he had rescued, and after his father's death he succeeds him as king.

This is a typical *Arabian Nights*-type fairy tale.

Notes

1. Stories involving two rival wives are found frequently in Arab folklore, reflecting the actual situation prevailing in a polygynous family. The rivalry between the co-wives is carried on by their sons. The sympathy of the tale lies with the neglected wife and her son.
2. What the "Bird of Power" is remains unexplained. It evidently is one of the mythical beings of Arab folklore, as are the flying magic "Camels of Love." See tale 24.
3. The ghoul of the Arab folktale is in most cases a friendly being. He has a frightening appearance but responds to kindness and proves to be helpful.
4. The sister of the ghoul is a *ghoulah.* She can be in either a dangerous or a friendly mood. Her preoccupation with ashes indicates her dangerous mood; handling sugar indicates her friendly mood. By suckling at her breast, the youth becomes the adoptive son of the *ghoulah,* and she is filled with love for him.
5. Like the *ghoulah,* so her children can be dangerous and have to be approached with caution. However, once they promise safety to the youth, they not only become friendly but are ready to serve him to the best of their ability.
6. As among humans, so in the ghoul family the youngest son is the best and most capable.
7. The ghoul, of course, can fly, as can all the fabulous beings in Arab folklore.
8. Forty is, again, the typical number of individuals in a group engaging in a joint activity, such as the forty thieves.
9. To tell his story means to explain why he did what he did.
10. The frequently used polite expression of willingness to do what the other person asks.
11. As in the case of the Birds of Power, here again the youth cannot resist the temptation to take what he was explicitly told not to take.
12. See note 9 above.
13. The ghoul is not only friendly and willing to serve the youth but also clever, knowing the way out of a difficult situation.
14. One of the characteristics of a ghoul is that he can change his shape to any other shape he chooses.

15. It was the youth's two brothers who cut the rope. What the listener suspected all the time is now confirmed: the two sons of the respected wife are evil and wish to kill their brother.
16. It was a miraculous horse, able to fly in the nick of time to wherever it was summoned by the rubbing of its hairs. The storyteller is not aware of the contradiction between this and the inability of the horse to find food and to get out of the well.
17. At this point the storyteller has forgotten that the youth himself wished to marry the daughter of the king of China.
18. The humiliated woman is, of course, the neglected wife, the mother of our hero.
19. Up to this point, we have not heard that the youth loved the girl who had given him the bracelet.

18
The Dull-witted Fisherman

Written and read over Jerusalem Radio by Dr. Isḥāq Mūsā al-Ḥusaynī, March 11, 1947.

In days of old there lived a dull-witted fisherman. Whenever he caught fish, he would sell it in the market at the cheapest price, so much so, that he became known among the people for his stupidity and carelessness.

Three of the merchants agreed among them to exploit the fisherman, and to buy the total of his catch for a few *dirhams*.

One day his wife said to him, "O Saʿīd, if you catch something today, sell it neither for a little nor for much."[1] He said to her, "Very well."[2]

In the early morning the fisherman went to the sea. He kept throwing out his nets until late afternoon, when he caught a big fish. He took it and brought it home. While he was on his way the three merchants saw him. They approached him and greeted him with the best greeting. He returned their greeting, and continued on his way. Thereupon they asked him to stop. They said to him, "Come, O Saʿīd, sell us the fish!" He said, "No. I don't want to, because my wife told me not to sell it, neither for little nor for much." They told him, "Leave that alone. That has no benefit. Sell us the fish." Thereupon they put a *bishlak*[3] in his hand, and took the fish from him. Saʿīd took the *bishlak* and went home.

When his wife saw him, she said to him: "What did you do, O Saʿīd?" He told her: "Here, take the *bishlak,* the price of the fish." She said to him, "Did I not tell you not to sell it?" He said, "Yes, you did say it. However, these merchants overpowered me. They bought the fish despite my wishes." She said to him, "Be careful not to return again like this." Thereupon he promised her to fulfill her wish the next time.

[Next day] he went out early in the morning to the sea as was his wont, and kept throwing out his net until noon, when he caught a big fish. However, as soon as he started walking home, he saw the three merchants waiting for him on the road. They greeted him and welcomed him, suggesting to him that he sell them the fish which he carried. But he refused, saying, "My wife was angry yesterday, and today I shall not sell the fish even if you pay me a thousand pounds."

They said to him, "Stop that talk, O Saʿīd!" They continued to treat him with kindness from time to time, until he became softened and flexible. Thereupon they took the fish and gave him one *bishlak.*

Saʿīd returned home, and his wife went to meet him, indulging herself in the hope of the fish. But behold, he was returning without it. She asked him what he had done. He told her what had happened to him with the three merchants, and how they had blocked his way, and insisted on buying the fish, so much so that he was forced to sell it.

She said to him, "But did I not order you[4] last night not to sell at whatever price?" He said, "That is correct, but they took it forcibly." She said, "Very well. Whatever has passed is dead. Tomorrow when the merchants meet you face to face, don't sell them the fish no matter what price they offer. If they harass you, fight them. Do you understand? Don't sell the fish. Don't sell it . . ."[5] He inclined his head in a gesture of agreement, and promised to bring back the fish, and would not spend any more time on this matter.

The following day he did whatever he had done on the previous days, and caught a big fish. As he was returning home, he encountered the three merchants who were waiting for him in the middle of the road. They greeted him, and accosted him, saying, "What, O Mr. Saʿīd . . ." But he answered at once, saying, "Watch out not to approach me. My wife has instructed me to fight you if you should try to take the fish from me." They said, "And what is our interest in the fish? We just want to have a word with you."

Saʿīd was confident, and approached them. They said to him, "Let us look at the fish, at its shape and beauty." Thereupon he handed the fish over to them. At that point they told him, "If you want to take the price of the fish, here it is. If not, don't bother us."

Saʿīd the fisherman started to cry and to sob.[6] Finally he said to them, "Well, give me the price of the fish." Thereupon they paid him one *bishlak,* and he took it and returned home.

When he arrived home his wife said to him, "Well now, O Saʿīd! What is behind you?" He recounted to her what had happened to him, and did so crying.[7] She said to him, "Don't worry, Saʿīd. Do you know those merchants?" He said, "Yes, I do."

In the early morning the wife accompanied Saʿīd, and both went to the market. He walked in front of her, and she followed him, until they arrived at the market. There he showed her the merchants, one by one. Afterward they returned home.

On the following day she said to her husband Saʿīd: "You go out now, and don't come back before four o'clock in the afternoon. Do you understand? Do not return before four o'clock in the afternoon!" And she repeated this to him several times.[8] (Upon the return he knocked on their door, she opened the door for him, and said to him, "Come on, go out now!")[9]

Her husband went out, and she was left alone in the house. She applied colors to her face, and on her hair perfume, and on the arms bracelets. She put on the finest clothes she had, until she appeared like the moon.[10]

She went to the store of the [first] merchant, and greeted him with peace. The merchant answered her with a greeting, welcoming her to his store, and asking her to sit down. Then she said with some coquetry, "Do you want me to sit here? Honor my small house!"[11] He said to her, "When?" She said, "At one o'clock this afternoon." They both agreed to meet at that time.

She then proceeded to the second merchant, and repeated the same actions with him, exactly as with the first one. She agreed to meet him at two o'clock that afternoon. She then moved on to the third merchant, and agreed to meet him at three o'clock that afternoon.

Thereafter she returned home, and started to count the hours and minutes until it was one o'clock. And behold, there was a knock on the door. She opened it, and our friend the first merchant entered. She greeted him and let him in into a nicely furnished room. She took off his jacket, and invited him to take a cozy seat. She started to prepare coffee for him, then put coals in the fireplace, and put a small jar on top of it. She started to blow gently on the coals so that the time would pass, apologizing for the delay in serving the coffee.[12]

She continued to do this until two o'clock in the afternoon, when there was a knock on the door. She rose quickly, pretending to be uneasy, and said to him, "My husband has arrived. Where shall I hide you?" She quickly led him by the hand to a dark room in the lowest part of the house, and hid him there.[13]

Then she hurried to the door, opened it, and the second merchant came in. She welcomed him, greeted him, and led him to the same living room. She was speaking gently and kindly to him, as she had spoken to the first merchant. She busied herself with various things during the entire hour. She expressed both regret and then apology for neglecting him, until three o'clock arrived, and there was a knock on the door. She again pretended to fear the arrival of her husband, and led him down to the same dark room. She put him beside his friend.

She returned to the door and opened it for the third merchant. She did everything exactly as she had done with both of his companions. She persisted in treating him nicely and indulged him until it was four o'clock, when her husband actually returned. She then led him to the dark room, where the three merchants sat holding their breath, without recognizing each other.

When her husband entered, she told him that the three merchants were sitting in the dark room, in fear and confusion. She then ordered him to go down and beat them up. Her husband took a stick, went down to the room, and remained there, and kept on beating them until all three perished.[14] Then he returned to his wife, and told her that he had beaten them to death. She went down to the room, and found them as he said they were. She told him, "I did not ask you to kill them. I asked you just to beat them up in order to scare them." He said, "What happened happened."

In the evening she dressed up, and went to the house of her neighbor, a man with a small brain. She said to him, "O, our neighbor, a poor man has come to us. Each time I get him out of the house, he returns to the house. Help me to get rid of him, and you will have your reward." He said to her, "Where is he?" She said, "There he is, sitting in the house."

She had already seated one of the merchants in a beehive,[15] and placed a tall conical cap (the cap of a dervish) on his head. The neighbor came, and carried him out on his back, and went to the sea where he threw him in,[16] and then returned to his house. In the meantime she had taken out the second merchant and placed him in a beehive, and put a high conical cap on his head. As soon as the neighbor returned, she went to him and said, "The poor man came back. What shall I do?" He said, "Did the evil one really come back?" She said, "Yes." The neighbor came and carried off the second one, thinking it was the first one. He threw him in the sea, in order that he should not return. In the meantime she did with the third merchant what she had done with the first two. She went to her neighbor to tell him that the evil one had once again escaped from the sea. The neighbor became very angry, and carried off the third one. He waded into the sea as far as he could, and cast him away forcefully.

By the time he came back, dawn was breaking, paving the way for the rising of the sun. When he reached his house he saw a man putting on his head a cap similar to the cap of a dervish, holding a lamp in his hand. Thereupon he attacked him, beating him on the head with a stick, and then carried him off on his back, saying, "May Allāh curse you, O you evil one! Did you manage to get out a third time from the sea? And from where did you get the lamp?" When he reached the sea, he threw him into it. Then he returned to his woman neighbor, telling her about the matter of the poor devil, and of how he had got out a third time, carrying a lamp.

Thereupon she was confident that her husband had really got rid of the wicked merchants. She gave some money to her neighbor. She went through the clothing of the merchants, and took whatever money or possessions were in them. Then she sold them in the market.

Her husband returned to his fishing, safe and secure. As for her, she returned to a more luxurious life, enjoying wealth and prosperity, obtained by her smartness, cleverness, and shrewdness. Both of them lived in comfort and ease.[17]

Comments

Even though this story was authored by Dr. Isḥāq Mūsā al-Ḥusaynī and the miraculous folkloristic elements of supernatural beings and happenings are absent from it, it still is written in the traditional style of the Arab folktale and contains many characteristic Arab folktale motifs. In fact, it is a composition containing, on the one hand, features depicting Arab life as it could be observed in a seaside Arab town (such as Jaffa) and, on the other, acts, reactions, and behavior patterns as can occur only in a folktale. The combination of these two types of elements endows the story with its specific charm.

Notes

1. As in many Arab folktales, here, too, the wife is presented as much more intelligent than her husband, and it is she who takes the initiative to improve their situation.

2. This first exchange of a few words between the husband and the wife establishes her superiority; she tells the husband what to do, and he accepts her instructions.
3. A small coin.
4. That a wife should address her husband in this manner is a folktale feature with no basis in the actual husband-wife relations in Arab society.
5. The wife's words and her repetition of her instructions show that the fisherman was indeed dull-witted and therefore had to be told a thing several times before he understood it.
6. The fisherman cries because he sees that despite his wife's explicit instructions, he is unable to resist the persuasion of the merchants. Crying is considered by the Arabs a most unmanly exhibition of weakness.
7. The fisherman again cries, because he is ashamed that he was unable to follow his wife's instructions. The wife now sees that she must take action.
8. The wife does not tell her husband what she intends to do.
9. The sentence in parentheses is out of place and is probably an erroneous and distorted repetition.
10. The folktale here leaves reality behind and leads us into an imaginary world, in which the wife of the poor fisherman has face paints, perfumes, jewelry, and fine clothes and is very beautiful.
11. Not only is the wife of the fisherman beautiful, but she knows how to behave in a seductive manner. Such a sudden change of character is a folktale motif with no relation to reality.
12. In the world of the Arab folktale, even if a man has an assignation with a woman, the quasi-ritual serving and drinking of coffee have to precede the sexual engagement between them. The same scene is described in tale 5. It is a reflection of the almost obligatory nature of the Arab custom of serving coffee to a visitor immediately upon his arrival.
13. The tale endows the poor fisherman's house with a cellar and a living room where his wife can receive guests. This is yet another intrusion of folktale elements into the otherwise realistic picture of the life of a poor fisherman and his wife.
14. The killing of people is a common occurrence in the Arab folktale. The fisherman gets carried away by his revengeful beating of the three merchants, and he does not (or cannot) stop until he kills them. The wife is only faintly annoyed by the killing of the three men by her husband, even though the only crime the three merchants had committed was to persuade him to sell them his fish for a low price—certainly not a crime deserving the death penalty. However, in the Arab folktale the killing of a person is often presented as not a more grievous act than, say, slapping him. Nor is it explained why the three merchants, who were friends and who previously were able to persuade the dull-witted fisherman to do what they wanted, do not resist his

murderous attack. In any case, this scene is definitely a folktale motif and has nothing to do with a depiction of reality.

15. The presence of a beehive (Arabic *qafīr*) in the house of the poor fisherman is surprising and puzzling. Nor is it clear what is meant by the woman placing the dead merchant in the beehive, which does not seem possible.
16. The folktale does not find it reprehensible that the neighbor throws the merchant, whom he believes to be a poor beggar, into the sea, thereby killing him, nor that he then kills yet another man, whose identity is unknown to him.
17. The folktale wastes not a word on the fact that the well-being of the fisherman and his wife was achieved at the price of murdering three merchants and the death of a fourth man.

Part Three

1982–84

19
The King and His Wife

Recorded by Yoel Perez, from the mouth of Sabḥa ʿAbbūd (age 56) of the ʿArab al-Ḥujeyrāt tribe, ca. 1984.

By Allāh, there was an emir, he lived in a house, his house was big, on the second story.[1] He and his wife lived on the second story.

A beggar came to him. He said to her, "Woman . . ."

This king [said], "Get up and give him alms, give this beggar, give him a loaf of bread, give him something."

She said to him, "By Allāh, that will not help him."

He said to her, "Why?"

She said to him, "The poor man [is poor] because of his wife, and the rich man [is rich] because of his wife. By Allāh, that will not help him."

The king said to her, "By Allāh, I shall divorce you, and give you to the poor man to see whether you will make him rich."

He divorced her and gave her to the poor man. She went and joined the poor man. The poor man had a small hut, he had nothing, he was begging for alms. She joined him, and he said to her, "Sit in the hut!"

She sat in the hut. While she was sitting in the hut, he was collecting alms. While he was walking, he passed a road, and behold there was a well. In the well there was one black woman and one white woman, and there was a man.[2] The one who was above, the beggar, looked at him, looked at everything there was in the well. He said to him, "You who are there above, which of the women is beautiful?"

He said, "By Allāh, my lord, love your beloved, even if he be a black slave." That is to say, [love] not the beauty but the heart.

He said to him, "By Allāh, take two pomegranates!" And he gave them to him as a present, that is to say, this [advice] was right: one should love in a person not the beauty, but his heart, the one whom he loves he loves.

He said to him, "Take this present from me, two pomegranates." He gave them to him.

He took them and gave them to his wife, to the wife of the king who sat in the hut. She cut the first pomegranate into two, and behold, a golden precious stone was in it. She went, sold it, and bought stones and built a palace like the palace of the king. She returned and opened the second pomegranate, and behold, there was in it another precious golden stone. She bought [things] like those that are in the house of the king, and more.

The beggar came to the land of the hut—there is no hut.[3] And she was on top, on the second floor, and the servants were with her. She said to them, "[Take] this most beautiful suit of clothes, go, wash that man. Wash him, clean him up, and bring him to me."

They tried to embrace him [to get hold of him]. He said, "Let me go, let me go!"[4]

They said to him, "No, we want to wash you and to dress you, and the queen said that you should go to her."

He said, "I don't want to!"

The main thing is, they took him and washed him, and dressed him in the suit, and brought him to her.

He said to her, "O, Allāh, from where is all this?"

She said to him, "I built it."

And he remained a month to walk about and to collect alms,[5] until he came to her.

She said to him, "Sit down. Did I make you rich? Allāh made you rich."

She delivered a letter in which she invited the king, her husband, and invited the vizier. The king came to her, and while he was walking, the king, he said, "Vizier! This is my house! This is my palace!"[6]

He said to him, "We have just now left your palace."

He said to him, "This is my palace."

He said to him, "No."

He said to him, "If not, this belongs to the Mistress Zabīdah." The name of his wife was Zabīdah. "I know her food. It is possible that she built this palace."

While they were sitting eating their midday meal, she passed the food around, and, behold, it was her food.

He said to her, "By Allāh, this is the food of my wife." [7]

She went, passed it around, and blessed them after the meal. She said to him, "O king of the time,[8] will you sign for me that the poor man [is poor] because of his wife, and the rich man [is rich] because of his wife?"

He said to her, "I shall sign." [9]

Comments

I begin this group of Arab folktales recorded in Israel in the 1980s with the story of "The King and His Wife" because it serves as a good example of several points made in the introduction concerning the insight these tales afford into character traits and values among the Arabs.

The first thing that strikes us is that the wife of the king appears to have a definite view of her own about the manner in which a couple makes its way in the world and the relative roles of husband and wife in achieving material well-being. As pointed out in the introduction, the Arab folktale frequently depicts the wife as more clever than her husband, as the one who takes the initiative and makes suggestions for the improvement of their situation. In the beginning of this story, the wife of the king is definitely not a downtrodden, intimidated woman but an individual who not only has strong views of her own but voices them openly. She does not hesitate to contradict her husband (by refusing to give alms to the beggar), and (although this is not explicitly stated but only implied) she refuses to budge from this position, even though it means being divorced.

On the other hand, the peremptory manner in which the king divorces his wife—it is a snap decision—is in conformity with the powers traditional Muslim religious law accords to the husband. The story clearly shows that when it comes to divorce, an officially sanctioned act, the husband can initiate and effect it at a moment's notice. Still, a certain tension is felt in the story between two aspects of the husband-wife interaction: in the power relations between the two personalities as they come to expression in the everyday conversation between them, the wife definitely holds her own, which does not harmonize with the official superiority with which Muslim religious tradition endows the husband.

That the husband (the king) not only divorces his wife but "gives her to the poor man" is pure story stuff. In the Muslim-Arab reality, a husband who divorces his wife has no say at all about whom she subsequently marries, or whether she remarries at all.

The new husband of the woman, to whom the king "gives" his wife, is described in the tale as a professional beggar. The figure of the professional beggar is again taken from traditional life in the Arab world, where begging was (and still is) an accepted, religiously sanctioned, venerable occupation. Almsgiving is an important religious duty, and beggars are able to eke out a living without becoming homeless, as they do in many modern American cities. While the beggar "works" the streets, his wife sits at home, in the hut, which is as much their home as the palace is that of the king.

Thus far, the story deals with the real world, from which it deviates only by certain modifications that do not strain the listeners' credulity. But in the next scene, when the beggar looks down into the well, he and, with him, the listeners get a glimpse of the wonderworld of ghouls and other extrahuman beings that populate most of the Arab folktales. That the well and the beings in it belong to a different world is not stated in the story but is evident to all its listeners, who are thoroughly familiar with the "fact" that wells, cisterns, and caves are gateways to the realm of the extrahuman, as it has been depicted in the Arab folktale for many hundreds of years.

However, even the wonderland of demons and ghouls reflects the sociocultural reality in which the storytellers and their listeners live. In this story, the three persons whom the beggar sees in the well mirror a configuration not infrequently encountered in the Arab world. There is a man (a ghoul), evidently white, and with him are two women, one white and one black, and the man is faced with the problem of choosing between them.

Ghouls in the Arab folktale are often presented as having problems that only a human can solve for them. The ghoul in the well has one that polygynous men were well known to be faced with in real life. The question he puts to the beggar means much more than meets the ear. The words he uses are "Which of the two women is more beautiful?" but what he actually means is "Shall I choose the white woman or the black one?" This is how the beggar understands the question, and it is this unspoken query behind the explicit one that he answers when he says, "Love your beloved, even if he be a black slave," meaning "Follow your heart, take the one you love, even if she is a black slavegirl."

While the tale offers this lesson, it does not go so far as to contradict the traditional Arab viewpoint that considers the white race more beautiful than the black. On the contrary, it accepts the Arab racial stereotype but advises that one listen to one's heart rather than consider mere beauty. In the Arab world, white skin in particular has always been considered more beautiful than dark skin. In many Arab folktales, the white skin of a girl is highly praised, and in the actual Arab world, other things being equal, the whiter the skin of a girl, the higher would be the bride price her father could expect to get for her.

Of course, individual attraction does not obey racial stereotypes, and cases of white Arab men who loved, married, and had children by black women are known from various parts of the Arab world. In this story, the ghoul in the well finds himself in a typical Arab dilemma: his thinking is dominated by the racial stereotype that holds that negroes are less attractive than whites, but at the same time he is attracted to the negro slavegirl whom he loves. It is in this quandary that he turns to the beggar, whose advice is: choose the woman you love, even if she is a black girl and therefore considered less beautiful than the white one.

The ghoul readily accepts the beggar's advice, and the story repeats the conclusion, "One should love not the beauty but the heart."

Having impressed the audience with this lesson, the story now returns to the never-never land of the fairy tale. The grateful ghoul gives the beggar two pomegranates, an apparently modest reward for the valuable advice—which, incidentally, allows us to suspect that the beggar of the story is not an ordinary mendicant but a man of wisdom, possibly a sage disguised as a *faqīr.* However, when the beggar gives them to his wife and she opens them, the pomegranates turn out to contain precious stones. There may be a hint here that the ghoul fully recognized the invaluable wisdom of the beggar's advice.

The beggar's wife instantly knows what to do with the newfound riches: she sells the stones and builds an exact duplicate of the palace of the king, her former husband. She accomplishes this—we are still in wonderland—within a single day, so that when the beggar comes home from a hard day's work of collecting alms, he does not find his hut but instead a sumptuous palace, on the second floor of which his wife waits for him.

The scene in which the poor, dirty beggar is being washed by a retinue of servants introduces a comic element into the story. His objection to being cleaned up reminds us of the screams of Eliza when, in the film version of Shaw's *Pygmalion,* she is subjected to the same indignity.

But ultimately the beggar is washed and dressed in fine new clothes and thus brought before his wife. In this scene, and from here on in the rest of the story, the wife is the dominant person, and the husband plays a distinctly subordinate role.

One more thing: even though he is now a rich man, the beggar continues to work the streets. Perhaps herein there is yet another hint that he is in reality a wise man for whom begging is his chosen way of life.

The next scene, describing a brief exchange between the beggar and his wife, is especially instructive. While she was still the wife of the king, the woman insisted that it was the wife who made her husband either rich or poor. But now, when she could claim that it was she who found the precious stones in the pomegranates and built and equipped the new palace, she does nothing of the sort but rather disclaims all credit and piously attributes their riches to Allāh alone.

What remains for the story to tell is the manner in which the wife proves that the position she took when she opposed her first husband (the king) was right. She invites him and his vizier, has them admire the fabulous duplicate palace she has built, serves him a rich repast—the king does not recognize her, but he recognizes her cooking—and thus demonstrates to him that indeed it is the wife who makes her husband rich or poor. The king signs a declaration to this effect, and the tale ends with the complete vindication and victory of the wife.

Notes

1. In the modest imagination of a poor Bedouin, a well-to-do man who lives on the second story of a house in a city must be an emir or, as he is styled a few sentences later, a king.
2. The man and the black and white women in the well are not ordinary human beings. As becomes evident from the gift the man gives to the beggar, they are benevolent jinns or ghouls.
3. The building of the palace and its furnishing with royal items are done in a miraculously short time. When the beggar returns home from his daily rounds, he finds his wife luxuriating on the second story, surrounded by servants.
4. A humorous detail. The beggar does not want to be cleaned up and dressed in fine clothes.
5. Despite his newly found riches, the beggar continues his alms gathering.
6. Here we learn that the palace the wife built is a duplicate of the king's palace.
7. The king does not recognize his wife, but he recognizes her cooking. In the story, the queen herself cooks.

8. An old royal title familiar from the *Arabian Nights.* Its meaning is something like "king of the present age."
9. The point the queen intended to make is not proven by the story. The beggar did not become rich because of his wife but because the jinn in the well gave him two pomegranates containing unimaginable treasures as a reward for his wise words about love. The wife's role is confined to cutting open the fruits and using the precious stones to build a palace. It seems that the story was told in a truncated form.

20
Ghouls in Switzerland

Narrator: Zahia Ghurayfāt (age 60) of the ʿArab al-Ghurayfāt tribe of Bayt Zarzīr, recorded by Yoel Perez, 1982.

There was a man who had three sons.[1] The three sons were studying in the school. They completed the twelfth year, and went to the university.[2] For their university studies they went to a city like Tel Aviv.[3] When they went they began studying.

In the city there was an emir.[4] The emir had a daughter. No man was allowed to see her when she went out into the streets of the city.[5] Guards surrounded her, and not a soul was allowed to remain in the city at that point.

The three brothers rented an apartment,[6] and took turns in going out at night to fetch food.[7] One day it was the turn of the oldest boy. The oldest boy went, the younger boys remained in the house. The guards called out, "It is forbidden to go out, stay at home!" When the boy went out, he saw the king's daughter going out, accompanied by twenty-four girls, and many guards were surrounding her.[8] When he saw her, the king's daughter saw him too. The king's daughter desired the boy, and the boy desired her.[9] After he saw her, he fetched the food and returned home.

The youngest brother said to the other two: "What would you wish me to be?" They said to him: "We wish you would become a doctor." He [the second] said to him: "And you, what would you wish me to be?" He said to him: "That you should become a lawyer."[10] But the oldest boy, he who had gone to the city, said to them both: "What would you wish me to be? Wish me that I marry the king's daughter."

In the gate there were guards, each of them watched out for strangers. They heard, they communicated with the king by wireless.[11]

The army came, surrounded the three brothers and seized them.[12] When they were seized, the king's daughter heard, and she knew that the boy wanted her.[13]

The king transported them in an airplane[14] and took them to Switzerland,[15] at twelve midnight. The daughter of the king followed them to the airport, and she rode and traveled with them.[16] She did not want her father, nor her brother, nor anybody else. She wanted the boy.[17] The three brothers rode [the plane], and the fourth was the king's daughter, and all of them traveled in the airplane.

There [in Switzerland] they had no houses.[18] They came and wanted to eat, the bridegroom[19] and his middle brother went to fetch food from the city. When they entered the city, it was forbidden to walk about at night.[20] They went to the market, and there was nobody there. Since there was nobody there they broke open a store, took food, and returned. When they returned, behold, the guards shot at the two, and they both died immediately.[21] She and their youngest brother remained alive.

In the morning—may I and you wake up in good health![22]—the guards were shouting, asking who in that city had lost two men. They were those whom the guards had killed. At twelve o'clock they buried them. This one knew that they were his brothers.

They [the emir's daughter and the youngest brother] left the strange city.[23] From there they went out to live in Switzerland.[24] And behold, there were his two brothers! When he passed by he recognized the boys,[25] and he returned. He said to her, "What has befallen us?" She said to him, "Nothing." They said to each other, "Where should we go?" They started to look for a house in Switzerland. They had neither food nor drink.

The guards started shouting,[26] "Who will enter this house? He who leaves it is a winner, and he who enters it is a loser!"[27] Who then would enter such a house, if the one entering it is a loser, and the one leaving it is a winner? He said to her, "Should we enter? What should we do?" They entered the house.

The woman neighbor came out, and said to her, "Do not enter the house! Many a time this house has caused families to die. It is impossible for a family to enter it and come out safely. All of them will die, O my sister. Do not go near that evil, you must not do it!" She[28] said to her, "My trust is in Allāh. There is nobody else for me to trust but Allāh."

This girl was weaving on a loom, the girl had been so hired.[29] Allāh alone knows what was the matter with her. The girl used to weave on the loom, and she filled the jar with water and started to weave on the loom. She remained awake until twelve midnight.

And behold, a big snake came,[30] and it stayed slurping from the jar until it drank all that was in the jar. When the snake saw the girl it poured back into the heart of the jar all that it had drunk from it. The poison of this snake would kill the sons of Adam [people] who would drink from that jar without realizing it, thinking it was only water.

For two, three days she did not drink from the jar, since she was smart. Once when the girl saw the snake she said, "This is the one who kills the sons of Adam. What should we do about it?" She waited until the snake came, then she awakened the man beside her,[31] so that he should see the snake that killed people. It was a ghoul, not a snake. At this point the snake jumped, and as the girl watched it just entered into the cave. It went inside, and when it went into the cave the girl closed the door behind it.[32] By the power of Allāh the snake was locked up with a rock that he [the boy] had put there. The youngest brother closed up the entrance tightly behind the snake.[33] He went to the blacksmith and said to him, "Would you make for me a sword of steel, and also a rifle of the finest model.[34] Would you make me an ax which is not surpassed by any other in the whole world? Because I want to cut off the head of the snake. By eventime they should be ready, and whatever the price, I shall pay it to you." He said, "Good."

People began to come and inspect the house. What did they do? They did not understand how they had remained well [safe] in the house. The people considered this most marvelous. Then the people realized what was going on: that the youth was going to have an encounter with the snake.

He stood near the door and armed himself, and the woman armed herself. And the snake came by, the man struck it with the iron. He [the snake] said to him, "Repeat!"[35] He said to him, "My mother did not teach me how to repeat." Then he struck it a second time. The snake said to him, "Don't strike me dead! I have three signs which will make you happy." He said to him, "What are the signs?" He said to him, "Pluck three hairs from me!" The snake said to him, "Pluck three hairs from its back." He plucked three hairs from its back. The snake said to him, "In the house in which I live there is a jar of gold. Watch when I go into the house, wherever I put my head there is a jar of gold. And I have a garden full of sour pomegranates and oranges all of gold, and over it is a whale[36] protecting it." He said to him, "Good."

The woman was with him. The snake said to him, "Watch out for that woman, because it is on her account that your two brothers went away. Therefore watch out for her. And the whale, when you encounter it first, give it the first hair, and for the first hair the whale will vouch for your safety."

The snake departed, the youth followed it. It entered the cave, and he entered after it. It said to him, "Burn the first hair so that the rock should not close on you." He burned the first hair, and the rock did not close, the rock remained open. When the rock remained open, he went and brought a shovel, a tractor with a claw. He went to the city and brought a winch[37] and lifted up the rock which weighed about six or seven tons. The whole city started to sing to the boy, rejoicing that he had killed the snake.[38] They went to the place where the snake had lived, and, behold, there was a jar filled with gold.[39] He took the jar of gold and said, "I want to see the garden." The fellow[40] went into the hole of the snake, and behold there was the garden in which there was a multitude of things. It had a whale, and the whale had two daughters,[41] what daughters! They were as beautiful as gazelles.[42] They were hanging by their hair.[43] When he saw them hanging by their hair, he said, "What is this?" They said to him, "What is it with you? Untie our hair!" He untied their hair, and said to them, "You have nothing to fear."

He burned the hair that he had taken from the snake. When he burned the hair the whale said to him, "By Allāh, if you had not thrown whatever you threw at me, I would have slain you,[44] and Allāh knows what would have happened to you, and I would have closed the rock upon you. But now you have become my son, and I shall die in two hours. Because you have burned this hair, in two hours I shall die. This sour pomegranate is of gold, the oranges are of gold, the grapefruit[45] is of gold, and under this dry tree there is a jar full of riches, and if you remove this jar full of riches from beneath it, you will survive, have everlasting livelihood, because it is full of gold."

There was a palace nearby. After the whale died, he [the youth] said to them [the whale's daughters], "What should I do with you now? I have with me the bride of my brother, and now I want to marry her. But now I have three of you. What should I do with you?" They said to him, "We don't know." He put all three of them in the house of the whale.

The emir's daughter looked around, and, behold, two men, her paternal uncle the vizier and her father, were passing through the palace. Their condition was frightening: they looked like beggars. The daughter could not definitely recognize them. She said, "These are the vizier and my father. I know them, and yet do not know them; I know them, and yet do not know them."

Thereafter the girls said to him [to the emir], "What are you looking around for, O my uncle?"[46] He said to them, "I think that one of you is my daughter. I had a daughter who looked like that, and she rode off on a horse. And there were three brothers studying in our city, she saw one of them, and they took her to Switzerland.[47] And I heard that two of them were killed, and that one and my daughter are well."

She said to him, "Here I am, your daughter!" He arose, embraced her and kissed her, and wept. She started to wash him and give him clothing. And he prepared the marriage contract for his daughter. She said to him, "I am still not married. The one I wanted died. This is his brother."

Her father made a marriage contract[48] with the brother. He said to her, "I don't agree that the contract should be only with you, but rather that the two women be included with you, three women in all." She said to him, "Agreed.[49] And may you live all your life in plenty."

Thereupon he drew up a marriage contract and married her, and her father rode the plane[50] and returned to his country.

Comments

This story is exceptional among the contemporary Israeli Arab folktales in that it combines many modern elements with traditional ones. The modern elements are realistic and reflect the influence of the present-day Israeli environment on the Arab society in which the tale developed, while the traditional ones hark to old Arab folklore motifs and are partly realistic and partly fantastic-miraculous.

The first part of the story is dominated by the realistic modern elements. The three brothers who are the heroes of the story complete twelve years of study, and then they move to "a city like Tel Aviv" to study at the university. All this is modern. But then the story switches to a traditional environment. The city in which the university is located is an Arab city, headed by an emir, who a few sentences later is termed "king." This king-emir has a daughter whom he keeps in total seclusion, as used to be practiced by the most traditional segments of Arab society. To make sure that no man can as much as glimpse his daughter, the king imposes a curfew on the city whenever his daughter goes out to take a stroll. A curfew, however, is an Israeli type restriction or security precaution, imposed on Arab cities in the wake of demonstrations, disturbances, or attacks.

Now the two milieus clash. The brothers, who live in an apartment they rented in the university city, must confine their shopping for food to the hours of the night, when the king's daughter is staying at home. Nevertheless, one night the oldest brother, out shopping, happens to catch a glimpse of the girl, who passes by surrounded by twenty-four of her maidens and a large number of guards. The girl, too, sees him, and the two, in typical traditional Arab folktale fashion, fall in love.

The brief conversation among the three brothers that follows also moves back and forth between the modern and the traditional. One of the brothers announces that he wants to be a doctor, the second that he plans to be a lawyer—two thoroughly modern occupations, much preferred by modern Israeli Jews, as well as by the upper crust of Israeli Arab society. But the third, the oldest brother, who caught a glimpse of the emir's daughter, has only one wish: to marry her, as is the wish of many heroes in traditional Arab folktales.

The king communicates with his guards in an up-to-date fashion, by "wireless" (that is, radio). At this point the story is incomplete. We are not told why the king arrests the three brothers, but we can guess: the guards noticed that one of them exchanged glances with the king's daughter. All three brothers are arrested and removed from the country, so that no more contact should be possible between any one of them and the king's daughter.

Next appears another modern feature: in the dead of night, the three brothers are deported by airplane to Switzerland. Why to Switzerland precisely remains unexplained. However, the king's daughter manages to sneak out of the palace and to board the same plane.

What happens after their arrival in Switzerland is described only vaguely. The brothers, we are told, have no relatives there—if they had, the natural thing for members of an Arab family would be to stay with them. They have to obtain food for themselves, and they do this by going out at night to the market, when all the stores are closed. Why they don't do their shopping during the day is not explained. In any case, they break open a store and steal food, and the guards shoot and kill two of them, the oldest one and the second oldest. The story does not explain why there should be an armed guard in the streets of the Swiss city and why there should be a curfewlike restriction there, too.

The story here omits an important development: it is not stated but only implied that after the death of the oldest brother, the king's daughter falls in love with the surviving youngest brother, who from now on takes the place of the oldest. Moreover, at this point the storyteller seems to have lost the thread of the story. The youngest brother and the king's daughter are now not in Switzerland but in "a strange city" from which they go on to Switzerland. Although the two elder brothers were killed and buried, now the youngest brother sees them alive.

As the youth and the girl are about to occupy a house, guards appear and warn everybody not to enter the house because it is unlucky. Nevertheless, the youth and the girl enter and also disregard the more explicit warning of a woman neighbor.

Now the king's daughter assumes a different character. She becomes a girl who is hired (by whom?) to spend all her day and half the night, until midnight, weaving on a loom. This is definitely a traditional folktale motif, as is that of the snake the girl sees three nights in a row coming and drinking all the water from the jar, then spitting it back and thereby poisoning the water. With these motifs, the story has definitely left the modern world of airplanes and radios and is back in the traditional wonderworld of the Arab folktale.

Having thus ascertained the reason for the death of all the people who lived in the house, the girl awakens the youth who sleeps next to her, and they recognize that the snake actually is a ghoul. They see that the ghoul-snake enters a cave—suddenly, there is a cave entrance in the house in which they are staying—and the resourceful girl quickly closes the door upon him, while the youth secures it by pushing a big rock against it.

Then the youth goes to a smith and asks him to provide him with an assortment of weapons: the finest sword, the finest gunpowder, and the finest ax—all this to enable him to kill the snake. At this point, the youth, who only a few days earlier had neither food nor drink, has unlimited resources and offers to pay the smith any price.

Only now are we told that the people of the neighborhood knew that the house was deadly because the snake killed everybody who tried to stay in it. The youth and the girl take up their position at the door. When the snake comes, the youth strikes him "with the iron"—we are not told whether it is with the sword or the ax.

With the next scene, we are even deeper in folktale wonderland. A widespread folktale motif has it that striking the monster once kills it, but striking it a second time revives it. When the youth strikes the snake, before it dies it asks the youth to strike it a second time. The youth strikes the snake a second time, and the grateful snake offers him three hairs from its head and three from its back, as well as jars of gold and fruits of gold.

Next, for good measure, the story throws in a whale which guards the treasures found in the snake's house.

The youth follows the snake into its cave and, on its advice, burns one hair which prevents the rock from closing after him. Here the storyteller has forgotten that earlier the youth himself had to shove the rock against the door of the cave, and represents the rock as blocking the door automatically.

The story next switches from the fairytale wonderland to the world of modern technology and heavy road-building machinery. Although the rock no longer blocks the door leading into the cave, nevertheless the youth goes to the city and brings a shovel, a tractor, and a winch to remove the rock, which, we are now told, weighed "about six or seven tons."

At some point in the course of this technical effort, the youth must nevertheless have killed the snake—even though it had turned from a deadly enemy into a friendly helper—because the whole city rejoices and fetes the youth for having killed it. The youth collects the jars of gold, and in the garden in "the hole of the snake," he finds two exceedingly beautiful girls, the two daughters of the whale, who are hung up by their hair, as are many captive maidens in Arab folktales. The youth unties them and burns a hair the snake gave him, which protects him from the whale. The whale adopts him as a son, but because the youth burned the magic hair, it must die two hours later. Thus, the whale is the second magic animal (actually, a human being in the shape of a whale) who befriends the youth and as a consequence must die.

The garden in the hole of the snake is at this point miraculously transformed into a palace. The two daughters of the whale and the king's daughter are installed by the youth in the palace. Suddenly, the king's daughter espies her father the emir and her uncle the vizier (who appears only here) "passing through the palace." The two men are dressed in beggars' clothes, and the girl cannot definitely recognize them. Nor does the emir recognize his daughter, but when she asks him, he tells her that his daughter "rode off on a horse" and was taken to Switzerland by three brothers.

The daughter identifies herself, washes and dresses her father, who thereupon declares himself willing to give her to the youth in marriage. But the youth insists on marrying not only her but also the two daughters of the whale. The emir's daughter agrees, and the youth, after a rather unsuccessful excursion into the modern world of universities, airplanes, radios, and heavy machinery, settles back into a traditional Muslim Arab marriage with three wives. As for the emir, he takes the next plane back to his own country.

At first glance, it is difficult to know what to do with this folktale, which appears to contain an indiscriminate mixture of modern and traditional elements. However, a careful analysis of the relationship between the two types of features shows that the sympathy of the story lies with the traditional rather than with the modern. The snake which is a ghoul, the cave which is a palace, the whale which is human and has two beautiful daughters, the magic hairs, the golden pomegranates, oranges, and grapefruit—these are the elements with which the storyteller is thoroughly at home, representing the world in which the heroes and heroines move with familiar ease. The modern world, the story tells us, impinges on our traditional lives, and since its intrusion cannot be helped, we must make use of whatever it has to offer, but we must not overestimate its value, we must not become captivated by it, and we must not let it dominate our lives. Looked at from this viewpoint, the story appears to be a masked cautionary tale, a plea not to allow modernism to occupy a more than secondary, limited place in the life of the Arab community in the midst of, or next to, the modern, technologically oriented Israeli majority. It is all right, the story seems to say, to make use of planes and radios when need be, but our proper place is in the palace and garden of traditional Arab life.

In the manner typical of the fairy tale, and the folktale in general, the story nowhere spells out this lesson. Nowhere does it say, "It is better to do this than that." It only tells what its protagonists did, the difficulties they encountered, the steps they took to solve their predicaments. It shows that living in a modern environment and utilizing modern equipment and machinery are ultimately unsatisfactory, and each time the protagonists find themselves in the former or make use of the latter, they quickly escape back into the reassuring wonderworld of the fairy tale in which they feel thoroughly at home and with whose threats and promises they know how to deal. The two older brothers, who go out to the streets of the Swiss city (trying to cope with the modern environment), are killed by the guards, even though their only crime is to be in the streets during curfew hours. It is from this inimical world that the youngest brother and the girl flee into the magic house with whose supernatural dangers (the snake-ghoul, etc.) they feel they can cope. It is also characteristic in this connection that it is by her return to a traditional Arab women's occupation, weaving on a loom, that the girl remains awake and notices the snake-ghoul coming and poisoning the water. It is only owing to this happenstance that she and the youth know they have to refrain from drinking it and thus stay alive. Against the bullets of the guards the protagonists are helpless. With traditional dangers, represented by snakes and ghouls—meaning the exigencies of traditional Arab life—they know how to deal.

Another important difference between the relationship of the protagonists to the realistic world on the one hand and to the wonderworld of the folktale on the other is in the role religion plays in the two realms. When faced with dangers or uncertainties in the wonderworld, they repeatedly invoke the name of Allāh, and, as the story shows, Allāh does not fail to help them. When faced with the dangers of the realistic world (the armed guards in the streets of the Swiss city), the protagonists do not invoke Allāh, as if they knew that such an appeal in that situation would be useless. Implied in this difference is the lesson that it is preferable to face the dangers of the wonderworld, that is, the traditional Arab world, in which Allāh can help than those of the realistic modern world in which religious belief and reliance are of no avail.

As the story progresses, it becomes more and more clear that the wonderworld stands for the traditional Arab life, in which the protagonists prefer to live. Unverbalized but embedded in the story is the lesson of what is the right thing to do for people who by birth and upbringing are identified with the heroes and heroines of the tale.

This is indicated also by the change in the girl's attitude toward her father's wishes relative to her marriage. In the beginning of the story, the emir's daughter is rebellious; she does not want to comply with her father's wishes concerning her relations with men. The father wants to prevent her from meeting any man, probably because he considers her too young to marry. The girl rebels, runs off, and manages to board the plane that takes her to Switzerland with the youth she secretly loves. Boarding the plane and flying to Switzerland with a lover who has a university education means leaving behind the traditional Arab milieu represented by the father and entering—and more than that, embracing—the modern world. However, as a consequence of this step, the girl's lover and his brother get killed, which can be taken as symbolic of the girl's inability to find her place in the modern world or to master its exigencies. After returning to the traditional world of the Arab milieu (symbolized by taking up weaving and by the various fairytale figures), the girl reencounters her father, and now she is ready to marry the youth her father selects for her. That this is a compromise for the girl, and not her own choice, is indicated by the words she utters when her father prepares the marriage contract for her. She says, "The one I loved has died. This is his brother." She does not say that she loves the youngest brother, but since her father wants her to marry him, she accepts him. The acceptance by the girl of the traditional place of the Arab woman is indicated even more emphatically by her consent to the youth's desire to marry two other girls at the same time. With this, the return of the rebellious girl into the fold of the traditional Arab family is complete.

A word needs to be said about the appearance of the emir and his brother as beggars. Why do the emir and his brother the vizier appear dressed in dilapidated clothes? I believe the story introduces this element in order to indicate that the emir and the vizier stand for the traditional Arab world which the girl had abandoned for the enticements of the modern world. When viewed from the "palace" of the modern world, the traditional Arab world appears to be poor, backward, dirty. But when her father reminds the girl of what she left behind and of the modern world having killed her lover, her traditional milieu appears attractive to her again, which is expressed by the girl washing her father and giving him new clothes. The rehabilitated father is one whose authority the girl is willing to accept.

In the course of her experiences and disappointments in the modern world, the girl also undergoes a process of emotional maturation. When she ran away from home, she had no consideration for her father or for the world he represented. She was all wrapped up in her desire to go after her lover, who symbolized for her the modern world and all its attractions. Now, after her adventures, or rather misadventures, in Switzerland, she is mature enough to value her father, the familiar Arab world he represents, and the position assigned to her by the traditions of that world.

Notes

1. In colloquial Arabic *wlād* ("children"). But since the noun is masculine, it is generally used in the sense of "sons."
2. The storyteller is familiar with the situation in middle-class Israeli families

where the general ambition is to have sons go on to university studies after finishing twelve years in elementary and high school.

3. The narrator does not want to define precisely the locality, but when wishing to speak of a city with a university he thinks of Tel Aviv, the biggest city in Israel.
4. Here it becomes clear that the narrator has traditional Arab conditions in mind: he speaks of an Arab city headed by an emir, whom he later alternately terms "king."
5. The background of this statement is the traditional urban Arab custom of secluding women.
6. Here and in subsequent details, the storyteller refers to aspects of modern urban life.
7. Why the brothers go out to purchase food at night is not stated.
8. Switch from the modern situation back to a traditional one.
9. Traditional Arab folktale motif: the youth and the girl glimpse each other from a distance and instantly fall in love.
10. The wishes to become a doctor and a lawyer reflect familiarity with conditions in the modern sector of Arab society in Israel.
11. The wireless (Arabic *lā silki*) again refers to modern conditions.
12. The soldiers arrest the three brothers because they overheard one of them say that he wanted to marry the king's daughter.
13. By now, the king's daughter not only desires the youth but knows that he, too, wants her.
14. Modern means of transportation known to the narrator.
15. The narrator must have had some specific reason for mentioning precisely this country rather than a larger and better known one.
16. The story here is inconsistent. The king's daughter, so carefully guarded, nevertheless gets away alone and boards the plane. In the sequel, the story contains many more inconsistencies, contradictions, and duplications, which seem to indicate that the narrator was not a first-class master of the craft.
17. What happens during the plane ride remains unstated, but now we learn that her love for him was greater than her love for her father, her brother, or anybody else.
18. In the Arabic *buyūt,* "houses" used in the sense of "relatives." The Arab expectation is to stay with relatives when away from home.
19. The relationship between the king's daughter and the youth has by now developed to the point where the narrator considers him her bridegroom.
20. The night curfew conditions known to the Arabs in Israel are here ascribed to the Swiss city.
21. Breaking into a store and being shot by the guards are familiar Israeli-Palestinian happenings attributed to Switzerland.

22. The flow of the story is interrupted by this interjection of a blessing, customary in Arab conversation.
23. After the oldest brother is killed, the youngest takes his place in relation to the girl.
24. The narrator has forgotten that the brothers and the girl had already reached Switzerland.
25. The narrative is inconsistent here. The two elder brothers were killed by the guards, and yet here they appear again alive and well.
26. The guards in the new city appear here without any introduction. Nor does the narrator tell about the intervening events which are self-evident: the boy and the girl found a house and were ready to occupy it.
27. The house is enchanted. Despite the warning, the boy and the girl enter it.
28. The emir's daughter.
29. "This girl" again refers to the emir's daughter. Again, a sequence of events has been skipped: the boy and the girl settled in the house, and the girl took up a traditional occupation of Arab women, weaving. "She had been so hired" is unclear.
30. With the mention of the big snake, which turns out to be a ghoul, the story switches from modern to traditional ambience, replete with such well-known Arab folktale features as snakes, ghouls, caves, and jars of gold.
31. The emir's daughter and the youngest brother sleep side by side as if they were husband and wife.
32. The woman takes the initiative, as in many Arab folktales.
33. The story here inconsistently attributes the closing of the cave to the youth, although it was already done by the girl.
34. In Arabic *mūdīl,* an example of a foreign loan word in the colloquial of Israeli Arabs.
35. The first strike kills the monster, the second revives it—a widespread folktale motif. See Motif C742 "Tabu: striking monster twice." In this story, the youth strikes the snake once, but before the snake dies, it asks him to strike it a second time. Despite his mother's warning, the youth complies. Now the snake, revived by the second blow, asks the youth not to kill it and promises him all its gold in exchange for sparing its life. In the sequel of the story, it appears that the youth subsequently does kill the snake.
36. Arabic *ḥūt* ("whale"). In the wonderland of the folktale, there is nothing impossible or even incongruous in a whale dwelling in a house. A "helpful whale" is known to folk literature (see Motif B472 "Helpful whale").
37. Arabic *shūfl;* Arabic *winsh.* Both are loan words in the Israeli Arabic colloquial. The whole sequel here is illogical: the door of the cave, which the girl (or the youth) had no difficulty in closing, now has become a rock that

closes automatically and the opening of which requires heavy machinery; the snake was alive but is now dead.

38. The circumstances of the snake's death remain unreported.
39. At this point, the narrator interjected, "The size of the jar, which is there outside, was the size of the jar of gold."
40. Here the narrator refers to the youth as *zalameh* ("fellow").
41. Now we learn that the whale was actually a wondrous quasi-human being with two beautiful daughters.
42. Arabic *ghizlān,* metaphor for an ideal of feminine beauty.
43. Captured women are frequently described in Arab folktales as hanging by their hair (see tales 24 and 26).
44. "If you had not said this and this, I would have killed you." A well-known folklore motif.
45. Arabic *qarfūt,* a phonetic approximation.
46. In the Arabic *Yā ʿammī,* a popular form of respectfully addressing an older person.
47. The narrator forgot that the brothers did not take the girl to Switzerland but that she voluntarily followed them to the plane.
48. This time, the emir's daughter, conforming to the traditional behavior expected of an Arab girl, readily agrees to marry the man selected by her father. Her behavior here contrasts with her earlier demeanor when she ran away with the youth to Switzerland in defiance of her father's wishes.
49. Polygyny is still considered desirable, or at least acceptable. The emir's daughter agrees to being only one of three wives of her bridegroom.
50. The story ends on a symbolic note. The emir takes a plane to return to his country; modern technology can—and should—be used to serve and maintain the traditional world.

21
The One-eyed Giant Shepherd

Recorded from the mouth of a 60-year-old Bedouin woman from the 'Arab al-Mazārīb tribe of Bayt-Zarzīr, near Nahalal, Israel, by Yoel Perez, 1984.

Once upon a time there were three young men, and what young men! Each of them stood with his shoulders high above all others, young men of great strength. One day they said to each other, "Come, let's go and roam about in the rocky fields, let us see the world!"

They set out. While they were walking on the road they saw a flock of sheep. What a flock! Each sheep—an elephant! Their shepherd believed that there were no sheep like them in the whole world.

The three young men said to each other, "This flock, where did it grow up? By Allāh, let's go after them and see who is their owner."

They went following the flock, and reached a cave. Its size was like the size of a house and more. The flock entered the cave, and behold, the owner of the flock came out of the cave, what an owner! His height was like that of an electric pole.[1] And he had one eye in his forehead, like this was his eye.[2] When they saw him, not a drop of brains remained in their heads,[3] even though they were courageous.

He said to them, "A thousand welcomes to those who come! For a long time I have not met young men like you. *Ahlan wa-sahlan* [welcome], honor me and come into my house!"

They entered the house. One of them was fat of body, the other average, the third thin. They entered the cave. He went and slaughtered for them the biggest of the sheep, and said to them, "Enjoy your evening meal!"

They began to eat, but their host did not eat with them. They said to him, "Eat!" He said to them, "I don't want to eat."

After they ate and had their fill, he took each of them in his hands, and pawed them over. He took the fat one in his hands, and said to him, "You are nice and fat, I shall begin with you. I shall eat you."

He had a spit in the cave. He pierced him with the spit and put him over the fire, and began turning him on the spit. He roasted him on the fire and ate him.

He locked the other two in the cave, a day, two days, three days. He slaughtered for them sheep and gave them to eat. He was waiting that they should get fat. But they lost weight, they became thinner. They were afraid to gain weight.

One day he got hold of the average young man, and said to him, "Today I shall eat you, before you expire and die." He took him, pierced him with the spit, roasted him, and ate him.

Who was left? The thin one was left. Every day he slaughtered for him a sheep and fed him, so that he should become fat. But he did not become fat.

One day he said to him, "I want to eat you, whether you are fat or not!"

The young man could not stand on his feet for fear, and said to himself, "There is no way out for me but to wait until he falls asleep, and then I can do to him what I want."

He waited until he fell asleep, and he himself did not sleep. He heated up a wire[4] on the fire until it became glowing red. He thrust it into his one eye, and burned it. He began to scream in his pain—he could not see. He was blinded!

The thin youth fled and hid among the sheep. He said to him, "Wherever you flee from me, you cannot open the door of the cave."

In the door of the cave there was a big stone, only the *ʿimlāq*[5] was able to move it with his shoulder. Nobody else was able to move the stone from its place, and he was inside. How could this thin man get out of the cave? He went and hid among the sheep, and found the skin of the sheep which the giant had slaughtered in their honor on the day of their arrival. He said to himself, "I shall wrap myself in this skin for my protection."

The sheep were locked in the cave—one day, two days, three days. He did not take them out, they were dying of hunger, they wanted to eat. One day the giant said, "I shall let them out one by one so that I can catch him."

The sheep went out, and he pawed them one by one. The turn of the thin man came. He put on the sheep-skin, and put the horns and the head over his own head. When he came near the door the giant caught him and sniffed at him. When he touched its horns, he said, "Ah! This sheep I slaughtered a long time ago." [6]

The thin man got out of the cave and returned to his family. He took along with him the whole flock of sheep. While he was going, the giant began to shout. What did he say? "For the sake of Allāh, leave me a few sheep, so that I can sustain myself on them."

He said to him, "You will no longer see life!"

He returned to his country and the flock of sheep with him.

He returned to his country after having been absent for four months. They said to him, "From where is this flock? What wonderful and fat sheep!"

He said to them, "This and this is the story."

They said to him, "This story is a lie! It is not true!"

He said to them, "Come and I shall show him to you in a certain place."

The Badw came, and became frightened. When they got there, more were those who died than those who escaped in peace. They died of the terrible sight, and those who saw it believed the story.

Comments

This story is a more recent version of the one recorded in 1910–11 by Hans Schmidt in Biʾr Zayt, Palestine (see tale 1). The two differ in several respects. In the Biʾr Zayt story, the three human protagonists were an urbanite, a fellah, and a Bedouin, with the story's sympathy lying with the Bedouin. In the present story, too, there are three human protagonists, but they are simply three stalwart youths, evidently from the same tribe of which the storyteller is a member, and the only difference among them is that one is fat, one is of average build, and the third is thin. Since the hero of the story is the thin youth, it appears that its sympathy lies with him, from which one might conclude that the ideal body figure among the Bedouin is the thin one. In accordance with Bedouin manners, the one-eyed giant is extremely polite and hospitable. He welcomes the young men and slaughters for them the biggest sheep he has. Only when it becomes evident that he himself does not eat of the dish he prepared does his behavior become suspicious.

After the *ʿimlāq* (giant) roasts and eats the fattest of the three youths, he gives ample food to the other two to fatten them up and finally roasts and eats the second youth as well, even though because of his fear he did not gain weight. Only when the giant tells the thin youth that soon he will eat him as well does the youth bestir himself to action. He heats a wire and blinds the sleeping *ʿimlāq.*

The youth happens to find the skin of the big sheep the giant had slaughtered for him and his friends when they arrived. He wraps himself in the skin and, thus disguised, manages to escape among the other sheep, though the giant paws each of them over carefully. In fact, when the old sheepskin is under his hands, the giant sniffs at it and recognizes that it is the skin of the animal he had slaughtered "a long time ago," but he still does nothing to stop the youth wrapped in it. This seems to indicate the stupidity of the giant.

Once outside the cave, the youth takes along all the sheep of the giant. Despite being blind, the giant notices this and begs the youth to leave a few sheep behind so that he should not starve. Although he is a man-eating giant, he nevertheless invokes Allāh. The youth does not fulfill his request but curses him and returns to his own country with the flock of fat sheep.

The story has a peculiar epilogue. When his people see the fat sheep and ask the youth how he got them, he tells them his story. But they do not believe him, until he takes them and shows them the place. Once there, they get so frightened that they try to run away, but many die of fright when they see "the terrible sight." What the terrible sight might be is not explained, nor do we learn why healthy and brave Bedouin should die of fright. One must assume that this ending is appended only in order to add greater importance to the story.

Yet another version of the same type of folktale was recorded by Yoel Perez in 1984 from the mouth of Muḥammad Ibrāhīm of the ʿArab al-Ḥujeyrāt tribe of northern Israel. It tells of a group of Bedouin who go to steal from a goatherd of a neighboring tribe, who keeps his animals in a cave. The goatherd sleeps at the entrance to the cave, but the thieves discover a hole in its ceiling, and through it one of them is let down into the cave on a rope. He ties up one animal after the other, and his friends pull them up through the hole. When, in the dark of the cave, the thief ties up by mistake the goatherd's donkey and his friends begin to pull it up, the donkey brays and wakes up the goatherd. The Bedouin on the outside all run away, abandoning their fellow tribesman to his fate. When the goatherd begins to let out his remaining goats one by one, the

Bedouin hangs on to the belly of a big he-goat whose hair on both sides hangs down almost to the ground, and thus he manages to escape. Moreover, he drives off many of the goats and arrives back at his tribe with a rich booty. There he finds his friends gathered in his father's house mourning his assumed death. See Yoel Perez, "*HaShātir wʿImlāq Polifem,*" in *Tevaʿwaʾ Aretz* (Sept.–Oct. 1985).

In this version, the animals are not sheep but goats, their owner is not a giant or a ghoul but a simple goatherd who does nobody any harm, and he is not blinded by the thief. Actually, the only feature common between this version and the others is the manner in which the thief escapes from the cave. The story tells with approval of the theft of the goats; the goatherd belongs to a neighboring tribe from whom stealing is a morally irreproachable act, a reflection on the Bedouin tribal mentality. Nor does the story censure the behavior of the Bedouin men in abandoning one of their ranks in the cave, instead of jointly overpowering the single goatherd, which they certainly could have done easily. Thus, the main interest this version holds for us is in the picture of the Bedouin mentality it allows us to glimpse.

Notes

1. Here the modern Israeli environment, in which the storyteller lives, intrudes. When she wants to illustrate the height of the giant, the first thing that comes to her mind is an electric pole.
2. The storyteller indicates with a gesture how large the giant's eye was.
3. That is, they lost their minds for fright.
4. Again, intrusion of modern Israeli conditions: the instrument the youth employs to blind the giant is not a stick, as in the traditional versions, but a wire.
5. *ʿImlāq* is an Arabic term derived from the biblical Hebrew ʿAmaleq, the hereditary enemies of the Israelites (Deuteronomy 35: 17), whose name appears in Arab tradition as *ʿAmālīq* or *ʿAmālīqa,* Amalekites, and also in Arab folklore telling of the evil king ʿAmlūq. See *Encyclopaedia of Islam,* new ed., 1: 429. In the Arabic colloquial, *ʿImlāq* means both Amalekite and "giant."
6. The blinded *ʿimlāq* recognizes that the skin is that of the sheep he slaughtered long ago but, like Homer's Polyphemus, is too stupid to draw the obvious conclusion that it is worn by the thin youth as a means of escape.

22
Ḥasan the Sharp-witted

Recorded by Yoel Perez from the mouth of a member of the ʿArab al-Marisāt Tribe, August 7, 1982.

There was a king who had only one daughter. There were no boys or girls beside her. The king loved his daughter as he loved himself. His most fervent wish was that she should marry an emir of the emirs.[1]

The king gathered emirs from all countries, so that they should ask for the hand of his daughter. But each time an emir would propose to the girl, she would reject him.[2] When she rejected the emir, her father became angry, because he was anxious that she should marry that emir. Not important which emir, the important thing was that she should marry an emir. The first emir came, and she rejected him. The second—she rejected him, and the third—she rejected him.

Finally he understood that his daughter wanted one whose name was Ḥasan. The emir was annoyed, because this Ḥasan was from the common people, and not an emir. Then the king started thinking that he would remove his daughter, the *emirah,* far away from Ḥasan, and remove Ḥasan from his daughter. But if she should learn of that matter she would become angry,[3] and if his daughter became angry, he would become upset mentally.[4]

The king had a vizier, a helper to the king. This vizier was very clever and cunning, like a fox. The vizier said, "Leave this matter to me. I shall handle this matter for you in my way. You will like it."

The king said, "Handle this matter, on one condition: that you remove Ḥasan from my daughter, and my daughter remains happy, and does not become angry."[5]

The vizier said, "Don't worry. I have a way."

The king asked, "How? Tell me."

The vizier said to him, "We shall bring Ḥasan, and tell him that the king wants to have him marry his daughter, on one condition. If you fulfill that condition, you will get his daughter."

The king asked him, "What is the condition?"

The vizier said to the king, "Listen, we shall take two pieces of paper. We shall write on one piece of paper 'Death,' and on the second piece of paper we shall write 'Life.' And we shall tell him, 'Listen, O Ḥasan, the king will give you his daughter if you pick the paper on which is written "Life." In that case the emirah will remain with you.' "

The king said to him, "How could you give him the two pieces of paper? Perhaps he will pick the piece of paper on which is written 'Life,' and there is a big chance that he will take the *emirah,* and that I don't want."

The vizier said to the king, "Don't worry. We shall tell him that what is written is 'Death' and 'Life,' but when we bring him in we shall write 'Death' on both pieces of paper: on this we shall write 'Death,' and on this we shall write 'Death.' In this manner the piece of paper which he will take in his hand will have on it 'Death.' "

The king said to the vizier, "I salute you! You are a faithful vizier, the one whom I can trust!"

The king agreed, and was happy and at ease.[6] On the second day he invited all his friends, and he invited the people of the city, and he invited Ḥasan to the feast. But the *emirah* learned of the trick right away from a spy, a servant who heard the conversation between the king and the vizier. The spy went to tell the *emirah,* and she sent a message to Ḥasan. She told him, the story is such and such. She explained to him what would happen,[7] and she urged him not to come to the feast.

The appointed time of the feast arrived. All the people were present. The vizier was waiting, the king was waiting, and the *emirah* was happy.[8] At the appointed time, behold Ḥasan came without fear. All the people were standing and watching and waiting to see what would happen.[9] The king was happy and the vizier was delighted.

He said to him, "Now we want to get rid of Ḥasan."

The king rose and delivered a speech before the people, and said, "Listen, O people, I am a just king, just with all the people. I have only the one *emirah* who is to me dearer than my soul. I am willing to give her to Ḥasan, who is from the common people. I am not high-handed. But I have one condition. Here are two pieces of paper. On one is written

'Life,' and on the second 'Death.' If Ḥasan picks the piece of paper on which is written 'Death,' we shall kill him, and he will have killed himself by his own hand. And if it is written upon it 'Life,' it means that I shall give him the *emirah.*"

They said to him, "Good."

Ḥasan took a piece of paper and instantly swallowed it, and said to the people, "I swallowed a piece of paper. Let us open the second. If it is written on it 'Death,' it means that I swallowed 'Life,' and I took life."

The king became confused, and the vizier knew and was confused, and they knew that Ḥasan was stronger, smarter, and more sharp-witted than they. On both pieces was written "Death," and there was no piece of paper of "Life."

They were forced to open the second piece of paper. They found that "Death" was written on it.

Now the people began to clap and say, "Ḥasan is the king! Ḥasan is the king!"

The king rose and said to the vizier, "You are not worthy to be vizier. You deserve that we should kill you. You are a cheat!"

Ḥasan took the king's daughter, and became vizier of the king.

Comments

This story belongs to the group of Arab folktales in which the supernatural is totally absent, and which in its entirety takes place in the real world, even though that real world is considerably altered in order to suit the purposes of the story. That is, while we encounter in it no ghouls, no speaking animals, no hidden treasures, no transformations of men into animals and vice versa, we are presented with a number of less blatantly unrealistic features. Thus, the hero is a young man of the common people who at the end of the story marries the princess and becomes vizier. He is opposed by a king who wants his daughter to marry an emir but who does not have the youth killed (as a typical Arab potentate would have done), resorting instead to a trick in order to prevent his daughter from marrying the youth. The daughter (the *emirah*) dares to oppose her father and rejects one after the other the princely suitors presented to her by the king. The king loves his daughter so much that he tries not to make her "angry" (that is, upset, sad) by forcefully removing the youth. The daughter has spies who inform her of the plot her father and the vizier hatch in order to kill the youth she loves. These are unrealistic features, but unrealistic on a different level from that of the supernatural miraculous elements.

All this adds up, despite the absence of the supernatural, to a kind of quasi-realistic wonderworld, removed from the "real" world in which the storyteller and his listeners live, not by miraculous features but by the different social order it depicts and on which it bases the events it relates. In this image of a different social order lies much of the fascination of the story for the listeners, who recognize in it their own world but in an altered state in which they would like to see it.

In addition, of course, there is the enjoyment the "common people" derive from hearing that one of their own ranks succeeds in standing up to the powers that be—the king and the vizier—and defeating them at a game the latter have devised for the purpose of destroying him. The hero does this by using his wits, and, without revealing that the king and the vizier have engaged in cheating (by writing "Death" on both pieces of paper), he manages to force the king to keep his given word and let him marry his daughter.

Folktales about the clever peasant youth who gets the better of the king are widespread all over the world (see Tale Type 921 "The King and the Peasant's Son"; Motif H583.1 "King: What do you see? Youth: One and a half men and a horse's head"–H583.6 "King: What are you doing? Youth: I boil those which come and go"). Their popularity, no doubt, is a result of the satisfaction the listeners derive from identifying with the youth and enjoying his victory over the king. However, there is a significant difference between them and this story. In type 921, the youth comes out the winner in the contest with the king by being able to solve various kinds of riddles; he gives answers that at first hearing are themselves impossible but which subsequently turn out to be not only correct but ingenious. In this story, the youth resorts to a trick that turns the king's and the vizier's dishonesty against them, and thus wins not only life but also the hand of the princess.

The identification of the listeners with Ḥasan and their gratification at his victory are expressed in the story itself in the cry with which the people greet the clever youth: "Ḥasan is the king! Ḥasan is the king!" This, of course, does not mean that the people intend to recognize Ḥasan as king by acclamation or that they want him to take the place of the old king but merely that they rejoice at his victory. "Ḥasan is the king!" is but an exaggerated formulation of something like "Ḥasan is victorious!"

In a like manner, when Israeli Foreign Minister David Levy won a political victory in 1990, his enthusiastic supporters feted him by crying, "David king of Israel! David king of Israel!"

Notes

1. *Emir* in Bedouin terminology is the title of a high-ranking tribal chief or the head of a tribal confederation. (The title of a minor tribal head is *sheikh.*) In other sectors of Arab society, *emir* is the title of a prince or a commander. In this story, it is used in the sense of a prince of a royal house. The king of the story wants his daughter to marry an "emir of the emirs," that is, a member of a royal family.
2. For a girl to reject a suitor chosen by her father is not as uncommon among the Bedouins as it would be among the villagers and townspeople. Such an attitude by a girl appears several times in the Arab folktale and can be taken as a reflection of the actual position of a girl in Bedouin society.
3. Arabic *bidduha taz*ʿ*al,* literally "her will is that she become angry," meaning "she would become angry."
4. Arabic *yu*ʾ*aththir* ʿ*alayhi nafsiyyan,* that is, "it will afflict him mentally."
5. This condition, stipulated by the king, shows how strong was his love for his daughter.
6. The assumption is that once the matter has been apparently entrusted to chance, the king will no longer be held responsible for the death of Ḥasan, and even his daughter will not be able to blame him for it.
7. Colloquial Arabic *shū biddu yasīr,* literally "what was its will to happen."
8. The happiness of the *emirah* lets the listeners suspect that she knew that Ḥasan had a way of escaping the danger.
9. See note 8 above.

23
The Prince Who Turned into a Deer

Recorded by Yoel Perez, from the mouth of Thaljeh Mūsā (age 65), of the ʿArab al-Ḥujeyrāt tribe, February 5, 1982.

There was an Arab [Bedouin] tribe. [In it was] an emir who had a son and a daughter. Their mother died. Their father married a woman. The children remained.

One day the wife of their father, what does she want to do with them? She wants to drive them away.[1] She let them be until they fell asleep. She said to the people, "*Yallah* [let's go], on the road, O men."

All the men wandered, they loaded up the camels, and all the men wandered.[2] And the children continued to sleep. The son and the daughter. Those [the men] got up at night.

In the morning the children woke up. There are no people. There is nothing. They froze in their place, they thought, and they sat. When they sat, what did she say to him? She said to him, "My brother, where shall we go?"

He said, "My sister, let's grab a road and go."

While they were walking on the road, they were dying of hunger and thirst. While they were walking they came to a grove. They said to it,[3] "My uncle, do you have a little bread?"

He said to them, "Certainly, grove, grove."

He gave them a piece of bread, a loaf of bread. They ate. They wanted to drink. They reached a second grove. They said to it, "My uncle, do you have water?"

He said to them, "No, by Allāh, my children."

[They reached] a third one. It said, "No, by Allāh, [but] before you is a spring, before you."

They came to the grove, and it was standing, sitting. It said to her, "Before you is the spring, but he who drinks of the spring, there are seven springs, he who drinks from the spring of the deer will become a deer, and he who drinks from the spring of donkeys will become a donkey, and he who drinks from the spring of the camels will become a camel, and from the spring of the wolves, the spring of the wild animals, from all the springs, each one has a spring."

"Where is the spring from which we should drink?"

He said, "There, opposite, drink!"

They, because of the great thirst, her brother almost died of thirst, [he was] the first to slurp from the spring of the deer, and drank. As soon as he finished drinking, and, behold, he is a deer.

She said to him, "My brother, what shall I do with you?"

He said to her, "I don't know, my sister."

He speaks, but he is a deer. She went with him, went, went, and came to a house of people. They turned toward the house, the house of an emir, the biggest house among those of the people. They came to the house.

It is a custom of the Arabs not to ask [anything] of a guest for three days, [such as] from where he came and where he goes.[4] After three days he said to his wife—the emir had no children, he had no children at all—he said to her, "Ask her, O woman, whether she wants to get married?"

She asked her. She said to her, "Will you get married?"

She said to her, "Marriage is a cover[5] for me. With him whom I shall marry I shall make a condition."

He said to her, "What is the condition?"

She said to him, "He should take care of my brother. My brother is miserable, and I want him to remain with me. He who will take care of my brother,[6] him I shall marry."

The emir said, "I shall marry her, why not?"

He invited the people, as is the custom of Allāh and His prophet, and married this girl, and her brother remained with her.

One day the people said, "The time of pilgrimage has arrived."

The emir said, "Let us go on pilgrimage."

Formerly they used to go on camels.[7] They would ride on camels and go. How long did they stay? Six months. He prepared to go. One day he came and said, "Let us go to take leave of her."

How did he leave his wife? He left her and she was pregnant, the sister of the boy was pregnant.

He said to her, "By Allāh, woman, watch over her, over the poor girl. This one, watch over her." That is to say, give her food, and if she gives birth, take care of her.

She said to him, "Do you need to command me, O emir? I shall take care of her more than necessary."

He said to her, "Good."

The emir arose, loaded the camel with the people who went on pilgrimage, and went on pilgrimage. He went on the pilgrimage two months, three, Allāh knows. The woman remained. Her months arrived, that is to say, the time of her birth. Her rival wife knew a pit, she knew a place where there was a pit.

She said to her, "My rival wife, I want to move the house,[8] tomorrow you will give birth, and the emir will return, and likewise this house is not nice. I want to move the house, also to a nice house, so that it should be spacious, and so that the emir should return from the *ḥajj* [pilgrimage] and the people should bless him."

She said to her, "Good."

That one arose, did not know that there was in it a pit, in that place. She brought a mat in such a shape, covered the opening of the pit with the mat, and they moved. They set up the house, one—there were one, two, three—three places in the house, three pillars.[9]

She said to her, "Good."

She arose and put her. The woman began to suffer the pangs of childbirth, she was about to give birth.

She said to her, "My dear, I don't want you to give birth here, I want you to give birth in this room, in this place, in the house here, here, I shall warm for you, and it will be good for you, I shall light a fire for you."

She said to her, "Good."

She put her on the mat upon the mouth of the pit, put her there and seated her down there. The mat sank into the pit, she fell into the pit. She covered the pit. She put over it a piece of iron and covered it, and moved the house,[10] she returned to the place where it was.

The woman gave birth. What did she bear? She bore a son. Her brother saw her when she fell into the pit, when she made her fall and put her in the pit. Her brother began to come to her, he began to go to the people to get alms,[11] he began to collect food from the people, and went and brought it to his sister, to the pit. What did he say to her? He said to her, "Your poor brother."

Then they pulled out the knife, as is the wont of the rulers, that is to say the hunters. One who had a rifle saw the deer and wanted to go to shoot him. But he fled.

He began to say to her, "Your poor brother." That is, "While I was going to come to you, your poor brother, they pulled out the knife," that is, "they pulled out [the knife] to slaughter him."

And she said, "What shall I do with you, my brother? I am in the pit."

He got up, and returned.

On the day on which the emir returned, what was she about [to do]?[12] She went and brought a lamb [of the] flock, and dug in the earth. First she brought the lamb, put it down, and put clothes on it, and wrapped it in shrouds, and called the people.

She said to them, "The wife of the emir died, come and take her so that we go and bury her."

They did not know what was in it, for this is how it is for a woman, a man is not allowed to see her,[13] everything is closed. They carried it and went, they dug a grave and put the woman in it—not the woman, the lamb, they put the lamb in place of the woman. The woman was in the pit, she knew nothing.

This emir returned from the pilgrimage. He said to her, "So-and-so, I don't see where is So-and-so."[14]

She said to him, "By Allāh, O emir, So-and-so gave you her life."[15]

He said to her, "O no, no, no! The poor one! If Allāh wishes! You did your duty with regard to her, you wrapped her in shrouds, and watched over her, you took care of her."

She said to him, "More than necessary, as you wanted it, and more than that."

That deer was sitting next to the fire. The people came and went to the emir and greeted him. It is of the customs of the Arabs to come and to go and to greet him.[16] And the deer was sitting.

What did he bring with him? He brought fig cakes, dry figs, fig cakes and raisins and dates and the like. He gave them to him.[17]

He said to him, "Take it all."

He, the deer, was eating, and took them into his hands. Where did he go? He ran to his sister and gave her the food.[18]

One day, while he was sitting, the emir got up in the morning in order to pray, and the deer got up and went out.

He said, "The deer, I don't know where it is going. All day long the deer is absent, I cannot find him. I want to know where the deer goes, where it goes during the day."

In the morning he gave him—he drank a glass of tea and ate, and that one took the food with him, put it in his hands, and went out.

He said, "By Allāh, I shall follow him, I shall go quietly, quietly, and follow him, and shall see where the deer goes."

This one got up, and the emir as well. The deer was before him and he after him, quietly, quietly, and he did not see him. He went quietly, quietly, he went to the opening of the pit, and gave [food] to his sister, and said to her, "Your poor brother, they pulled out the knife, as is the wont of the rulers." [19]

He was looking at him, and, behold, the woman sits there, and the child naked in her lap, sucks from her, and she is in the pit.

He said, "You are here?"

She said to him, "I am here." [20]

He got up, returned to the people, said to them, "Who loves the emir?" [21]

They said, "What happened, O emir?"

He said to them, "Come to the well, follow me, somebody fell in the well, somebody fell in the well, follow me, follow me."

The people went after him, and, behold, it was his wife.

He said to her, "So-and-so![22] Where? Did you not say that she died? What was it that we buried?"

She told him.

The people got up, and came, and went, and brought her out and her son.

He went and dug up the lamb, and took it out, and said to them, "Who loves the emir? Let him bring a bundle of wood and a little fire."

He wanted to burn her, to burn his wife. He got up, burned his wife, and there remained he and his new wife and the deer,[23] and they remained and enjoyed themselves.

Comments

This folktale is an Arabic variant of Tale Type 450: "*Little brother and little sister:* The boy is turned into a roe by the cruel stepmother. Lives with his sister in the forest. The king marries the sister. Her stepmother usurps her place as wife. Disclosure, punishment, and reunion."

However, it differs from type 450 in some significant details, several of which reflect the Muslim Arab environment. Although in the beginning of the story it is the stepmother who manages to drive away the brother and the sister, subsequently the rivalry is not between stepmother and stepdaughter but between the older and the younger co-wives of the emir. The rival wife does not merely usurp the place of the sister but plots to kill her. The opportunity is provided by the months-long absence of the emir on a pilgrimage to Mecca. The punishment of the evil co-wife is death by burning.

Apart from these specific Muslim Arab features, our story differs from type 450 in other details. It is not the stepmother who turns the boy into a deer; his metamorphosis comes about as a result of his drinking from a magic spring, while his sister is able to withstand her thirst and does not drink. The groves the children encounter are personified; they speak and give warnings. The children remain faithful to each other: the sister does not abandon her brother who turned into a deer, and the brother, even though his life is in danger from hunters, feeds his sister who cannot get out of the pit into which her co-wife put her.

As is the case with several other folktales in this collection, recorded in the 1980s, the second part of the story is incoherent and fragmentary, and shows evidence of the impatience of the storyteller, who seems to rush to reach the story's end.

Notes

1. Stories about the wife who wishes to drive the child or children of her rival out of the house are as old as the Bible. See Genesis 21: 10.
2. The story does not explain how it came about that the wife of the emir was in charge of the household. It says only that she ordered the people to break camp and move off, so that when the children wake up in the morning they find themselves alone and abandoned. The motif of abandoning children in this manner recurs in other Israeli Arab folktales.
3. The grove is conceived of as a person. The children speak to it, and it answers them. They address the grove as "My uncle," the customary form of address by a younger person to an older individual, related or not.
4. The storyteller feels it is necessary to explain what is (or was) the old Arab, i.e. Bedouin, custom.
5. Cover in the sense of protection. The girl, having no father to protect her and having only a brother who had turned into a deer, is willing to marry in order to be protected.
6. The story does not make clear but lets the listener feel that the girl has informed the emir that the deer is her brother.

7. Again, the storyteller feels the need to explain what was the custom in former times.
8. Moving the house means to strike the tent and move it to another place.
9. The three pillars are three tent poles. The newly pitched tent was a large one.
10. Once the girl fell into the pit, the co-wife again moved the tent back to its old location.
11. The girl's brother, although he has the form of a deer, behaves in a human fashion; he gathers food and thus keeps his sister alive.
12. The story returns to the emir's older wife. Before the return of the emir, she arranges a fake burial, saying that the younger wife had died.
13. Another explanatory comment on an old Arab custom.
14. The storyteller does not bother with inventing names for the two wives, so she refers to them as "So-and-so."
15. Meaning she died while giving birth to his child.
16. Yet another reference to an old Arab custom.
17. The emir is goodhearted. He gives tasty food to the deer.
18. The storyteller imagines that the deer had hands in which it could carry food to his sister.
19. The deer-brother still suffers from the trauma of almost having been killed by the hunters.
20. The discovery of his wife and child by the emir and the woman's reaction to his appearance at her pit are described with laconic brevity.
21. "Who loves the emir?" is the customary introductory sentence when a ruler or leader asks a service from his followers.
22. The emir confronts his older wife with her evil deed and orders her to be burned.
23. One would expect that at the end of the story, the deer-brother will somehow regain his human shape, but it does not happen.

24
Pomegranate Seed

Recorded by Yoel Perez, from the mouth of Zahia Ghurayfāt (age 60) of the 'Arab al-Ghurayfāt tribe of Bayt Zarzīr, September 11, 1982.

O honored listeners to the words, shall we tell a tale, or shall I sleep?[1] Let's tell a tale.

There was a woman who was not able to become pregnant, and she could not bring forth children. Her husband was a working man.

One day a merchant came and was hawking his goods, saying, "Pomegranate for pregnancy! Pomegranate for pregnancy!"[2] The woman came, took a mug full of pomegranate seeds, and said, "O Allāh, Allāh be praised and exalted! With Your might and by Your miracles and Your exalted state and Supreme Being, let me have a daughter or a son like the seeds of this pomegranate, red and good. Praised be Allāh sublime, who is mighty with His ability, power, and supremacy."

Twenty years later[3] she gave birth to a daughter whom she called Pomegranate Seed. The daughter was very pretty and beautiful. Her beauty was incomparable. When anyone saw her, he would say, "Pomegranate Seed is more beautiful than her mother!"

Then her mother became jealous and angry, whenever she heard that her daughter was more beautiful than she. Then her father started to like the daughter more than the mother. The mother, upon hearing this, would ask him, "Why do you love the daughter more than me?"

He said to her, "Because she is more beautiful and better than you."

Subsequently she started to ask the stars, "O stars, who is more beautiful, I or Pomegranate Seed?" The stars replied, "Pomegranate Seed." Then she asked the moon, "O moon, who is better, I or Pomegranate Seed?" The moon replied, "Pomegranate Seed." She asked, "O Arabs, who is better, I or Pomegranate Seed?" They said to her, "Pomegranate Seed."

In the end she asked all the people, and all of them preferred Pomegranate Seed. Then she said, "I want[4] to spill the blood of the girl and to slay her."

The mother prepared provisions for a journey, and said to her daughter, "We want to go to your uncles."[5] The daughter said to the mother, "No, how can we go? I don't know my uncles."

The mother said to her, "I want to introduce you to your uncles."

Then she took the daughter through mountains and valleys in which there was nothing except hyenas and ghouls, and other such creatures. They both stayed in an area full of rocks until night fell, the sun set, and the world became dark. There was no moon.

The mother said to her daughter, "Let's go to sleep." The daughter said to her mother, "My hair is joined to yours, my flesh is tied to your flesh, and I shall sew my dress to yours, and your arm will be beneath my head, and my arm will be beneath your head."[6]

The girl remained asleep until the sun rose upon her, and she became hot. She woke up to find that nobody was beside her. She started screaming, "Mother! Mother! Mother!" There was nobody near her.

Then a *ghoulah*[7] came and said, "May Allāh watch over you, O darling Pomegranate Seed! Allāh be with you! May the safety of Allāh be with you, and whoever forsakes you will be forsaken by Allāh! From where did you come to me? From the gate of happiness to the gate of hell?"

The girl said to her, "I was brought here by good fortune and by luck." Thereupon the *ghoulah* took the girl with her.

The *ghoulah* was roaming freely with the gazelles, and she took the girl along with the gazelles to a cave, to a natural cave, like the ones used by goats. She let the gazelles into the cave, and brought the girl in as well. She warmed her and dressed her. She said to her, "You are my daughter, by the covenant of Allāh, and whosoever betrays you will be betrayed by Allāh! For I have been looking for you for a long time, O Pomegranate Seed!"[8]

The *ghoulah* roamed with the gazelles, and every day she would take the gazelles with her as she roamed about. [When she returned] she would shout, "O Pomegranate Seed! Open the door for the gazelles!" And Pomegranate Seed would clear the door for the gazelles.

The *ghoulah* led the girl in the cave, and all of a sudden she saw houses in the interior of the cave. The *ghoulah* showed her a door and a faucet, and told her that she was allowed to open them, but warned her that whatever room was closed she should beware of opening it.[9] She gave her the keys to the entire place.

Once the *ghoulah* was absent, the girl went around and started to open the places which she had been warned not to open. She opened the first faucet, and dipped her finger into it. All of a sudden, her finger was all gold, and then the gold stuck to her finger. She tried to remove the gold from the finger, but could not. She opened another place, and all of a sudden there were two girls there, hanging by their hair. She did not speak to them, but closed the door, and while doing so she injured her finger, and wrapped it up.

The *ghoulah* came back, and said to Pomegranate Seed, "Open the door for the gazelles! They give milk from their horns, they give milk from their teats. O Pomegranate Seed! Open the door for the gazelles, they give milk from their horns, they give milk from their teats!"

She opened the door, and, behold, the finger of Pomegranate Seed was wrapped up. The *ghoulah* asked her, "Why is your finger wrapped up, O my darling?"

She said to her, "It was injured."

The *ghoulah* knew the truth, and she said to her, "Let me see it!"

The girl said to her, "No, it hurts me."

"Let me see it!"

"No, it hurts me!"

The *ghoulah* said to her, "Did I not tell you not to open that door?" [10]

However, the matter was of no importance, since the girl was dear to her.

One day a merchant was hawking his goods, shouting, "Buckles, combs for sale!"

It was the first time that a merchant came to this place on a donkey.

Pomegranate Seed looked at his wares, because she had much gold to spend. She asked his permission to take his merchandise. He asked her, "Are there any human beings in this place?"

She said to him, "I am a human being, I am Pomegranate Seed."

He said to her, "Pomegranate Seed used to live in our neighborhood, but her mother took her and shed her blood."

She said to him, "I am Pomegranate Seed. Is my mother still there?"

He said to her, "Yes."

She said to him, "I want to entrust you with a little gold to give to my mother." [11]

He said to her, "Good."

She gave the merchant a little gold wrapped in an envelope, to deliver to her mother.

Her mother was very upset about her daughter. She wanted to kill her, she no longer wanted to have a child. She wondered, saying, "I abandoned her among the debris of rocks, and yet she is still alive! I want to kill her!"

She said to the merchant, "Return to me!" She bought a poisoned comb [12] for her daughter, and when the merchant returned, she gave it to him for her daughter. She told him, "I entrust you with it for my daughter. Let nobody else open it, except my daughter, and when you arrive there let her wash and clean herself, and make sure that she combs her hair."

The merchant set out on his rounds, carrying his gold and his property. He went to Pomegranate Seed, and told her, "This is what your mother entrusted to me!"

Thereupon she heated up water on the fire, and washed her hair. Then she started to comb it. The first time she combed her hair the teeth of the comb broke on her head. The second time her fingers were broken. The third time Pomegranate Seed died.[13]

The *ghoulah* came back from afar, and started to shout, "Pomegranate Seed! Open the door for the gazelles!"

Nobody answered. The *ghoulah* said [to herself], "If I find her asleep, she is safe, may Allāh be with her, and may the trust of Allāh be with her! But if I should find her alive and awake, by Allāh, there is nothing else I can do but eat her, eat Pomegranate Seed!" [14]

The *ghoulah* went to open the door, and there was Pomegranate Seed dead.

"O darling! O Pomegranate Seed! O Pomegranate Seed! O Pomegranate Seed!"

Pomegranate Seed did not answer. The *ghoulah* put rugs and carpets on the floor, dressed Pomegranate Seed in the finest clothes of the most expensive kind. The gold that the *ghoulah* heaped on Pomegranate Seed could not be heaped on the backs of the camels of love.[15]

She said, "O camels of love! I beg your trust, don't descend unless you are told the phrase,. 'By the life of whoever is on your back!' Only then descend!"

The camels of love flew. There were some children playing football in the field. Among them was a poor man. He was saying, "Come down, O camels of love!" But the camels did not come down. The poor man then said, "By the life of whoever is on your back, come down, camels of love!" The camels of love came down.

When they came down, the poor man said to them, "Keep all the money and gold, I want to take only the girl! I shall ask my mother to wash her, and we shall bury her."

The youth,[16] took the property and the gold, and the rugs and carpets, and he took Pomegranate Seed and brought her to his mother. He said to her, "O my mother!"

She said to him, "O my son!"

He said to her, "Heat up some water, O my mother, and wash this young woman. I found her dead on the back of the camels of love. Let us wash her and bury her."

She said to him, "Yes, O my son!"

Thereupon she started to light the fire, and she brought a pot that resembled a jar of copper, and brought water and heated it. She carried in the girl and spread a mat under her, and started to wash her for burial. Who would be willing to bury her? As she was washing her, the woman shook the girl's head, and behold there was there four or five teeth of a comb set in her head. She plucked out the first one, whereupon Pomegranate Seed said, "Ouch!" She plucked out the second one, and again Pomegranate Seed said, "Ouch!" Then she plucked out the third one, and she said, "I witness that there is no God but Allāh, and I witness that Muḥammad is the messenger of Allāh!"

When she said that, the woman said, "This [girl] was dead, and now she has come back to life!" She brought clothes for her, and dressed her, and she woke up, and behold, she was Pomegranate Seed!

The woman stopped showing her to the Arabs [i.e., she hid her], fearing that somebody would see her and take her to marry his son, or that the king would take her for his son.

Day after day the old woman would go to the water, and Pomegranate Seed would ask her, "Let me go with you to the water!"

But she said to her, "No, O my darling!"

One day the king's son saw her and fell in love with her. He told his father and mother, he said to them, "I want the sister of the poor boy!"

They said to him, "He has no sisters."

He said to them, "I shall never get better if I don't get that girl!" [17]

They went to the old woman and told her.

She said to them, "This is my son's wife, and her story is such and such and such. She is not my daughter."

They said to her, "We want her even so, even if by force!"

The old woman took the girl and went to the king's son. He was told her story, from its beginning to the end. The king's son did not stop wanting to go to see the girl. They told him, "Allāh sent her as a gift to the poor man; it is a sin for you to take her away. You can take any girl you want."

He said, "Yes, of course!"

He came and gave the poor man fifty sheep, fifty goats, and fifty cows, and gave him property. He then married Pomegranate Seed, and brought her to the poor man.[18]

Comments

All in all, this folktale is remarkable on several counts. Instead of the familiar jealousy of the evil stepmother who plots to kill her stepdaughter because she is more beautiful (see Tale Type 709 "Snow White"), we have here the true mother of the girl who repeatedly tries to kill her. Along the lines of Bruno Bettelheim's psychological approach to the fairy tale, we might say that this story concretizes the girl-child's fear of her mother whom she perceives as an overwhelmingly powerful competitor for the affection of her father, and as an elderly woman jealous of her own youthful charms, which she perceives as superior to those of her mother. In any case, the appearance of the true mother as the villain, instead of the more commonly encountered stepmother, is unusual and could be interpreted as evidence of the greater tension between mother and daughter in the Arab family than is the case in European families reflected in the typical widespread Tale Type 709 "Snow White."

Likewise unusual in this story is the almost totally benevolent character of the *ghoulah,* who takes in the daughter and behaves most lovingly toward her (with the exception of the one scene in which she feels that if the girl has again disobeyed her, she would have no choice but "to eat her"). In many Arab folktales the *ghoulah* is an ambivalent figure, both good and bad, and it is rare that she appears to be so overwhelmingly good and truly motherly as in "Pomegranate Seed."

An interesting (and unexplained) feature in the story is the appearance of "the camels of love," on whose backs the *ghoulah* sends the (apparently) dead Pomegranate Seed back to the world of humans for burial.

The end of the story, the marriage of the girl to the prince (as emended), is the typical happy ending of the Arab folktale.

A shorter variant of this story was recorded by Yoel Perez from the mouth of Sarwah Yasin Ḥajājrah on November 18, 1984. In it, the heroine's name is Jabīnah (derived from *jubn,* meaning "cheese," so that the name means something like "Cheesewhite"). The roles of the mother and the *ghoulah* are the same, but instead of the camels of love, it is a bird that takes Jabīnah back to the human world, to her mother, with whom Jabīnah lives happily ever after.

The name Jabīnah as that of a folktale heroine appears repeatedly in the stories of the Israeli Bedouins.

Notes

1. Customary introduction to telling a tale, intended to arouse the interest of the listeners.
2. The pomegranate, which is full of seeds, is believed to help a woman become pregnant. It appears in other Arab folktales as well, e.g., in the modern Egyptian story in which a man becomes pregnant as a result of eating pomegranates. See Richard M. Dorson, "The Falcon's Daughter," *Folktales Told Around the World* (Chicago: University of Chicago Press, 1975), p. 159.
3. The time element is frequently disregarded in the Arab folktale.
4. "I want to" in Arabic usage means "I shall" or "I have decided to."
5. In colloquial Arabic *khawāliki* ("your maternal uncles"). The mother's brothers belong to a different tribe, and the daughter has not yet met them.
6. The daughter is afraid in the forbidding environment but trusts that her mother will protect her.
7. *Ghoulah,* the feminine of *ghoul,* is a female demon. They appear very frequently in Arab folktales. She has a distinctly ambivalent character. On the one hand, she is frightening and dangerous and is believed to eat human beings; on the other, she can be extremely kind and helpful. In this story the *ghoulah* appears as a totally kind, protective person, who is everything for

the girl that her mother is not. Moreover, she is very religious: she constantly invokes Allāh.

8. This statement of the *ghoulah* places her in a parallel situation with Pomegranate Seed's mother: both had yearned for a long time to have her as their daughter; but while the real mother is evil, the *ghoulah* is good.
9. The well-known motif of the forbidden chamber (Tale Type 311).
10. The *ghoulah,* of course, knows that the girl entered the forbidden chamber, but since "the girl was dear to her" she does not punish her.
11. Although Pomegranate Seed knows that her mother intended to kill her, she still loves her mother and sends a lavish present to her. This attitude of a child toward an evil mother recurs several times in the Arab folktale.
12. The attempt to kill the girl with a poisoned comb is a motif in the "Snow White" tale; see Tale Type 709.
13. We know, of course, that she only seemed dead, but the statement that she died intensifies the interest in the outcome of the story.
14. This is the only indication in the whole tale that the *ghoulah* belonged to the race of beings who eat humans.
15. In the Arabic transcription *jimāl al-hawā* ("camels of love"). However, possibly the storyteller intended to say *jimāl al-hawā*ʾ ("camels of the air"). In any case, the reference is to mythical animals that can fly in the air and understand human speech. Cf. tale 27.
16. Only now do we learn that there was a youth in charge of the camels of love.
17. Implied in this statement of the king's son is that he fell ill because of his passion for the girl.
18. The end of the story is confused. We would expect that the king's son, after having compensated the poor man with lavish gifts, would marry the girl and bring her to his own parents.

25
The Uncles and Their Nephew

Told by Fāleḥ al-Rashā'ideh (age 30) of the Rashā'ideh [Rashayda] tribe of the Negev, Israel, recorded by Yehudah Katz, 1984.

In times past there were Badw [Bedouin] east of the Jordan, not found here. There was one among these Badw, the Badw in Jordan, the Shaʿlān,[1] they are of the Shummar, the ʿArab Shummar.[2] They had a Sheikh, his name was Ibn Rashīd.[3] He said to the people of his tribe, "O people!" They said, "Yes?" He said, "Let none of you light fire, and let none make coffee, and when you go out on a raid and one of you gets hurt, don't take him back with you." They said, "At your command!" They accepted this instructions.

They had a nephew in another tribe who had killed somebody. He had shot somebody and killed him. Where did the youth flee for fear of the avenger of blood? He fled to his mother's brothers,[4] the Banī Shummar, at Ibn Rashīd, to them he fled.

When he fled to them, the Badw were wont to go out every year twice or three times on raids,[5] Allāh is the one who knows. They raided, they roamed about in raids. They said, "We are going out on a raid." Who were they who prepared to go out on a raid? The men, the uncles of the boy who had come to them. They were seven brothers. He said, "In the name of Allāh, I too want to go with you on the raid, O my uncles!" They said, "O nephew, stay here and rest, don't go, and we shall not deprive you of your share in the booty."[6] He said, "No, by Allāh, O uncles, I want to go with you!" They said: "Let's go, we and you, to Allāh's open spaces!"

They went, a month, two months,[7] and reached the country of the Ḥuwēṭāṭ[8] to the east of the Jordan. They were of the Badw of al-Saʿudiyya, or of the ʿIraq,[9] while they themselves were of the Badw of Jordan around Karak.[10] They came to them.

When they looked from the head of a tall hill to see the camels, and behold the camels were grazing, pink ones, white ones, reddish ones and yellow ones, and they were grazing. They fell upon them, took and led away of them what they took, and left. The guard who watched over the herd began to cry out: "O Ḥuwēṭāṭ, they took the camels, pursue them, O sons of Ḥuwēṭāṭ!"

They pursued them, overtook the men who rode off with the camels. [They said:] "Get off the camels, get off, surrender!" They said: "Impossible!"[11] They [the Ḥuwēṭāṭ] shot at the boy and broke his leg, of the boy who had come with them, their nephew. They shot at him and broke his leg.

He said: "O, my uncles, I am wounded. Let Allāh make your way smooth, go, let Allāh make your way smooth! Return home. I am wounded, leave me!"

They said: "No! How could we leave you? Your uncles are with you, and they should leave you? They will not leave you!"

They brought acacia wood, peeled off its bark, tied it around his leg and bandaged it. They cut off two branches, made of them a stretcher, and took it upon their shoulders.[12] They said, "Up, ride, arise, let's go!"

They lifted him on their shoulders and went on carrying him. And for three months, from the Ḥuwēṭāṭ until they reached Ibn Rashīd, they walked for three months. There was among them one uncle, the eldest of them, the eldest of the group. When they were marching, and were traversing a distance of ten or fifteen kilometers, he went ahead, and brought water from some place, and kneaded and baked, and then met his brothers and gave them to eat, to them and to his nephew. When he saw an animal, he shot it and brought them the meat and fed them. He also carried the stretcher when his turn came, he did not let the others carry more than he did. His name was Hdēb, their eldest brother was called Hdēb.

They continued to travel for three months, until they reached home, reached Shummar, and put down the stretcher, and, behold, their brother [i.e., nephew] was limping on his leg. He was able to walk on it, but had a light limp. The bone grew together during the trip, while they were carrying him on their shoulders.

They[13] said: "We must let you know, O Ibn Rashīd, that So-and-so and his brothers brought home with them a wounded of theirs, they carried him three months."

He said, "Call them to me, I want to cut off the heads of all of them right now!"

They came. They said, "What is it, O Ibn Rashīd?"

He said, "How did you bring back with you a wounded when you raided the Ḥuwēṭāṭ? You brought with you a wounded, they could have destroyed all of you! There would have been one [lost], but not all of you! You are seven and he is [only] the eighth! No! They would have killed him, but not all of you!" [14]

They said to him, "O Ibn Rashīd, he is our nephew. Allāh forbid, if we had left our nephew, it would have covered us with shame."

He said, "Now I shall cut off your heads." [15]

He [the nephew] said, "O Ibn Rashīd, I want to say to you two words, and after I have said them to you do to me what you want!"

He said, "Speak!"

Said the youth, he who was wounded, he whose broken leg had healed, he said: [16]

Yesterday morning I sat on a heap of stones on the lookout for the enemy,
    And today I cannot leave the door of the tent.
We fell upon Zimlah and in the direction of al-Ṭor
    Upon pink and yellow camels and herds of white camels.
The camels' owners overtook us on their steeds,
    Strong mounts which broke in like into a herd of swine,
They attacked us in masses, it cannot be denied,
    And we prevailed upon them to grant us our lives.
I said to my uncles, "This is my fate in the world, and what happened,
    And go in peace, O noblest of heroes!"
They said, "Get up, ride, and put your things on the backs of the marchers,
    Take your place on the shoulders of the heroes."
My uncle al-Ihdēb is the strongest of the marchers,
    Carries a weight greater than his share and does not complain.
Two take care of me, praise to my uncles, there is in them no fear or fault,
    Like camels carrying a load, crossing a steep incline like a smooth path.
Two take care of me, and two are next to me,
    And the two are with me like a she-camel with her calf.
For ninety nights I am on shoulders with patience,
    While I am on the shoulders of heroes.
I am amazed that no change is seen on their faces,
    They are like Badw going to a wedding feast.[17]

Ibn Rashīd said, "And this is what your uncles did? For three months, they carried you on their shoulders and brought you home?"

He said, "By Allāh, by Allāh, my uncles carried me and brought me home."

He said, "Since this is what they did, I forgive them. And I permit that in the future if a Badw goes out with them and gets wounded, they should bring him home."

And peace be upon you.

Comments

This story is of considerable value, not for its interest as a folktale but because it opens a window on the folklife, mores, and values of the nomads of the North Arabian Syrian Desert as they existed until the middle of the twentieth century and were fondly remembered by the young Rashā'ideh storyteller as late as the 1980s. It is a fictionalized story of an unsuccessful raid conducted by a group of seven brothers from the Shaʿlān subtribe, whom the storyteller considers a part of the large Shammar (here pronounced Shummar) tribe, located in the Kerak (here pronounced Karak) district to the east of the Dead Sea, in Jordan.

The story starts by telling that Ibn Rashīd, the sheikh of the Shaʿlān, issues three prohibitions to members of his tribe: not to light fire, not to make coffee, and not to bring back from a raid any member of their party who was wounded. It is the last of these three prohibitions that is at the heart of the story. The points of the first two prohibitions are not explained—they lie outside the interest of the story. The tribesmen accept the edict of their sheikh, but, as it develops in the course of the story, their sense of loyalty to a wounded family member overrides their respect for the word of their sheikh, and they disobey it.

The scene now shifts to another, unnamed tribe, into which a sister of the seven brothers married. She had a son, who shot to death a man of his own tribe, seemingly unintentionally, and had to flee so as to escape the victim's avengers of blood. He flees to his mother's brothers, who take him in hospitably.

At this point, the story diverges into stating that the custom of the Badw of those days was to go out on raiding parties twice or three times a year. When the brothers next plan to go on a raid, the nephew (who remains unnamed throughout the story) asks them to take him along.

Thinking that he wants to have a share in the booty, the brothers suggest that he should stay put and they would still let him have a share. But the nephew insists, and they give in.

The story does not state what mounts, if any, the eight raiders used. It only says, "they went . . ." The one to two months the party spends in getting to their destination is clearly a folkloristic exaggeration. In any case, they finally reach their goal: the country of the Ḥuwēṭāṭ, a widespread and powerful tribe whose main concentration is in southern Jordan and northern Saudi Arabia. The storyteller is vague about the location of the tribe and identifies the Ḥuwēṭāṭ as being Badw of either Saudi Arabia or Iraq.

Once the raiding party espies from a hilltop the beautiful pink, white, reddish, and yellow camels of the Ḥuwēṭāṭ, watched over by a single guard, they swoop down and abduct as many animals as they can. The guard alerts the tribesmen, who mount their horses, pursue the raiders, overtake them, and, in order to force them to dismount from the stolen camels, fire at them. One bullet hits the nephew in the leg and breaks it. This seems to have been sufficient warning for the raiding party. They dismount, and the Ḥuwēṭāṭ, following an old nomadic code of chivalry, let them go otherwise unharmed.

The nephew, who evidently was aware of the decree of Ibn Rashīd, begs his uncles to leave him behind and make good their escape. But the seven brothers are of one mind that the loyalty they owe their wounded nephew takes precedence over their tribal duty to obey their sheikh. They improvise a splint and a stretcher and set out homeward carrying the wounded youth on their shoulders.

At this point, the valor of the eldest of the seven brothers, Hdēb (Hudayb), becomes evident. He marches ahead of the others, hunts game, cooks it, provides water, and with all that takes his full share in carrying his nephew.

Here it becomes clear that the raiders have no mounts. They must walk all the way, and thus it takes them no less than three full months to reach home—again, of course, a storylike exaggeration: if they walked every day as little as ten to fifteen kilometers, as the story seems to imply, they could have reached Kerak from Ḥuwēṭāṭ territory in a fraction of ninety days.

In any case, they were on the way long enough for the leg of the nephew to heal, so that he was able to walk, even though with a limp.

Having arrived home, one of their fellow tribesmen notifies Ibn

Rashīd that the brothers disobeyed his orders and brought back with them their wounded nephew. Ibn Rashīd is enraged, commands them to appear before him, and explains to them (for the first time in the story) that his intention in issuing that order was to make sure that only the wounded man, and not all of his companions, is killed by the enemy. The brothers defend themselves by arguing that it would have been a shameful deed to leave their wounded nephew behind. Ibn Rashīd is not appeased and orders their heads to be cut off—a story motif not in accordance with the actual tribal mores which do not vest such powers of execution in a tribal chief.

The nephew then asks Ibn Rashīd's permission to speak and launches into reciting a *qaṣīdah,* a poem in the traditional Bedouin style, in which he describes the bravery and self-sacrifice of his uncles. The wounded youth's plea and poem soften the sheikh's heart, and he not only forgives the seven brothers but rescinds his order and allows thenceforward a wounded member of a raiding party to be brought home. Thus, the story is ultimately a quasi-mythical reaffirmation of the raiders' moral duty to bring back a wounded comrade, even though they thereby endanger their own lives.

Notes

1. Shaʿlān is the name of the princely family of the great Rwala tribe. See R. Patai, *Society, Culture and Change in the Middle East* (Philadelphia: University of Pennsylvania Press, 1971), p. 152.
2. Shummar is the local variant pronunciation of Shammar, the name of one of the most powerful tribes of the Syrian-Iraqi desert (see ibid., p. 90). The storyteller is in error in stating that the Shaʿlān are of the Shammar. In fact, the Rwala (of which the Shaʿlān are the princely family) belong to the ʿAneze tribal confederation, a Qaysī (northern) group, while the Shammar belong to the rival Yamanī (southern) moiety (see ibid., pp. 207–8, 210).
3. The Rashā'ideh, or Rashayda, of the Negev referred to in the story seem to be a branch of the tribe of the same name in the Sinai Peninsula. The Rashayda of the Sinai are a Hteym (variants: Hiteym, Hutaym, Heteym) vassal tribe (see ibid., p. 252).
4. A feature taken from real life: If a man gets involved in a blood feud within his own tribe, he flees to another tribe to take advantage of its protection. If he has maternal relatives (such as mother's brothers) in that tribe, the protection he enjoys is much stronger.
5. The storyteller is conscious of the changed circumstances, and explains that

this used to be the custom. To go out on a raid for the purpose of capturing camels or other animals from an inimical tribe was considered an honorable and, in fact, a highly praiseworthy undertaking which gave the young men of the tribe an opportunity to demonstrate their bravery.

6. His uncles reassure the youth that even if he does not go with them on the raid, they will let him have a share in the booty just as if he had been with them.
7. To spend one or two months in seeking a tribe to raid is a gross exaggeration in the story. In reality, raiding expeditions were of very short duration.
8. On the Ḥuwēṭāṭ (Ḥuwaytāt, Ḥwētēt) tribe and its feuds with neighboring tribes, see Patai, *Society, Culture and Change,* p. 254.
9. In fact, the Ḥuwēṭāṭ roamed as far east as the border area between Saudi Arabia and Iraq.
10. The city of Karak is located some twelve miles to the east of the southern tip of the Dead Sea.
11. Verbal exchanges between enemy groups prior to engaging in actual fighting were part of the behavior pattern observed by traditional Bedouin tribes.
12. This detail indicates that the Ḥuwēṭāṭ deprived the raiding party of its mounts, so that the seven brothers had to walk and carry their wounded nephew on their shoulders.
13. The speakers are members of the seven brothers' tribe, who inform their chief of the return of the raiding party.
14. Only here does Ibn Rashīd explain the reason for his decree: by carrying with it a wounded member, the life of the entire raiding party was endangered. It is better to lose one man than eight.
15. The punishment for disobeying the chieftain is death.
16. The youth intones a *qaṣīdah,* a poem in the traditional form, in which he extols the bravery of his uncles who carried him for three months on their shoulders. For a description of the *qaṣīdah,* see *Encyclopaedia of Islam,* new ed. (Leiden: E. J. Brill, 1978) 4: 713–16.
17. A longer version of this *qaṣīdah,* as well as this story in its entirety, were published by Shafīq ʿAbdul-Jabbār Kamālī in his *Al-Shiʿr ʿInda al-Badw* (Poetry among the Bedouin) (Baghdad: Matbaʿat al-Irshād, 1964), pp. 318–25. According to him, the author of the story and the *qaṣīdah* is Majīd al-Rabudh of the Shammar tribes, and the event itself took place ca. 1890.

26

Seven Brides for Seven Brothers

Recorded by Yoel Perez, from the mouth of Sabḥa ʿAbūd (age 56) of the ʿArab al-Ḥujeyrāt tribe, November 27, 1980.

Once upon a time there lived a man and he had seven sons. They were his sons. They said to him, "It is our wish to marry seven sisters."

Their father said to them, "From where shall I bring you seven sisters? Go and seek!"

They rode on horses, and went to search, and they went on the road. They went and went in the wadi. They had a tent, they set up the tent, and settled down in the place, one day. Every night one of them kept watch over them, kept watch over them and over the horses.

One night the youngest one of them got up. The light went out. When the light went out, he said, "What? Shall I awaken them in the night? It would be a pity to awaken my brothers and to ask them for matches."

He looked around, eastward and westward in the night, and behold, there arose a small light. He went in the night toward the light, went, went, went, went, the light was far. When he arrived, and behold, the light was in a cave, and on the cave there was a big closed stone, forty [were required] to remove it, and forty to close it. Allāh helped him, and he removed the stone and entered, and lay down among them.[1] When he was lying among them in the night, they wanted to go out to steal, they left the house open. He began to eat, he ate of each plate a little, and lay down among them.

When they got up, one of them said, "Something is missing from my plate."[2] "And I, something is missing from my plate." "And I, something is missing from my plate; who is this, by Allāh? Who is this here with us? Get out, Allāh and the protection of Allāh be upon you, we shall not betray you. Get out!"

He got out, and said to them, "It is I."

He said to them, "*Yallah* [let's go]! Come on, let us go to seek theft, let us go to the treasury of the king to steal it." This is [what he said. They said,] "Good."

They went in the night. He went before them. When he went before them he said to them, "I have with me forty stones, each time I throw a stone, let one [of you] come out."[3]

He entered the rooms, and behold in the first room there was a girl, and in the second there was a girl, and in the seven rooms—in each room a girl. The youngest—he looked, and behold the room in which was this girl, and above her head was a snake which was about to bite her. He arose, killed the snake, and imprinted the palm of his hand with the blood on the door of the room, that is to say, he put the palm of his hand on the door of the room of the girl.

And each time he threw a stone, one came out, and he killed him, removed his head, killed him—all the forty. As for the girl, he took her ring, he took from the youngest girl, from above whose head he killed the snake, he took the ring and gave her his own ring. He arose, killed the forty.

The king got up in the morning. What is this in his house? Forty men? Fear! Who, who, who? They began to search. There is someone? Each time somebody came, they brought him. They said, "Who?"

She said, "I know him." The girl, who, who, who? Each time somebody came she was standing under the palace and watching.

He said to her, "Who?"

She said to him, "Bring another one, bring another one."

What? None was left.

She said to them, "Search around the city."

There was nobody. They brought his brothers. They said to her, "These [men] we found outside the city."

She said to them, "No. Bring another one!"

They said, "They have no more brothers!"

She said to them, "Search!"

They found their brother.

She said to them, "Bring this one!"

When they brought him, she recognized him.[4] They brought him, put him next to her, and they sat next to the king.

He said to him, "Your honor, O king, we are seven brothers and we want seven sisters."

He said to him, "I have seven daughters."

He gave one to each one. They remained with him for a month.

They said to him, "Now it is our wish to return, to ride to our father."

"By Allāh! Return!"

Each of them rode on his mare, and each of them brought her along.

When they were on the road, the bride of the youngest one forgot something in the house.

She said to him, "I want to return to bring it!"

He said to her, "No, I shall return to bring it."

He said to them, "Good, wait for me here!"

This was the youngest one. When they were waiting for him, they did not notice that the girl who was sitting with them got up, a cloud came, and snatched away the girl and took her. When it took her, the boy came, he said to them, "Where is the girl?"

They said to him, "A cloud came and snatched her away."[5]

He said to them, "Good, what shall we do?"

He said to them, "You stay here, I shall go to search for her."

He went. While he was going, going, he came to the sea. He looked, and behold, there was a girl. She said to him, "Turn over that stone, and enter under the earth, and come to me!"

He arose, turned over the stone, and went out to her. She said to him, "What are you looking for?"

He said to her, "A cloud came and took away my bride."

She said to him, "Good, do you have a mare?"

He said to her, "Yes."

She said to him, "Go, try, see whether the mare jumps on the face of the sea."

He went, tried, trained the mare, and she got up and jumped.

She said to him, "Go and jump on the face of the second sea! Enter the house, and in it there is a black horse and a white horse. Kiss the black horse on this side and that, and you will find the girl hanging by the hair of her head.[6] A monster took her."[7]

He got up, went to the horse, kissed it and said, "By your life, give me!"

He came to the girl, cut off her hair, and let her ride behind him on the horse, and crossed the sea. The monster jumped up, but found nobody, he pursued him from behind, from behind . . .[8]

He came to his brothers, they rode on the horses, he and they, and he returned to his mother and father, and arranged a wedding and married her.

Comments

Apart from the folkloristic motifs contained in it, this folktale is of interest because it exemplifies considerable storytelling ineptitude. In fact, it can be taken as a demonstration of the degeneration of the storytelling skill that in the past gave us such marvels as the stories contained in the *Arabian Nights,* and that, even in the mid-twentieth century, still produced stories of great interest and intricacy, as shown by several recorded in Palestine-Israel and contained in this volume.

We can only speculate on the factors that brought about this decay. Possibly, or even probably, one factor is the changed conditions of life in modern Israel, where technological civilization penetrates even the traditional seminomadic Arab villages and creates an atmosphere unfavorable to the patient development of the details of a folktale, to the attention required to unroll its events, to the stylistic refinements, and to the other features that make a folktale attractive, well rounded, balanced, and rich. In this folktale one feels an impatience, which in turn leads to jumps from one subject to the next without the required introductory explanations. Thus, for instance, the storyteller simply forgets to mention that the young brother finds forty thieves asleep in the cave, that he tells the forty thieves to enter the king's palace one by one in response to his throwing out a stone—which he does in order to be able to kill them one by one—that the cloud was actually a monster who kidnapped the girl, and so on.

Of course, we must not conclude from this story, and from several others like it, that the Arab storytelling skill is about to die out in Israel. Much depends on the talents and inclinations of the individual storyteller, and next to such truncated stories as this one, one can still find others in which the traditional mastery of the Arab *qaṣṣāṣ* is still fully present. This volume contains several stories of this valuable variety.

Notes

1. The storyteller forgot to mention that upon entering the cave, the youth finds forty thieves asleep.
2. This is the familiar motif of noticing that something is missing from the plate and concluding that somebody must be hiding in the place.
3. The idea, rather ineptly expressed, is that each time the youth throws out a stone, one of the thieves should enter the palace of the king.
4. Only now do we find out that the girl, whose life the youth saved by killing the snake, was not asleep but observed him doing this and thus was able to recognize him. The bloody handprint of the youth on the door, which evidently was meant to serve as a sign of identification, has in the meantime been forgotten.
5. A moment earlier, the storyteller had said that the brothers did not notice that a cloud snatched away the girl. Yet now they report the event to the youngest brother.
6. Captured girls hanging by their hair appear several times in the Arab folktale (see tales 20 and 24).
7. Now we learn that it was not a cloud that snatched away the girl but "the monster," *al-ḥūt*. Actually, the primary meaning of *ḥūt* is "fish," "whale."
8. At this point, the storyteller evidently lost patience, and in the very next sentence she concludes the story by telling briefly about the happy arrival of the youths and their brides and their wedding.

27
Wadīʿah

Recorded by Yoel Perez, from the mouth of Maryam Muṣṭafa Ṭabbāsh of the ʿArab al-Ḥilf—Ṭabbāsh tribe, August 23, 1982.

There were Arabs,[1] the Arabs were encamped. Formerly they used to have houses of hair [tents].[2] Among them was a woman, she had seven sons, she had no daughters. She became pregnant, was about to give birth. Those sons wanted a daughter. We, in former times, did not have hospitals and the like.[3] They had a midwife. The woman gave birth, and the women were with her, and with her was the midwife who cut the umbilical cord.

They [the sons] said to her, "If you give birth to a daughter, put for us a sign on top of the house, put for us a vial of kohl for painting [the eyes], as a sign."[4]

And they went away.

She gave birth to a daughter. She said to the women, "Can you put for me the mirror and the vial of kohl on top of the house?" For the sons.

The sons went to play, to hunt. They were young men, not children.

They [the women] went. And, behold, they did not put it, they put a sword. They [the sons] had told her, "If you give birth to a son, put a sword." Those women cheated her, they put a sword.

The sons came and found a sword. They returned, looked, and went to a faraway land, like from here (the place where I am telling the story) to Afula, even farther than Afula, Jenin,[5] Allāh knows. They went from her, found a place and settled down. They began to eat, to drink, they brought, they set up, and they put, until the daughter grew up. What did her mother call her? Wadīʿah.[6]

The girl grew up, she started to go to school.[7] They said to her, "We have brothers, and you have no brothers."[8] Her mother had ceased giving birth. "We have brothers, and you have no brothers."

She went to her mother crying, sobbing. She said to her, "I have no brothers." She said to her, "You have seven brothers, but your brothers, I don't know where they went."

This daughter grew, she reached the age of ten, twelve, fifteen. I don't know, Allāh knows.[9]

One day, this daughter, it came to her mind to seek out her brothers. Alone she went in the fields, she made bread, loaves of bread. We used to make it in fire. She made it of barley and wheat and vetch and lentils and beans, she made out of all of them flour, she made out of each one (out of each kind) a loaf of bread. She took it along on the way, and she went thus, she—Allāh knows in what hour she went. When night came, she slept, she did not know [the time].

One day Allāh brought her to the house in which lived her brothers, to the place, to the house. She entered the place, there was nobody there. She found everything placed in the cupboard, Allāh knows what she found. She sat down, ate. She found there a cat, she found a cat and stayed there. She prepared the evening meal, she knew that men lived in that house, that there were no women in it. She prepared food, and waited, and hid herself, hid herself behind the cupboard, Allāh knows where.

One [brother] came to prepare the afternoon meal, he wanted to cook. He came, he found the cooked meal, ready and covered. He searched, there was nobody, no living soul. He gave to the cat so that it should eat of the meal, he wanted to see whether the food was poisoned or not.[10] The cat ate and fell asleep, nothing happened to it.

His brothers came, all the six of them, from outside. He brought them the meal, they ate of the food and drank water, and Allāh knows what they did. They said, "Let us get up and search." They searched for her, they said to her, "You are the one who prepared the food? Allāh's protection be upon you! He who betrays you, May Allāh betray him![11] Come out! Who are you? A ghoul or a human being?[12] What is your position?"

She came out, and, behold, she was a girl like an apple. When she came out, she sat down with them. They said to her, "What is your name? And from where are you? From where did you come?"

She told them and said to them, "I lost my seven brothers—like you."

They said to her, "What is your name?"

She said to them, "My name is Wadīʿah, and the name of my

mother is . . . She said to the women, 'Put the vial of kohl and the mirror on top of the house,' but they put there a sword, the sword was a sign that she gave birth to a son."

They embraced her, and kissed her, and said to her, "We are your brothers!"

They became known to each other, and they stayed. They stayed, Allāh knows, a month, more or less. They wanted to take her back, let her go back with them to the house.

Before she returned to the house she began to sweep and to wipe. She found a seed of *ḥummuṣ,* of this shape, squashed it, and ate it. She found it, and nothing else beside it. This one [a feminine person, a *ghoulah*?][13] began to tell her, "Give me of what you have eaten."

She said to her, "This was a single seed of *ḥummuṣ* which I found while I was sweeping, there is none other."

She said to her, "Give it to me, or else I shall pour water upon the fire."

There are no Arabs who have no fire and matches or kindling wood.[14] She was putting the kindling wood on the fire, and left it there, the fire continued to burn all day long. She had none [*ḥummuṣ*]. The girl did not pay attention. The cat went and put water on the fire.[15] She [the girl] intended to prepare food for her brothers, and, behold, there was no fire. She looked, she stood, and, behold, like among the ʿArab al Kaʿabiya[16] from afar, she looked, and, behold, [something] like smoke, Allāh knows, and upon it a spark of fire. She, at four o'clock, began to go, to run. She went, looked, and, behold, a *ghoulah* was sitting [there].[17] She went to the *ghoulah* and found her grinding wheat to prepare a meal. She said to her, "Peace be upon you!"

She said to her, "Upon you be peace! Were it not that peace is evident in your words, I would have allowed the wild animals to hear the breaking of your bones"—that is, she would have eaten her.[18] "What do you wish?"

She said to her, "I want a spark of fire."

She said to her, "Good."

What did the *ghoulah* do? She took a little *salīqa* [wheatgroats], which she was preparing at that time, it was still green (not dry), she made it and put it.

She said to her, "Take a little burgul while it is still fresh, we eat it."

She said to her, "No."

She said to her, "But surely!"

She put it in her pocket, and it made a hole in her pocket. The girl went, she ran, and they [the kernels of burgul] were dropping behind her. She continued [to run] from the door of the house of the *ghoulah* to the door of her own house.

One day in the afternoon the *ghoulah* followed their footsteps.[19] She [the girl] did not tell her brothers. She prepared an evening meal and sat down. In the morning her brothers went to work. Next morning she [the *ghoulah*] came to her. Behold, she came to her. They, her brothers, killed the husband of the *ghoulah,*[20] and brought his head, and put it in a box, in a carton, Allāh knows, and were playing with it. She [the *ghoulah*] came, sat down next to the girl, they talked, she and the girl, and they were satisfied, that is, in a nice manner, not rudely.

She sat with her, and said to her, "Give me a comb so that I can comb my hair here with you."

She went to the cat and said to her, "Go, bring me a comb."

The cat said to her, "I shall go and bring you the head of the old one in the basket."[21]

The girl said nothing to her.

The *ghoulah* said to her, "Give it to me."

She [the girl] gave it to her, when she looked at it, she recognized it. She said, "Ah!"

This one, the *ghoulah,* when she went away from her, in the afternoon, what did she do? She stuck a nail of blood and a nail of poison in the threshold, and Allāh knows. The girl went out, the nails got stuck in her, she remained in the door.[22] Her brothers returned from work, found the house dark, there was no basin for taking a shower in the house. They found their sister. What should they do? They said, "This our sister, we cannot heal her on earth, one must put her on 'the camel of the air,'[23] and Allāh is omnipotent!"

This "camel of the air" is like a big bird. They—Allāh knows—brought silken kerchiefs and dressed their sister, as Allāh wanted. The "camel of the air" came, they put their sister on it and said to him, "Go! If somebody tells you, 'Descend!' don't descend, but if someone tells you, 'By the life of what you are carrying, descend!' then descend."

It did not descend. There was [there] an old shepherd of a small flock, he said to it, "By the life of that which is on your back, descend!" It descended. He looked, and, behold, it was a girl.

He said, "I shall take her, we shall gain some profit.[24] Let us give her shelter (let us bury her). It is a pity to leave her like this."

He had an old wife, and had no children. He had neither a son nor a daughter. He took her to the old woman.

He said to her, "Come, see this girl, how beautiful she is. Pity [upon her]."

He dug deep to bury her in the ground. She began to wash her, she began to do her this, to dry her feet, to wash them. And behold, she removed the first nail. The girl sighed.[25] She remained with them, Allāh knows how many days. She recovered, they let her be. She began to think, "You, what is your position? From where did you come? From where? From where?" She told them the truth. The girl remained with them.

One day the son of the emir saw her, he asked them for her, Allāh knows, he took her, Allāh knows. [After] a year, more or less, she gave birth to a son. She bore a son, and stayed. One day, who wanted to betray her? A *jinniya* [a female jinn].[26] One day she came to her, when the boy was a little grown, this one, the *ghoulah,* blew, and behold, she was a dove flying in the sky, hovering, hovering.

The child said, "O flock of doves, have you seen my mother?"

She said to him, "Your mother is with the last flock. She is crying over you and over her seven brothers."

One day, Allāh knows, her husband came, did something to her, Allāh knows, hunted her, Allāh knows what he did to her. They took her to the sheikh, there were healing sheikhs, Allāh knows, they did to her from the Koran,[27] from something else, Allāh knows, they began to do to her, from here, from there. The girl recovered, she became healthy. She related to them and told him [her husband], "I shall not remain here with you, I must go to search for my brothers in another place."

They rode on a horse, formerly there were no automobiles.[28] She went, searched for the horses and her brothers, and, behold, they found her brothers. They found her brothers. They took her and went, they brought her brothers to her. They recognized each other, she and they, and they went to their family.[29]

Comments

The story begins in a well-constructed manner and goes on satisfactorily until close to its end, when it simply falls apart and peters out in almost meaningless general and vague statements. Also, the concluding part of the story is fragmentary; new characters appear without any introduction and with no connection to what went before. The impression is that toward the end of the story, the storyteller reached the end of her patience and rushed to finish it without paying any attention to logic or continuity.

On the other hand, interesting in this story is the time distance repeatedly indicated by the storyteller. She emphasizes that in olden times, when her story took place, the Arabs (i.e., Bedouins) used to live in tents, in contrast to the houses in which they live now; they had no hospitals, but a midwife helped the woman in childbirth; when sick they went to a healing sheikh who restored them to health by reading conjurations from the Koran; they used to have fires going in their lodgings all day long; they used to ride on horses and had no motorized vehicles. These remarks help to establish the distance between then and now with reference to features of the material culture, changes in which are readily acknowledged. No such time distance, however, is established or even hinted at when it comes to supernatural features. The storyteller does not find it necessary to state that "in former times" her people believed in ghouls and *ghoulahs,* in "camels of the air" that understood human language, in poisoned nails that kept a person in a deathlike state as long as they were stuck in his or her foot, in cats that obeyed (or so it seems) the unspoken command of the *ghoulah,* and so on, or that in former times such supernatural creatures used actively to interfere in their lives. These, as well as the prince who marries the girl at the end, are standard features of the folktale, apparently as valid in the present time as they were in days of old when the events related in the story were supposed to have taken place.

Notes

1. The term *Arabs* is used in the specific sense of nomadic Arabs, Bedouin.
2. Reflection of the changed situation: the tribe no longer dwells in tents but in stone, brick, or mud-brick houses.
3. Again, reference to the changed situation: nowadays the women go to the hospital to give birth.
4. See Tale Type 451 "The Maiden who Seeks Her Brothers"; I "The Brothers and Their Sister"; and Motif T595 "Sign hung out informing brothers whether mother has borne boy or girl"; N344.1 "Wrong sign put out leads to boys' leaving home."

5. Reference to the Jewish town Afula and the Arab town Jenin, both not far from the locality where the storyteller lives.
6. *Wadīʿah,* a girl's name, meaning "deposit," "pledge."
7. Reference to modern conditions: in past times, few boys and no girls of a Bedouin tribe went to school.
8. To have no brothers puts a girl in an inferior position. Brothers are the natural protectors of a girl.
9. Whenever the storyteller refers to something about which she does not know the particulars, she uses the phrase "Allāh knows."
10. Having found a prepared meal and no trace of the person who prepared it, the brother is afraid that perhaps somebody intended to poison them.
11. The brothers, of course, don't recognize their sister whom they have never seen before. By invoking Allāh's protection, they reassure her that they will not harm her.
12. The question "Are you a ghoul or a human being?" is frequently asked in the Arab folktale of a person encountered in a strange situation.
13. The sudden appearance in the tale, without any introduction or transition, of a female person, possibly a *ghoulah,* shows a certain ineptness of the storyteller.
14. The changed situation in which the tribe, settled in a village, finds itself prompts the storyteller to insert the remark about the custom—no longer observed—of having matches and kindling wood on hand all the time.
15. This statement about the cat intends to indicate that it was not a simple cat but rather a kind of magic animal. This is made even clearer later.
16. The ʿArab al-Kaʿabiya are a tribe.
17. The intention of the storyteller, rather ineptly expressed, is to say that after walking a long distance, the girl enters a house where she finds a *ghoulah* grinding grain.
18. With these words, the storyteller explains the phrase used by the *ghoulah,* "I would have allowed the wild animals to hear the breaking of your bones."
19. The unexpressed assumption is that the *ghoulah* was able to follow the girl by tracking the kernels of burgul that dropped from her pocket.
20. The husband of the *ghoulah* appears without any introduction.
21. The magic cat can speak and brings to the girl the head of the *ghoulah*'s husband cut off by the brothers.
22. It is unstated but understood that the girl died or appeared to be dead.
23. "The camel of the air," yet another character appearing without any introduction, is evidently a magic, flying camel, able to speak or, at least, to understand human speech.
24. The word *profit* is used here in the sense of merit, earned by performing the pious deed of burying the girl.

25. Just as the story does not say explicitly that the girl died, so it does not say that she revived, only that she "sighed."
26. The incident with the girl's son and his being kidnapped by a *jinniya* is inserted in a rudimentary form and disrupts the story line.
27. The healing of the girl by readings from the Koran and other traditional methods ties in with her deathlike sickness caused by the poisoned nail.
28. Yet another reference to the distance between the present conditions and those of the past in which the story takes place.
29. In this conclusion of the story, the girl is imagined as being unmarried; otherwise, she would return not "to her family" but to that of her husband.

28
The Two Hunters

Recorded from the mouth of Shaḥādah Ḥayyām (age 75) of the ʿArab al-Saʿdiah [Seʿdiya] tribe, transcribed by Yoel Perez, September 2, 1982.

There were two friends, each of them from a certain tribe, Allāh knows which.[1] They said to each other, "Let us behave honestly with each other in our hearts and intentions and in our minds, whether awake or asleep, and on every occasion when we want to go out to hunt and to shoot."

When they went to hunt and to shoot, they were absent for a month or two, and each of them would take along provisions enough for two or three days. Provisions mean food.

As they were walking on the road, they became hungry. They put down their rifles, and sat down, they ate, near a well of water, a cistern of rain. They had brought along a jerry-can. They drew water and ate. Both of them ate from the provisions of one of them. They ate, drank, and continued to walk, walk, walk, until they became hungry again.

One of them said to the other, "Let's open your provisions." The other said, "No, let's finish your provisions. Then we shall open my provisions." So they ate everything that one of them had. He had nothing more left. Both of them ate twice. They ate lunch and dinner.

Let us say they slept that night near that well, until the morning, beside that desolate place. They started to walk very early in the morning, at four o'clock. From three in the morning they started to walk. They walked, walked, walked, walked. They became hungry and wanted to eat. One of them said to the other, "Open your provisions. We want to eat." The other said to him, "No, no. You finished your provisions. I won't let you eat of my provisions."

[The first hunter said,] "O bad, o good! Fear Allāh! There are no stores, no market, nor cities from which to buy. There are no Arabs from whom we can beg. No towns from which we can beg. Where will I go to eat?"

The other said, "I don't care if you die."

He ate, and put the rest back in his bosom. He ate, ran away, and left the other alone. This poor man was yellow from hunger, and went to sleep hungry. Too bad. He could not walk any more. He remained asleep until the sun set, and the world became night. Because of hunger he could not walk, and his brother, his companion, had abandoned him. As for him, he had had good intentions. Poor man, for him the world was honest, while the other had only used his tongue. He only spoke with his tongue. He did not mean what he said.

The man slept at night. It was very cold at night. At night it became cold. He started to walk, and all of a sudden he saw a cave in the mountain. He entered the cave and slept.[2]

While he slept, behold wild animals came, among them a wolf, a fox, and a hyena. They were companions[3] who would always gather in that cave. They sat down and told stories. That poor man, because of his fear, got a headache. He had a headache, went inside, and hid himself because he was afraid that they would eat him. He was afraid of them, and started to listen to them. They started to talk.

One of them said to the other, "O, you, Abū Ḥasan [the fox], are you full or hungry?" He said to him, "By Allāh, I am full. (Abū Ḥasan al-Ḥuṣaynī is the fox)."[4] He said, "And you, O Abū Sirḥān (the hyena)?" He said to him, "As for me, by Allāh, I am full. I found a camel, and ate of the camel, and am full."

Who was left? The wolf. He [the hyena] said to him, "And you, Abū al-dhiʾb, are you hungry?" He said to him, "No, by Allāh, my brother. I came across a herd of sheep, and the shepherd took a sheep and gave me one of them, and I ate, until I became full, and left over some of it."

They said, "Allāh be praised. All of us are full."

So they spoke to each other, and he was listening to them, and looking at them. He became happy. He said, "Were they hungry, they would want to look here and here, wishing to eat me."

He made a count, namely until it became daytime. That is, now it became two o'clock, three o'clock. The wild animals started to scatter among the rocks.

Now, out came male and female mice, of the big ones, one after the other. Each one of them carried a golden *lira*[5] out from the cave, in which there was a treasure, and they were running around all over the floor of the cave. There was a floor there. They brought out and piled up the *liras,* until there was a heap this high.

The wild animals were talking among themselves, and were spending a sleepless night. Abū Ḥasan [the fox] said to them, "In the morning they [the mice] will want to start playing with these pieces of gold. How they will entertain themselves, O, Abū Sirḥān [the hyena], O Abū al-dhi'b [the wolf]!" Thus they were telling stories to each other.

The pile of gold became this high, they came and tumbled the gold pieces, and played with them. Then they built up the pile again in the same place as before. They were talking among themselves, and all the time the man was listening. He thought that when the mice would go out in the morning, when the day would start, they would again do the same thing: they would bring out the gold, and pile it up. The man said to himself, "If somebody were to hit them with a bone, or a stone, or anything, he could take all the gold." Thus were the wild animals talking at night. He let them make a pile, and then he got hold of that piece of bone, and hit them. They ran away, and the pieces of gold remained piled up. He put them in his handkerchief, tied it up, and hid it in his breast pocket. Nobody knew about it, except Allāh.

The man became relaxed, and since he had just found a treasure, and the like, he was ready to do things. He started walking. He walked and walked. And behold, there was a city, a city like this city. He said, "Perhaps I shall meet somebody who will give me food. I shall have more strength. Perhaps I shall buy something in a store."

He came to stores and houses, and everything was there. He went into a certain store, and bought, and ate and drank. How wonderful became his health! The gold pieces were in his breast pocket. Nobody knew about them but Allāh.

Thus he reached his own town. He bought a piece of land, and built a palace,[6] and opened stores with his gold. He opened everything, and built many projects and factories. Thus he became an *efendi.*[7] He started to enter high society. People started to invite him. He had influence. He remained a good man as he was before, and had good intentions. He did not cause problems. But he had been poor. He did not have the fame of being a great person, or of being a *bey.*[8] He did not have fame, but property makes the person, and it gave him fame. They started having parties, and had gatherings, and invited him. He went. He became known to the viziers, and started to be acquainted with the viziers and the king. They held elections, and he became king.[9] See, how Allāh does what He wants! When he became king—how wonderful a king he became! The government now was in his hands. The gold treasure was in his hands. Everything was in his hands.

One day they went out. In days of old they would go out in a carriage, a wagon with horses—it means that the horse pulls it in the street.[10] This carriage was like a royal one. He was sitting, and near him were the viziers on both sides. He was respected, and the people lined up along the road, wishing him well.

All of a sudden, he passed by some porters carrying bags and other similar things. The king used to pass by everybody, poor or rich, good or bad, gypsy or poor, he passed by everybody. And behold, he recognized his companion who had been with him, who did not give him food when he was a young man, when they were going out, who did not let him eat with him. And behold, there he was, carrying a heavy weight on his back, and he was barely able to carry it.

He said to him, "Hey, you dog—far be it from the listeners![11]—come here!"

His companion looked at him, and said, "O, king of the time![12] I did nothing wrong!"

The king said to him, "Yes, you did! And throw down that bag from your back!" And he hit him with a whip.

The king never hit anybody. All the people looked at him. Why did the king hit this man? They told him, "The king never hits anybody, nor does he ever become angry!"

The king said, "Yes, I remember, when we sat near a certain place, next to a certain well, you ate from my provisions, but you did not let me have from your provisions."

He [the porter] said, "What has brought you to this high position?"

The king said, "Whoever Allāh is with has no fear. I have mercy, and have never ill-treated anybody, and praised be Allāh! Allāh has lifted me up, and gave me a high rank, with Allāh, since to be of the rank of a king is not simple. Yes, there is a Hereafter in the world, and the Hereafter is good."[13]

[The poor man said:] "What did it bring you, and what did it not bring you?"

The king said, "This is my good deed that has brought me [reward]. Mercy is good, and if you are straight with Allāh, He will give you."

The poor man said, "Good. As for me, even if you kill me, or peel off my skin, I shall not leave you alone. I shall go with you."

The king took him and said to him, "Come, you will be a servant in this house, here and there. You will sweep for me this *sālūn* [salon], and make a cup of coffee. It means, that you will be a servant."

He went with him, and they sat like this until the *dīwān* [council] was concluded by the king.

Although he was a king, since the other man had been his companion, his heart took pity on him. He said to him, "Come, I want to tell you. It was so and so and so with me. When you left me alone, I went into a cave where you left me. I found a cave and spent the night there. In came wild animals, and they talked in front of me, thus and thus, and all of a sudden mice came out, and brought gold and piled it up. I hit them with a piece of bone, and took the gold. Allāh, praised be He and exalted, lifted me up, and I arrived at this rank."

The other man said, "Yes, by Allāh, I will go and do as you did, and maybe I shall become like you." [14]

He knew the place where they both had been. He went straight there. He was looking around, and all of a sudden there was this cave, exactly as he [the king] had described it. He went inside the cave. The time was evening, afternoon. He went inside the cave and, all of a sudden, there came the fox, and the hyena who was nicknamed Abū Sirḥān, and the wolf, and they all sat down. One of them threw himself at the door of the cave. The other fell down. The third one fell on top of them. They said to each other, "What is the matter? Woe, O my brother, I am hungry." Abū Ḥasan [the fox] said, "O my brother, Abū Sirḥān, I am hungry." The wolf said, "Woe, my brother, Abū Sirḥān, I am hungry, since I have not eaten for two days. Each time quails came, they flew off, and I haven't eaten anything."

Abū Sirḥān said, "I came to the herd of camels, and the small camels were behind their mothers.[15] I tried to eat one of them. They did not let me. They chased me. I ran away."

As for the wolf, he said, "I came to these sheep, and their owner is very powerful, he was with them, and their owner was standing there, and he had a rifle. Each time I came near them, he would shoot with the rifle. I have not eaten, and have not tasted anything for two days."

He said to him, "By Allāh, O Abū Ḥasan, you are less heavy than we, go have a look at the cave. Perhaps you will find someone left behind, or something like that."

He started to sniff at the odor. Then he started to draw near the door. What? He said, "I have found." He asked him, "What did you find?" He said, "I found a big man, like this." So each of them took a slice of the man, and he died and disappeared. May you have safety and live![16]

Comments

The teller of this story is distinguished by his style: he uses very brief, abrupt sentences and likes to repeat them in a somewhat altered form. In other words, he has an individual style of his own.

The two human protagonists of the story are hunters who enter into an alliance of friendship, but one of them is evil and lets his companion starve. Three animals also figure in it: a wolf, a fox, and a hyena, who meet in a cave and hold conversations. The three animals are entirely humanlike, which is emphasized by the human names of two of them: the fox is called Abū Ḥasan, the hyena Abū Sirḥān, and only the wolf is called Abū al-dhiʾb (Abū Dīb), which means "Father of the Wolf." The three animals are also humanlike in their religiosity: in their talk, they frequently say "By Allāh," "Allāh be praised," and so on.

Caves in the Arab folktale are associated with treasure. In this story, the cave in which the good hunter finds shelter and in which he overhears the talk of the three animals is full of gold *līras* (pounds), which the mice who live in the cave heap up in front of him. He drives off the mice, ties the gold in his handkerchief, and leaves.

Reaching home, the hunter buys land, builds himself a palace, opens stores, and, utilizing the modern conditions in the country, builds "many projects and factories." His riches make him famous, and—in accordance with a mixture of traditional and modern conditions—he is elected king.

When the new king recognizes his old hunting partner among the poor people, at first he gets so angry that he hits him with a whip, but then he forgives him and employs him as a personal servant. He even tells his former companion how he got rich.

The other hunter thereupon goes to the cave hoping that he, too, can enrich himself with the gold. But it so happens that the fox, the hyena, and the wolf, who return to the cave at the same time, not having found food for three days, are starving, and when they "sniff at the odor" of the man, they fall upon him and devour him.

The story does not end by stating the lesson one can learn from it, but it could well be this: what is lucky for one man can be disastrous for another, and betrayal of friendship leads to misfortune.

Notes

1. The phrase indicates that the storyteller does not know the names of the tribes, but Allāh knows.
2. By entering the cave, the hunter moves from the real world into the world of the fairy tale in which animals speak and behave like human beings.
3. I know of no other folktale telling of friendship among the fox, the wolf, and the hyena.
4. Explanatory comment by the storyteller.
5. *Lira* was the Arabic (and Hebrew) term for the Palestinian pound during the British mandatory period.
6. A characteristic act attributed by the Arab folktale to a person who unexpectedly becomes rich: he buys a piece of land and builds a palace.
7. *Efendi* is the title of a well-to-do Arab urbanite.
8. *Bey,* or *bak,* or *bek,* is a government official in Turkish times, also a title of courtesy.
9. A curious mixture of modern and traditional features. The storyteller, living in Israel of the 1980s, knows that high office can be achieved only by being elected, yet at the same time the highest position to which a man can aspire is for him still that of a king. Hence the hero of the story is elected to kingship.
10. Horsedrawn carriages are so rare in the environment of the storyteller that he finds it necessary to explain that such carriages were used in olden times.
11. An interjection to spare the listeners' feelings, which are offended by the mention of a dog.
12. Traditional phrase in addressing a king, familiar from the *Arabian Nights.* It means "king of the present age."
13. Meaning it can happen that the reward, usually preserved for the Hereafter (*ākhira*), is reaped already in this world.
14. This is a recurrent motif in the Arab folktale: the evil person goes to the

place where the good person found his treasure but as a consequence is killed.

15. A detail from the actual Bedouin experience: the hyena (or the wolf, or the fox) cannot attack a baby camel if it stays near its mother.
16. After mentioning that the man was eaten by the wild animals, the storyteller finds it necessary to counteract the bad influence this reference can possibly have by wishing safety and long life to his listeners.

Afterword

To bring this selection of Arab folktales from Palestine and Israel to a close, a few remarks seem appropriate concerning the place of these tales within the global spectrum of oral folklore of which they unquestionably form a part.

Folktales not only belong to a large variety of genres but also are characterized by a great fluidity of type which makes their classification extremely difficult. Nevertheless, students of folklore have repeatedly tackled the problem of how to classify folktales, and most have found themselves in agreement about the three main classes into which narrative folklore can be grouped:

1. *Myth,* which is an account containing sacred truth and usually explaining some important feature in the physical or social environment. Example: Theseus and the Minotaur.
2. *Legend,* which is adorned history, usually associated with some local feature or event that is believed to have taken place. Example: Lot's wife and the pillar of salt.
3. *Fairy tale* (or, better, *Märchen*), which is fiction, usually a popular story, and meant to be entertaining. Example: Hänsel and Gretel.

None of the above categories is absolute. In most cases, all one can say of an item of oral folklore is that its preponderant content places it in one of the three categories.

Within this classificatory scheme, the Arab folktales presented in this volume (and the Arab folktale in general) belong to the *Märchen* category.[1] Typical in this respect is the oft-found introductory sentence, which says that the story we are about to hear "was neither here nor there" or asks, "Shall we tell a tale or shall I sleep?" or states in some other form that what follows is not an account of things that actually did happen. This, however, does not mean that myth and legend are altogether absent from the world of Arab folklore. Quite to the contrary: historically, Arab folklore comprises stories that qualify as myths and others relating incidents from the life of Muhammad and other saintly figures of Arab history that definitely belong to the realm of legend. The fact remains, however, that pure myths and legends do not seem to figure among the stories current in twentieth-century Arab folklore; at least, they are absent from the folklore repertoire recorded in Palestine and Israel in the three periods of 1910–11, 1946–47, and 1982–84.

As far as the typology of their content is concerned, Arab fairy tales (*Märchen*) contain many of the motifs known from the folktale storehouse of other peoples. Apart from the specific coloration provided by local conditions, customs, and values, they do not differ essentially from these; in the comments and notes appended to the stories, I point out many such correspondences, as well as the reflections of local conditions in the tales themselves. A thorough study undoubtedly would find many more correspondences to folktale motifs present in other cultures.

Structurally, the Arab folktale falls into three types, two of which are distinct and the third of which is mixed. There are, first of all, those folktales that tell of the adventures of ordinary human beings, their trials and tribulations, the struggles between good people and bad people (usually ending with the triumph of the good), the difficulties emerging in plural marriages involving one man and two women, competition or even hostilities between half-brothers, and the like. In this type of folktale, poverty often plays a crucial role, and the outcome to which it leads is usually the attainment of riches by the poor protagonist, occasionally paralleled by the impoverishment of the wealthy one. These stories are typically based on real-life situations, and their *Märchen* character is supplied by the grossly exaggerated changes in life conditions they describe: the poor beggar becomes king.

A second, very different type of Arab folktale consists of stories that tell of encounters between ordinary humans and fabulous supernatural beings—jinns, ghouls, *ghoulahs,* ʿafrīts—and/or likewise fabulous supernatural occurrences that the human protagonists witness, participate in, or bring about. A salient characteristic of these stories is the absence of a sharp dividing line between the human and the demonic worlds: simply by entering a cave or a palace or by descending or falling into a well or cistern, the human hero enters an environment populated by demons, but as a rule he has no difficulty establishing contact with them. The lack of any clear demarcation between the human and the demonic scenes, and between the human and demonic beings, becomes most apparent in those episodes in which the human protagonist unexpectedly encounters a stranger, and his or her first reaction is to ask, "Are you a human or a ghoul?" As long as the ghoul (or any other demonic being) so chooses, the humans with whom he or she is in contact, or to whom the ghoul is married, have no way of knowing that they are faced with a demon.

Ghouls share with humans the quality of being pious Muslims. Both frequently and emphatically invoke the name of Allāh and express their gratitude to him. Demons are like humans also in respect of fertility and mortality: they can marry—either other ghouls or human beings—and can produce children with them. And they can and do die; in several stories, we hear of ghouls or *ghoulahs* being killed by humans. On the other hand, ghouls have magic or miraculous powers that make them much more powerful than humans: they change shapes at will, fly through the air, flit across great distances in a trice. Most ghouls, in most cases, are friendly to humans and, if the humans know how to approach them, are willing to help them out of difficulties. It seems no exaggeration to say that, apart from having a few unpleasant traits such as enjoying human flesh in their diet, the ghouls of Arab folktales are creatures endowed with qualities ordinary humans would love to have.

A special subcategory of the Arab folktale is the animal tale, in which animals speak like human beings, have human desires and needs, and are grateful to humans who help them when they are in trouble. There are also a number of tales in which animals appear only incidentally, but we are told that they can speak, that they have greater knowledge than humans, that they can fly (even if they are not birds), and that they are helpful.

As stated above, many Arab folktales are of a mixed type. In part these relate actions of ordinary humans in ordinary circumstances, and in part they take those humans into situations in which they encounter magic creatures, rocks that move at a verbal command, and other features of a fantasy world. Evidently, the Arab storyteller is not a taxonomist; he is unaware of mixing in one and the same story two or more disparate elements, thereby presenting problems to the folklorist but augmenting the enjoyment of his listeners.

As we have seen, in the Arab folktales recorded in modern Israel, another, newer kind of mixing of disparate elements occurs: the protagonists of these stories travel with total unconcern from the modern world with all its accoutrements to the traditional-miraculous one, and back again. For a folkloristic purist, such an admixture may seem to be a degradation of the folktale; for the broader-minded student of the folktale, it appears as a manifestation of the folktale's vitality in being able to extend its boundaries and incorporate phenomena of the modern world that have become as much parts of everyday life as were those manifestations of old that gave rise to beliefs in jinns and ghouls and other supernatural beings.

But despite its adaptability and perseverance in a technologically advanced environment generally unfavorable to the retention of folk traditions, the Arab folktale has no guarantee of survival. It thus presents folklorists with two major tasks. The more urgent one is to collect and record as expeditiously and as extensively as possible the Arab folktales that at present are still remembered by elders in city, village, and tribe. The second task is to study what is recorded, analyze and classify it, and thus incorporate the folk tradition of the Arabs into that great global treasure house of human culture that contains the folktales of all the world's nations.

Note

1. For a discussion of the Palestinian folktale genres and their taxonomy, see Ibrahim Muhawi and Sharif Kanaana, *Speak, Bird, Speak Again: Palestinian Arab Folktales* (Berkeley: University of California Press, 1989), pp. 1–8.

References

Aarne, Antti, and Stith Thompson. *The Types of the Folktale: A Classification and Bibliography*. 2nd ed. FFC No. 184. Helsinki: Academia Scientarum Fennica, 1961.

Bettelheim, Bruno. *The Uses of Enchantment: The Meaning and Importance of Fairy Tales*. New York: Vintage Books, 1989.

Bushnaq, Inea. *Arab Folktales*. New York: Pantheon Books, 1986.

Dorson, Richard M. *Folktales Told Around the World*. Chicago: University of Chicago Press, 1975.

Doutté, Edmond. *Magie et religion dans l'Afrique du Nord*. Alger: A. Jourdan, 1909.

Edmunds, Lowell. *Oedipus: The Ancient Legend and Its Later Analogues*. Baltimore: Johns Hopkins University Press, 1985.

Edmunds, Lowell, and Alan Dundes, eds. *Oedipus: A Folklore Casebook*. New York: Garland, 1983.

Ginat, Joseph. *Women in Muslim Rural Society: Status and Role in Family and Community*. New Brunswick, N.J.: Transaction Books, 1982.

Granqvist, Hilma. *Marriage Conditions in a Palestinian Village*. 2 vols. 1936. Reprint, New York: AMS Press, 1975.

———. *Muslim Death and Burial: Arab Customs and Traditions Studied in a Village in Jordan*. Helsinki-Helsingfors, 1965.

Haddawy, Husain, trans. *The Arabian Nights: Sinbad and Other Popular Stories*. New York and London: W. W. Norton, 1995.

Jaussen, Antonin. *Coutumes des Arabes au pays de Moab*. Paris: V. Lecoffre, 1908.

Kamali, Shafīq ʿAbdul-Jabbār. *Al-Shiʿr ʿInda al-Badw*. Baghdad: Matbaʿat al-Irshād, 1964.

Mernissi, Fatima. *Beyond the Veil: Male-Female Dynamics in a Modern Muslim Society*. New York: Schenkman, 1975.

Muhawi, Ibrahim, and Sharif Kanaana. *Speak, Bird, Speak Again: Palestinian Arab Folktales*. Berkeley: University of California Press, 1989.

Patai, Raphael. *Society, Culture and Change in the Middle East*. Philadelphia: University of Pennsylvania Press, 1971.

Perez, Yoel. "*HaShātir wʿImlāq Polifem.*" *Tevaʿwaʾaretz,* Sept.–Oct. 1985.

Pierotti, Ermete. *Customs and Traditions of Palestine Illustrating the Manners of the Ancient Hebrews.* Cambridge: Deighton, Bell, 1864.

El Saadawi, Nawal. *The Hidden Face of Eve: Women in the Arab World.* Boston: Beacon Press, 1982.

Schmidt, Hans, and Paul Kahle. *Volkserzählungen aus Palästina.* Göttingen: Vandenhoeck und Ruprecht, 1918.

El-Shamy, Hasan M. *Folk Traditions of the Arab World: A Guide to Motif Classification.* 2 vols. Bloomington: Indiana University Press, 1995.

Thompson, Stith. *The Folktale.* New York: Holt, Rinehart and Winston, 1946.

———. *Motif-Index of Folk Literature: A Classification of Narrative Elements in Folktales, Ballads, Myths, Fables, Mediaeval Romances, Exempla, Fabliaux, Jest-Books, and Local Legends.* 6 vols. Bloomington: Indiana University Press, 1955–58.

Westermarck, Edward. *Ritual and Belief in Morocco.* London: Macmillan, 1926.

Wetzstein, I. G. "Sprachliches aus den Zeltlagern der syrischen Wüste," *Zeitschrift der deutschen morgenländischen Gesellschaft* 22 (1868): 69–194.

Type Index

Tale Types are from Antti Aarne and Stith Thompson, *The Types of the Folktale: A Classification and Bibliography,* 2nd ed., FFC No. 184 (Helsinki: Academia Scientarum Fennica, 1961).

Tale Type 333 "The Glutton [Red Riding Hood]," 9
Tale Type 450 "Little brother and little sister," 213
Tale Type 451 "The Maiden who Seeks Her Brothers," 244*n*4
Tale Type 550/I[b] "Object of the Quest," 153*n*4
Tale Type 551 "Search for the Golden Bird," 153*n*4
Tale Type 676 "Open Sesame," 145
Tale Type 709 "Snow White," 9, 222, 224*n*12
Tale Type 921 "The King and the Peasant's Son," 206
Tale Type 931 "Oedipus," 41
Tale Type 954 "The Forty Thieves," 139*n*14
Tale Type 1137 "The Ogre Blinded (Polyphemus)," 33

Motif Index

Motifs are from Stith Thompson, *Motif-Index of Folk Literature: A Classification of Narrative Elements in Folktales, Jest-Books, and Local Legends,* 6 vols. (Bloomington: Indiana University Press, 1955–58).

B. Animals

Motif B472 "Helpful whale," 195*n*36

C. Tabu

Motif C742 "Tabu: striking monster twice," 195*n*35

H. Tests

Motif H583.1 "King: What do you see? Youth: One and a half men and a horse's head," 206

Motif H583.6 "King: What are you doing? Youth: I boil those which come and go," 206

K. Deceptions

Motif K603 "Escape under ram's belly," 33

Motif K1011 "Eye-remedy," 33

N. Chance and Fate

Motif N344.1 "Wrong sign put out leads to boys' leaving home," 244*n*4

Motif N471 "Foolish attempt of second man to overhear secrets," 145

T. Sex

Motif T412 "Mother-son incest," 41

Motif T595 "Sign hung out informing brothers whether mother has borne boy or girl," 244*n*4

Index

ʿAbd al-ʿAzīz ibn Muḥammad ibn Saʿūd, 57*n*3
Abraham, 16
ʿAlī Bābā and the forty thieves, 144–45, 146*n*5
Allāh: invoking in time of danger, 192
Allāh, Gate of, 146*n*2
Al-Shiʿr ʿInda al-Badw (Poetry among the Bedouin) (Kamālī), 231*n*17
Animal tales, 257
ʿAqāl, 81, 87*n*16
Aqrās (flat loaves), 79, 86*n*4
ʿArab al-Kaʿabiya, 241, 245*n*16
Arab folktales. *See* Palestinian-Israeli Arab folktales
The Arabian Nights: Sinbad and Other Popular Stories (trans. Haddawy), 33
Arab society: autocratic rule, 24; belief in pleasures of Paradise, 24; ceremonial mourning rituals, 24–25; crime of seduction, 66; fatalism, 24; feminists, 13; racial stereotype of black race, 178; respect for old age, 24; subordinate status of women, 13, 20; traditional hospitality, 66, 210; views of death, 23–24; view that white race is more beautiful than black, 178
Argonauts, myth of, 74–75

Badal (substitute or exchange marriages), 21
Badawī. *See* Bedouin
Balqa, 101, 104*n*1
Banī Ḥamdān, 57*n*4
Bedouin, 4, 37, 43*n*35; hospitality, 83, 88*n*30; literacy, 116*n*6; of North Arabian Syrian Desert, 225, 228, 230*n*2; part-time agricultural activities, 88*n*31; position of chief, 115; position of women among, 84–85, 207*n*2; pride in maternal relations, 109; raiding as honorable activity, 65, 67*n*17, 79, 85, 86*n*3, 103, 105*n*19, 225, 230*n*5; self-perceived superiority to townspeople, 109, 115; social organization and juridical institutions, 83–84, 85; survival through luck and cleverness, 33; traditional attitudes and values, 55–56; traditional image of noble chieftain, 65; typical tent of, 86*n*5, 101, 104*n*9
Begging, as venerable occupation, 178
Bettelheim, Bruno, 11, 222
Bey, 249, 253*n*8
Bird of Power, 155, 157, 162*n*2
Black people: black slave and white woman in folktales, 52, 55, 90, 94; racial stereotype of in Arab society, 178
Blood revenge, 23
Bread: *aqrās* (flat loaves), 79, 86*n*4; *shrākh* bread, 80, 86*n*6
Bride price, 126, 132*n*11
British mandatory period: official currency of, 146*n*1, 253*n*5; transitional situation between traditional and modern conditions during, 121*n*1
Burton, Richard: translation of *Arabian Nights,* 4–5
Bushnaq, Inea, 5

Camel, tying of, 89–90, 93*n*10
Camel of the air, 242, 245*n*23
Camels of Love, 162*n*2, 220–21, 224*n*15
Caves: associated with ghouls, 178; associated with treasure, 248, 252
Clarke, Arthur C., 8
Clashing rocks, motif of, 72, 74–75, 76*n*21
Close Encounters of the Third Kind (Spielberg), 8
Coffee, quasi-ritual serving and drinking of, 170*n*12
Crying, of a man, 166, 170*n*6
Cyclops (Euripides), 32

Damm buṭlub [yaṭlub] damm ("Blood demands blood"), 23
Death: matter-of-factness of in Palestinian-Israeli Arab folktales, 23–24, 56, 75, 168, 170*n*14; views of in Arab society, 23–24; violent, in Palestinian-Israeli Arab folktales, 22–26
Death of a Princess, 23
Dervishes, 135, 138, 139*n*9
Divorce: power of husband to initiate and effect, 177; triple, 110, 116*n*4

Efendi, 249, 253*n*7
Emir, 207*n*1

Fairy tale (Märchen), 11, 75, 255
"The Falcon's Daughter," 41
Fatalism, 23–24
Fellahin, 31, 67*n*8, 67*n*12, 99*n*9
Feminism, 130
Fiqh, 130
Flammarion, Camille, 8
Folktales: infrastructure of, 9–10; reflection of sociocultural environment of society, 10, 11; three main classes of, 255. *See also* Palestinian-Israeli Arab folktales
Forster, E. M.: *Aspects of the Novel,* 22
Forty: days in seclusion, 137, 139*n*13; individuals in a group, 157, 162*n*8; thieves, 117–20, 137, 139*n*14, 141, 233, 234

Gate of Allah, facing, 146*n*2
Genesis, 98*n*1
Ghoulah, 97, 99*n*9, 99*n*10, 218; assuming shape of woman, 87*n*29; benevolent and motherly, 222–23, 223*n*7; as either dangerous or friendly, 156, 162*n*4, 223*n*7, 241
Ghouls, 31–32, 162*n*6, 162*n*7, 185; bursting with anger and dying, 32, 35*n*15; changing shape at will, 158, 162*n*14, 257; found in wells and caves, 178; friendly and helpful, 96, 98, 156, 162*n*3, 257; as pious Muslims, 257; as snake, 185, 189; with long hair and nails, 96, 99*n*6, 156; with problems only humans can solve, 178
al-Ghūl, Fāyis, 2
Giants *(ʿImlāq),* 150, 197–99
Ginat, Joseph, 20
Granqvist, Hilma: *Marriage Conditions in a Palestinian Village,* 18–20, 21, 25
Gressman, Hugo, 6
Gypsies, 128–29, 131*n*4, 132*n*18

Haddawy, Husain, 4
Ḥidaydūn, 35*n*15
Honor, 11, 20
al-Ḥusaynī, Isḥāq Mūsā, 2, 120, 169
Ḥuwēṭāt, 229, 231*n*9

Ibrāhīm ʿAlī Ibāhīm, 35*n*15
Iraq, 22
Ishmael, 16

Jabīnah, 223
Jacob, 16
Jinn, 46, 48, 49*n*12, 70, 75*n*6, 87*n*23, 243
Job, Book of, 43*n*38
Jordan, 225, 228

Kahle, Paul: *Volkserzählungen aus Palästina,* 2
Kamālī, Shafīq ʿAbdul-Jabbār: *Al-Shiʿr ʿInda al-Badw* (Poetry among the Bedouin), 231*n*17
Karak, 225, 231*n*10
Katz, Yehudah, 3
Khaṭīb, 38, 42*n*12, 59, 66*n*3, 96, 98*n*5
Khayyāṭ, Laṭīf, 3
al-Kinānī, Sheikh Aḥmad, 1
Kufr, 12

Lang, Fritz, 8
Legend, 255
Levy, David, 207

Maʾdhūn sharʿī, 130
Madness, and prophetic powers, 139*n*10
Maghrebite, 102, 103, 104*n*10
Märchen (Fairy tale), 75, 255
Marriage, in Palestinian-Israeli Arab folktales, 17–18, 21; dominance of wife over husband, 45–47, 135–39, 139*n*4, 145, 146*n*6, 165, 169*n*1, 170*n*2, 177, 180; interchangeability of brides or bridegrooms, 56; problems among co-wives, 95–97
Marriage, traditional Arab: bride price, 126, 132*n*11; financial aspect, 19, 21; importance of alliance of families, 20–21; importance of wedding, 21–22; interchangeability of brides or bridegrooms, 20, 21; marriage patterns and position of women, 20; practical attitude toward, 19, 20
Marriage Conditions in a Palestinian Village (Granqvist), 18–19, 21, 25
Menstrual impurity, 66
Mernissi, Fatima: *Beyond the Veil: Male-Female Dynamics in a Modern Muslim Society,* 13
Moral code, traditional Arab, 22–23
Mourning rites, 25, 102, 104*n*15
Muḥammad Ibrāhīm, 200
Myth, 255

Narghile, 38, 42*n*21

Odyssey (Homer), 32–33
Oedipus motif, 40, 41, 43*n*31

Palestinian-Israeli Arab folktales: about encounters between ordinary humans and supernatural beings, 256–57; about ordinary human beings, 256; ambiguity of power relations between sexes in, 12–15, 35; animal tales, 257; autocratic rulers in, 24; blood revenge in, 23; capital punishment in, 22; concept of honor in, 11, 20; externalization and concretization of emotions in, 11–12, 61, 66; hand movements of storyteller, 104*n*13, 201*n*2; impact of modern environment on, 26, 236; invoking name of Allāh in time of danger, 192; liberties

Palestinian-Israeli Arab folktales (*continued*)
taken by translators of, 4–6; of Märchen category, 255–56; marriage arrangements in, 17–18, 21; matter-of-factness of death in, 23–24, 56, 75, 168, 170*n*14; miraculous features of, 26; mixture of modern and traditional elements, 187–88, 191–93, 195*n*30, 201*n*1, 201*n*4, 250, 253*n*9, 257–58; mixture of realistic and fantastic elements, 48, 257; quasi-realistic, 115, 206; reflection of traditional Arab sex mores in, 64–65, 66; as representative of *mentalité* of society, 7; rhyming in, 98; shifting of guilt away from human agent in, 6, 12, 57*n*11, 89, 93*n*9; structural types of, 256–57; wide range of storytelling skills in, 3, 47
—Motifs and themes: antiracism, 152–53, 175, 179; black slave and white woman, 52, 55, 90, 92, 93, 94; boy is turned into deer, 209–13; child's devotion to evil mother, 15–16, 73, 224*n*11; clashing rocks, 72, 74–75, 76*n*21; clever and resourceful women, 14, 32, 35*n*10, 45–47, 49*n*19, 65, 85–86, 123–30, 131, 132*n*21, 144; clever man outwitting forty thieves, 117–20; clever peasant outwitting king, 206; competition between poor brother and rich brother, 145; competition between wives in plural marriages, 155, 162*n*1, 211; cruel stepmother abandons children, 209, 214*n*1, 214*n*2; dominance of wife over husband, 45–47, 135–39, 139*n*4, 145, 146*n*6, 165, 169*n*1, 170*n*2, 177, 180; evil person goes to seek treasure that good person found but is killed, 145, 253*n*14; falling into pit or well, 53–54, 58*n*26, 80, 175, 211; forty, number, 69, 75*n*5, 162*n;* forty days in seclusion, 137, 139*n*13; forty individuals in a group, 157, 162*n*8; forty thieves, 117–20, 137, 139*n*14, 141, 233, 234; forty thieves hidden in forty jars, 145; girl's decision to marry a certain youth, 71, 76*n*20, 184, 203, 207*n*2; girl's rejection of suitor chosen by her father, 203, 207*n*2; helpful whale, 186, 195*n*36; homicide and violent death, 22–26; "If you had not said this and this, I would have killed you," 96, 186, 196*n*44, 241; internal struggle between good and evil, 6, 12, 52, 55, 61; love at first sight, 126, 132, 151, 153*n*2, 183, 188, 194*n*9; marriage of seven sons to seven sisters, 37, 41, 41*n*2; miraculous birth, 69, 74; mother's attempt to kill her child, 73, 76*n*11, 218, 220; noble and chivalrous Bedouin chieftain, 65; pact between young girl and youth to regard her as sister, 49*n*16; Polyphemus, 32–33, 197–99; power of husband under traditional Muslim religious law, 177; raiding as honorable activity, 65, 67*n*17, 79, 85, 86*n*3, 103, 105*n*19, 225, 230*n*5; ridicule of class distinctions, 130–31; ridicule of marriage customs, 131; sons on quest for remedy for their father, 152, 153*n*4; striking a monster twice, 185, 189–90, 195*n*35; tying up loser in a game, 60, 67*n*10, 72, 76*n*22; unfaithful wife, 89–

92; woman wearing men's clothing or reverse, 54, 58*n*27; women hung by hair in captivity, 34, 34*n*8, 186, 190, 196*n*43, 219, 235, 237*n*6. *See also* Ghoulah; Ghouls
Patria potestas, 14
Perez, Yoel, 2, 3, 33, 223; *"HaShātir w'Imlāq Polifem,"* 200–201
Pierotti, Ermete, 19
Pilgrimage, 59, 66*n*2
"Pillars of Faith," 66*n*2
Polygyny, 16–17, 155, 162*n*1, 187, 196*n*49
Polyphemus, 32–33, 197–99
Pomegranate: for pregnancy, 217, 223*n*2; with precious stones inside, 46, 176
Prayer: midday, 67*n*4; spring as favored location for, 82, 87*n*22

Qāḍī, 17, 45, 131
Qaṣīdah, 227, 231*n*16, 231*n*17
Qaṣṣāṣ, 1–2, 3, 14

Rabudh, Majīd al-, 231*n*17
Raiding, among Bedouin, 65, 67*n*17, 79, 85, 86*n*3, 103, 105*n*19, 225, 230*n*5
Raṣd, 46
Rashā'ideh, 225, 230*n*3
Rhyming, in Palestinian-Israeli Arab folktales, 98
Rivlin, Joseph J., 33
Rwala, 230*n*2

El Saadawi, Nawal: *The Hidden Face of Eve: Women in the Arab World,* 13
Samuel, Edwin, 2
Sand-diviner, 39, 43*n*28, 135, 139*n*8
Sa'ūd 'Abd al-'Azīz, 57*n*3
Saudi Arabia, 22
Schmidt, Hans, 2, 3, 33
Schmidt and Kahle, 5
Science fiction, 8–9
Seduction, severity of crime in Arab society, 66
"Seven Brides for Seven Brothers," 41*n*2, 233–36
Shahrazād, 14
Sha'lān, 228, 230*n*1
Shamma, 32, 35*n*12, 40, 43*n*32
Shammar, 225, 228, 230*n*2
Sharārī, 102, 104*n*17, 110, 116*n*5, 130, 132*n*22
Sharī'a, 12
Sheep's brain, 62, 67*n*22
Sheikh, 207*n*1
Shihāda, Ilyās
Shrākh bread, 80, 86*n*6
Siḥ'r (charm), 102, 103, 104*n*14
Sindbad the Sailor, 33
Singer *(shā'ir),* 57*n*9
Slaughtering, 76*n*25

Tents, of Bedouin, 86*n*5, 101, 104*n*9
Thousand and One Nights (Arabian Nights), 3, 4, 92, 94*n*15, 144, 236
Triple divorce, 110, 116*n*4

Urbanites, 31
'Urf, 12

Verne, Jules, 8
Volkserzählungen aus Palästina (Kahle), 2

Wasm (tribal mark), 81, 87*n*14
Wells: falling into, 53–54, 58*n*26, 80, 175, 211; as realm of extrahuman, 175, 178
Wells, H. G., 8
Whale, 186, 195*n*36

Women: desirability of white skin of, 94n16; dominance of wives over husbands, 135–39, 139n4, 145, 146n6, 165, 169n1, 170n2, 177, 180; fellahin, 99n9; hung by hair in captivity, 34, 34n8, 186, 190, 196n43, 219, 235, 237n6; menstrual impurity, 66; as more clever and resourceful than men, 14, 32, 35n10, 45–47, 49n19, 65, 123–30, 131, 132n21, 144; mourning rites, 25, 102, 104n15; position of among Bedouin, 84–85, 207n2; provocative behavior, 125, 132n7; subordinate status of in Arab society, 13, 20; as weak, 53, 58n23, 91

Yūsif, Jirius Abū, 2

Books in the Raphael Patai Series in Jewish Folklore and Anthropology

The Myth of the Jewish Race
revised edition, by Raphael Patai and Jennifer Patai, 1989

The Hebrew Goddess
third enlarged edition, by Raphael Patai, 1990

Robert Graves and the Hebrew Myths: A Collaboration
by Raphael Patai, 1991

Jewish Musical Traditions
by Amnon Shiloah, 1992

The Jews of Kurdistan
by Erich Brauer, completed and edited by Raphael Patai, 1993

Jewish Moroccan Folk Narratives from Israel
by Haya Bar-Itzhak and Aliza Shenhar, 1993

For Our Soul: The Ethiopian Jews in Israel
by Teshome G. Wagaw, 1993

Book of Fables: The Yiddish Fable Collection of Reb Moshe Wallich Frankfurt am Main, 1697
translated and edited by Eli Katz, 1994

From Sofia to Jaffa: The Jews of Bulgaria and Israel
by Guy H. Haskell, 1994

Jadīd al-Islām: The Jewish "New Muslims" of Meshed
by Raphael Patai, 1998

Saint Veneration among the Jews in Morocco
by Issachar Ben-Ami, 1998

Arab Folktales from Palestine and Israel
introduction, translation, and annotation by Raphael Patai, 1998

www.ingramcontent.com/pod-product-compliance
Lightning Source LLC
Chambersburg PA
CBHW051537230426
43669CB00015B/2636
9780814327104